Overcoming Disadvantage in Education

Governments, local authorities, school leaders and teachers all over the world want to improve the educational attainment and participation of all students, and to minimise any systematic differences in outcomes for social and economic groups. A particular concern is for those students from backgrounds that may objectively disadvantage them at school and beyond. However, considerable effort and money is currently being wasted on policies, practices and interventions that have very little hope of success, and that may indeed endanger the progress that is being made otherwise. The poor quality of much education research evidence, coupled with an unwillingness among users of evidence to discriminate appropriately between what we know and what we do not know, means that opportunities are being missed. At a time of reduced public spending it is important that proposed interventions are both effective and efficient.

Overcoming Disadvantage in Education is unique in the way that it:

- shows where the solutions to underachievement and poverty lie
- combines primary (new), secondary (official) and published (review) evidence
- distinguishes between those possible causes of underachievement that are largely fixed for individuals, and those that are modifiable

There *are* evidence-informed ways forward in handling under-achievement and increasing social justice in education. This book shows the most likely approaches, and where further work could yield further benefits.

This book will be a key text for students, developing academic researchers and supervisors in the social sciences, and for those research users charged with improving educational outcomes.

Stephen Gorard is Professor of Education and Well-being, Durham University, UK.

Beng Huat See is Research Fellow at The University of Birmingham, UK.

Overcoming Disadvantage in Education

Stephen Gorard and
Beng Huat See

Routledge
Taylor & Francis Group

LONDON AND NEW YORK

First published 2013
by Routledge
2 Park Square, Milton Park, Abingdon, Oxon OX14 4RN

Simultaneously published in the USA and Canada
by Routledge
711 Third Avenue, New York, NY 10017

Routledge is an imprint of the Taylor & Francis Group, an informa business

© 2013 Stephen Gorard and Beng Huat See

British Library Cataloguing in Publication Data
A catalogue record for this book is available from the British Library

Library of Congress Cataloging in Publication Data
Gorard, Stephen, author.
Overcoming disadvantage in education / Stephen Gorard and Beng Huat
See.
pages cm
ISBN 978-0-415-53689-9 (hardback) -- ISBN 978-0-415-53690-5
(paperback) -- ISBN 978-0-203-74166-5 (e-book) 1. Educational
equalization. 2. Children with social disabilities--Education.
I. See, Beng Huat, author. II. Title.
LC213.G68 2013
379.2'6--dc23
2013002575

ISBN: 978-0-415-53689-9 (hbk)
ISBN: 978-0-415-53690-5 (pbk)
ISBN: 978-0-203-74166-5 (ebk)

Typeset in Galliard
by Saxon Graphics Ltd, Derby

MIX
Paper from
responsible sources
FSC
www.fsc.org   FSC® C013604

Printed and bound by CPI Group (UK) Ltd, Croydon, CR0 4YY

Contents

Contents

Preface

Governments, local authorities, school leaders and teachers all over the world want to improve the attainment and participation of their students at school. They also want to minimise any systematic differences in school outcomes between social and economic groups. However, considerable effort and money is being wasted on policies, practices and interventions that have very little hope of success and that may even endanger the progress that is being made otherwise. The poor quality of much education research evidence, and the unwillingness among users of evidence to discriminate appropriately between what we know and what we do not know, means that opportunities are being missed. At a time of reduced public spending and increased public unrest, at least in the UK, it is important that proposed interventions are both effective and efficient. There *are* evidence-informed ways forward in handling under-achievement and increasing social justice in education. This book shows the most likely approaches, and where further work could yield further benefits.

This book synthesises and summarises the full body of existent evidence on how to overcome disadvantage at school, with a special focus on the role of poverty in educational attainment and post-compulsory participation. The summary of each approach will be inclusive and critical. This book represents a bold attempt to uncover how to break the stratifying links between the socio-economic background of individuals and their educational futures.

Overcoming Disadvantage is unique in three ways, showing where the solutions to disadvantage and the poverty gradient may lie, and where they do not. It combines primary (new), secondary (official) and published (review) evidence in a way that has never been attempted before in this area. All of these types of data are synthesised for the first time, to find out how to overcome disadvantage in education. The book adopts a clear model of causation in social science – consisting of association, temporal sequence, intervention and explanatory mechanism. It then uses this model to assemble and audit the evidence of all types relevant to the plausible causes of disadvantage. Very few possible causes have sufficient evidence for a complete explanatory model. The final way in which this book is different is that it clearly distinguishes between those possible causes of disadvantage that are largely fixed for individuals – such as their sex, health record or family background – and those that are modifiable – such as the school attended, area of residence or their motivation. The main focus of the book is on the latter list, since only these can be of use to anyone wishing to improve the educational chances of the most disadvantaged in society.

Overcoming Disadvantage is a research-based book, relevant for courses at master's level and above in social policy, social work, sociology and education. It will also be of considerable interest to researchers, practitioners and policy-makers in these areas. Despite its original approach, the book is written in an accessible and engaging manner, suitable for its readership. Terminology and technical issues are kept to the minimum needed for a reader to understand the research issues and to form their own critical judgements. Full references are given to the technical background for those who wish to learn more.

The authors would like to thank the ESRC, British Academy, Nuffield Foundation, Joseph Rowntree Foundation, Educational Endowment Foundation, European Commission, Royal Society and the Department for Education for funding the research that forms the basis for this book. The authors are grateful to many colleagues, especially Sandra Cooke, Peter Davies, Rita Hordosy, Nadia Siddiqui, Emma Smith and Carole Torgerson for their work on some of the datasets quoted here.

List of figures

List of tables

Chapter 1

What is disadvantage in education?

Introduction

This first chapter rehearses some of the evidence showing that educational outcomes and opportunities are heavily stratified by student background, and argues that this can lead to needlessly low achievement for some young people from the most disadvantaged backgrounds. Suggesting practical and policy solutions to overcome such disadvantage necessitates an understanding of the causal influences at play. The next section presents a four-criterion model of causation – association, temporal sequence, controlled testing and explanatory mechanisms – whose elements must be present in order to describe a relationship as 'causal'. The four elements then become a basis for classifying, judging the relevance of and synthesising different kinds of evidence in the remainder of the book. This chapter also proposes a distinction between those causal factors that are largely beyond the control of anyone, and those that could be modified in a practical way. It is the latter that must be the focus of work that has any chance of improving educational outcomes for those who are currently disadvantaged. The chapter ends by outlining the structure of the rest of the book. The book shows what can, and cannot, be done with limited resources. Some of the things that could be done are so clear and so simple that they should be a rebuke to any society that has not acted on them.

One of the main reasons why developed countries have universal, compulsory, state-funded education for children is so that individuals are not disadvantaged by their family background, parents' education, ability to pay or educational resources at home (Harris & Gorard 2010). Schooling is intended to reduce the influence of social, familial and economic background, so promoting social mobility and a just and equitable society. The same is true to a certain extent across Europe and more generally across the developed world (EGREES 2005). Any school system is a huge and costly intervention that does not have to be financed by the state, as evidenced by the history of the private sector and of church schools in England. The reason for state responsibility is to try and ensure that all citizens get an equivalent experience. Similarly, one of the main reasons for widening participation in post-compulsory education and training has been to increase equality of opportunity in the system, so reducing the link between social, ethnic or economic origin and the life outcomes for all individuals.

Unfortunately, it is not at all clear that this laudable aim has been achieved in Europe, the US, Pacific Rim or elsewhere, despite huge tax-payer-funded expenditure. In a review of policies and programmes aimed at closing the ethnic gap in school-readiness among young US pre-schoolers, Duncan and Magnuson (2005) found that differences in socio-economic resources account for half of the differences in test scores. Internationally, studies show that attainment at school is still strongly related to student characteristics such as their ethnic origin and first language, whether they or their parents are recent immigrants (Behnke et al. 2010), family structure (Battle & Coates 2004), parents' occupations (Li & Lerner 2011), parents' educational level (Magnuson 2007), income (Feinstein et al. 2004), the number of books at home (Mwetundila 2001), the degree of geographical isolation of their home and where they attend school (Fuchs & Wobmann 2004). The key influences on a child's educational attainment in the early years include parental education, low income, unemployment, early motherhood and low mother qualifications (Mensah & Kiernan 2010). In each of these studies and thousands more like them it is the most disadvantaged students that tend to perform the worst.

In England, children start school with different levels of resource and quickly display strong patterning of their attainment by family origin (Gorard & See 2009). School attainment at every subsequent age and stage reveals these same patterns (Gorard 2000). Table 1.1 shows that young people in England defined as living in poverty (free school meal/FSM-eligible) are much less likely to gain a C grade in either English or maths in their age 16 GCSE assessments. This is also true for all years, subjects, grades and phases of education.

Table 1.2 illustrates the same kind of variation for three ethnic groups. Young people of Gypsy/Romany origin are very unlikely to obtain a C grade or higher in these two key subjects, or indeed any others. In summary, the aggregate scores and qualifications for students from less elevated social classes, those living in poverty, in some deprived areas and for some ethnic minority groups are considerably lower than average. This is despite a system set up purportedly to prevent this.

Table 1.1 Percentage attaining at least grade C or equivalent in GCSE, England, 2005/06, by eligibility for free school meals (FSM)

	Maths	English
FSM-eligible	27	31
Not FSM	55	61

Source: NPD/PLASC

Table 1.2 Percentage attaining at least grade C or equivalent in GCSE, England, 2005/06, by ethnicity

	Maths	English
Gypsy/Romany	7	8
White UK	52	57
Chinese origin	81	67

Source: NPD/PLASC

The same patterns continue into immediate post-compulsory education, and thence into opportunities for higher education (Gorard et al. 2007). Families remain a key determinant of educational performance in later lifelong education and training of all kinds (Gorard et al. 1999a). In the large-scale study by Selwyn et al. (2006), young adults in England and Wales who left education at the earliest opportunity had parents who had themselves left school at the age of 14 (on average). Individuals who stayed on after the compulsory phase, on the other hand, had parents who had continued in school until at least age 16. In the same study, 95 per cent of adults whose parents were in professional 'service' occupations had continued on in education or training after leaving school. Over 50 per cent of adults with parents in unskilled or semi-skilled occupations, on the other hand, received no education or training after leaving school. These are illustrations of a deeply-rooted pattern of inequality and social reproduction, which is evidence that the education system in any country, far from overcoming such inequalities, may actually assist families in reproducing their relative economic and societal advantages.

There is perhaps no more important issue facing education and society today. Understanding the reasons for the poverty 'gradient' is particularly relevant for policy and practice in order to find appropriate approaches and suggested behaviour changes to help reduce it. There is considerable activity being undertaken to improve educational outcomes for disadvantaged children and thus close the gap, but as this book shows, there is currently little systematic attempt to see if any of this works. The situation demands a better approach, both practically and ethically. Practitioners and policy-makers need to take much more notice of research and development that can help them achieve this simple goal of creating a fair education system. More urgently and crucially, researchers need to change what they do and start providing the kind of evidence that practitioners and policy-makers can use safely. As succeeding chapters show, this means caring more about finding the correct answers to their research questions than about what those answers are. It means the end of absurd divisions and schisms in research, and instead the use of all available evidence to help those facing disadvantage. It means greater concern about the design of research. How to overcome disadvantage in education is a clear causal question. It needs to be treated as such. This calls for a more honest system of reviewing and disseminating research findings that is critical in its evaluation of research quality. This book is part of the answer.

Fixed and malleable causes

To understand disadvantage in education one needs to understand its causes. A claim that something acts as a cause of something else is a very strong one; this is partly because it cannot be observed directly. Gorard (2013) proposes a four-criteria model for establishing the feasibility of a causal model, building on the prior work of Hume (1962), Mill (1882) and Bradford-Hill (1966).

1   For X (a possible cause) and Y (a possible effect) to be in a causal relationship they must be repeatedly associated. This association must be strong, clearly observable, replicable and it must be specific to X and Y.
2   For X and Y to be in a causal relationship, they must proceed in sequence. X must always precede Y (where both appear), and the appearance of Y must be safely predictable from the appearance of X.
3   For X and Y to be in a causal relationship, it must have been demonstrated repeatedly that an intervention to change the strength or appearance of X then also strongly and clearly changes the strength or appearance of Y.
4   For X and Y to be in a causal relationship, there must be a coherent mechanism to explain the causal link. This mechanism must be the simplest available without which the evidence cannot be explained. Put another way, if the proposed mechanism were not true then there must be no simpler or equally simple way of explaining the evidence for it.

Clearly such a model is not intended to deny the existence of mutual causation, or of one-off events being caused. If each criterion is seen as necessary, though not individually sufficient for a causal model, then any evidence relevant to at least one of these criteria for any model can contribute to the search for a cause. No one study is likely to be able to address all four criteria at once. In order to propose any intervention to overcome disadvantage in education such a robust causal model must be identified first; however, this in itself is still not enough. There are plenty of causal models that might seem convincing but lead to conclusions that are impractical, ludicrously expensive, unethical or have damaging unintended side effects. Therefore, the practical malleability of any proposed causal factor is also crucial.

It is possible to envisage moving public funding from secondary to primary schooling, amending the rules for allocating school places or abolishing homework, for example. These are all malleable factors, and if the evidence is that these changes would improve the situation, then they can be considered. There is a wide range of possible reasons why early disadvantage turns into lower attainment at school. They include factors such as living in high poverty districts, and residential segregation by parental education. They include possible institutional causes such as school, teacher and peer effects, and segregation by poverty between schools. There are family and individual issues such as parental involvement, the early environment for children and student motivation and behaviour. It is these determinants that are the focus of this book – not because they are necessarily the most important scientifically but because they are modifiable and the most appropriate for anyone seeking to overcome disadvantage in education.

On the other hand, there is a further range of possible reasons why disadvantage is related to poor educational outcomes, of a kind that are not always susceptible to change via direct intervention. These include an individual's birth characteristics and those of their family, such as sex, ethnicity, first language, learning difficulties, long-term health issues, inherited talent and parental education and occupation. Attainment at school is also strongly predicted by an individual's prior attainment (Noble et al. 2006). This stems from an early age, perhaps even from birth. If taller children, those born in the winter, girls or US immigrants of Chinese origin are more successful at school then there is not a great deal that can be done about these factors envisaged as causes. It may be that being born in winter genuinely causes success at school, but this is an unhelpful finding because it is not about a malleable factor.

Very young children from the highest socio-economic status (SES) families have markedly higher rates of success in problem-solving compared to children from middle and lower SES families (Ginsburg & Pappas 2004). Such a difference in early ability or talent might be innate, or produced partly by a combination of poor early diet, higher stress experienced by low SES children and lack of access to a cognitively stimulating environment (Kishiyama et al. 2009). In reality, it is almost impossible to judge between these fixed and malleable accounts. There is evidence of both types of cause at once (Haworth et al. 2011). Twin studies tend to suggest that some educational outcomes are largely genetically determined (Nielsen 2006, Trzesniewski et al. 2006). In the unusual situation where children have been randomly allocated to parents, much behaviour appears to reproduce that of the adopting parents. However, school attainment and graduating from college are more like obesity and height in being strongly linked to biological parents (Sacerdote 2004). Perhaps hereditary general ability is the basis of early inequalities, but as children learn to adapt and adjust to their environment its relative importance declines (Gottfredson 2004), especially for impoverished families (Turkheimer et al. 2003).

It is not clear how much can be done about some of these factors in the short to medium term. If they are deemed unfair or unwarranted, one can only intervene to change something else to try and remedy the problem. Fixed determinants are taken into account in this book, to help understand educational outcomes and barriers to improvement, but they are not the main focus.

The structure of the book

Chapters 2 and 3 outline the sources of evidence used in the rest of this book, its limitations and the nature of the analyses undertaken. These chapters explain why the results of this book are as they are, and why the conclusions drawn may differ from standard accounts that misuse or ignore relevant evidence.

Chapters 4 to 11 then present a summary of available evidence relevant to family influences, school intakes, the role of teachers, individual attitudes and lifelong patterns of occupation, education and training, among others. Each chapter focuses on one of these issues at a time.

The final chapter then pulls all of these findings together, and presents a summary of the most promising evidence-informed approaches for overcoming disadvantage in education.

Chapter 2

The quality of existing datasets

Introduction

This is the first of two chapters that outline the evidence base for the remainder of this book. It is important both because, as standard, it provides readers with a basis for judging the security of the findings, and because it explains why those findings are original and different to what is often merely assumed to be true. This chapter presents a brief definition of terms relevant to educational outcomes and social disadvantage, and a summary of some relevant existing datasets. Existing and official statistics are much more complete, longer-term and larger in scale than anything that even a very full programme of primary research can provide. They are vital to the task of describing patterns of attainment and participation in education. Of course, they also have well-known limitations. They were usually collected for a different purpose to that for which they are used here, and they do not tessellate with or complement each other well, even when set in the same time period and geographic region. One such example for the UK is that individual student records for schools use poverty as an indicator of parental background, whereas individual student data for higher education uses parental occupation. Both measures are useful but they are not equivalent and neither can be converted to the other. Another important issue for this book is that the datasets for different countries do not match. This book makes use of primary international datasets and reviews of evidence worldwide (Chapter 3), and makes reference to results from international studies such as Trends in International Mathematics and Science Study (TIMSS), Programme for International Student Assessment (PISA) and Progress in International Reading Literacy Study (PIRLS), and teacher effectiveness work in the US. The most comprehensive datasets used in the book are from the UK or England. However, there are further crucial limitations to even these high-quality and world-leading datasets that are not usually acknowledged by other commentators. These problems are covered in some detail in this chapter, and they begin to show why the results in this book will be a challenge to some established beliefs, in areas such as widening participation and school and teacher performance. The chapter therefore provides a caution about how far existing data can be stretched without providing misleading results.

Educational outcomes

The educational outcomes of interest in this book are of three main types. The first and most obvious for policy-makers is attainment. Attainment can be considered as an individual's level of success in educational assessments of any kind. Key indicators include a young child's school readiness, such as the ability to read letters of the alphabet and count to ten, performance in standard national tests or the level of qualification gained by the end of compulsory schooling. The second major type of outcome is the individual's subsequent educational and work trajectory after the end of compulsory schooling. Participation includes what young people do when they have the choice to leave formal schooling, their immediate post-compulsory participation in education, university or college and their employment and training. Currently less likely to be the focus of policy are the wider outcomes of education. These include the values learnt from schooling, willingness to trust and help others, civic participation and perhaps most importantly enjoyment of learning and of life. For this book, the first problem encountered when dealing with any of these outcomes is that they are difficult to define and measure, as illustrated here.

Attainment

There are huge and well-documented issues of comparability in assessment scores between years of assessment, curriculum subjects, modes of assessment, examining boards and types of qualifications, among other issues (Lamprianou 2009). Maintaining or even judging standards is very difficult even within one country (Crisp 2010, Stringer 2012). There are frequent high-profile errors, such as when 45 per cent of candidates were awarded the wrong grade in an extreme case in the UK (Stewart 2009), which sometimes mask the lower level of 'everyday' error. Aggregating qualifications or comparing them over time and place adds further problems. Moderation will be imperfect, so one must assume a reasonable level of error in any assessment data of the kind used in this book.

Participation

Learning is largely an individual and internal process that takes place every day, not requiring a course, a teacher, a curriculum, an institution, fees, registration or certification (Livingstone 2000). One can participate in an educational course without learning much, and one can learn a lot without participating (Gorard et al. 1999b). People obtain much of their education through private reading, informal sources such as friends, cultural institutions such as museums and art galleries, library drop-in centres, free basic-skills provision, job-seeker training, liberal evening classes and courses delivered entirely by technologies such as television or computer (European Commission 2001, Selwyn et al. 2006). However, policy tends to promote a form of learning in institutions that yields to political and other control (Marsick & Watkins 1990), and then assumes this is the only learning of value (Billett 2010). This is an important point, and one that should not be forgotten. However, for the purposes of this book, the focus is on more formal episodes of participation. Even with participation in the kind of educational opportunities that require enrolment, deciding that a particular social group is or is not under-represented in education at any stage is a daunting task if undertaken properly.

To establish under-representation requires a definition of the stage or episode of education that the under-representation is in, a good measure of the purportedly under-represented group and knowledge of the prevalence of that group both in the relevant population and in the educational episode. Just some of the problems in these four steps were illustrated using entry to university or higher education (HE) as a topical example (Gorard 2008a). As shown later, simply identifying a sub-group of potentially disadvantaged students is hard – whether in terms of parental education, social class, disability or ethnicity. There are analytical compromises to be made about what participation is. Does it involve completion or merely acceptance on a course, for example? What exactly is HE? Does it include HE courses in FE colleges, FE courses in HE institutions, postgraduate students and those involved in professional training such as postgraduate teachers and social workers, those involved in short courses such as HE-based continuing professional development or those taking degrees by correspondence or via the internet? What is the relevant population of potential participants? Does it include all ages, even though some age groups are very unlikely to participate? Or is it better to bias the findings through a focus on the young and the full-time? Does the relevant population only include the country of the university itself, and if so is it possible to separate out any students from elsewhere? Whose domicile counts, anyway? Is it the residence of parents, or of the potential students themselves or some combination of these? All of these and many other decisions must be made just in order to compute the simple proportion of any social group participating in any stage of education. A different decision about any of them could completely transform the result.

Psychological constructs

A lot of research discussed in later chapters is based on psychological constructs such as attitudes, aspirations, motivation and self-concept, which are probably the most problematic of all of the indicators and measures discussed so far. They have no legal definition, and nothing external to calibrate them with. There are huge problems in their 'measurement' and analysis (Gorard 2010a). None have any real validity beyond the traditional weak argument that IQ is what IQ tests measure. They are invented explanations, useful only in so far as they can predict or explain other outcomes. Even in those situations where the measures correlate highly with something explicit (such as a revealed behaviour) there is a danger of tautology. A problem with trying to establish a causal relationship between something like expectations and subsequent attainment is that expectations are based on students' forecasts, as in the question: 'How far do you think you will get in school?' Such expectations may be simply survey-induced utterances that do not have real meanings in the everyday lives of adolescents (Morgan 2004). If educational expectations are actually forecasts, then associations between expectations and attainment cannot be given a causal interpretation (Alexander & Cook 1979). Attitudes are also often, when tested in non-tautological conditions, an inaccurate proxy. For example, students' reported attitudes to science at school are weakly but inversely related to their subsequent choice of studying science subjects or not (Gorard & See 2009).

Indicators

Also needed for any investigation of disadvantage in education are some indicators of possible disadvantage. Some of the more common and useful are described here. To these one could add the sex of the student, their first language, any disability, how long they have lived in their country of residence, their parental education, income, where they live and many other factors. All are discussed in the substantive chapters of this book. It is important to note that the indicators of possible disadvantage used in this book, such as eligibility for free school meals, are here for monitoring purposes only. They are used to uncover differences that are systematic, as opposed to merited or inevitable differences in outcomes. They are not presented as the explanation for the difference. The levels of disadvantage, their meaning and prevalence vary considerably around the world. The official definition of poverty in the UK is very different in all these three senses from the experience of poverty in sub-Saharan Africa, for example. The indicators below are therefore best considered as likely indicators of only relative disadvantage in education (Chapter 12).

SES

Classifications of socio-economic status (SES) vary over time and place and between studies. Widely-used systems have been based on occupational prestige, skill, the nature of work, educational requirements and even social distance. The classification of individuals into occupational classes or groups is a matter of judgement over which even experts disagree, even when the classification is standard (Lambert 2002). The categories themselves are arbitrary, and they interact with each other and with other categories such as sex, ethnicity, first language, health, disability and geography (Gorard 2001). An alternative is to use aggregated measures of socio-economic status for the area in which an individual lives, since it is usually easier to get standardised measures for an area than to get data on individuals. However, this does not overcome the difficulties of classification or even the problem of missing data, since as many students are likely to have missing address data as any other item. It tells us nothing about the individual other than the kind of small area they live in. Some of the most deprived families actually live in heavily polarised areas in inner cities, which the average scores disguise. It is a clear example of the ecological fallacy.

Analysis with existing datasets and studies is limited to the available SES variables. Different studies use different indices of SES and not surprisingly produce somewhat different results. A further key problem in examining trends in social categories over time is that the variables collected, or the coding used for the same variables, also change over time. Consequently it is often difficult to make genuine and straightforward comparisons over time or between groups. Perhaps most significantly for this book, it is not clear whether any classification by occupation (or any other indicator of disadvantage) should be of the potential student or of their parents. For example, it seems absurd to try and base the occupational classification of a student on their own work history when they may never have been anything other than a full-time student in education. It is no less absurd to base the current occupational classification of a mature HE student on the previous occupation of their parents.

FSM

Several developed countries offer similar free or reduced-rate school lunches to students at state-maintained schools if the student is known to be from a financially disadvantaged background. The official procedures for entitlement to a free meal and for registering and then taking that meal have traditionally offered social science researchers a useful, wide-ranging and pre-existing indicator of potential student disadvantage (Harwell & LeBeau 2010). Eligibility for free school meals (FSM) in England has several key advantages as an indicator of generic disadvantage for social policy research. It is officially and routinely collected annually for nearly every student, has a relatively simple legal binary definition, is strongly related to educational and other outcomes and has been collected since 1989, giving analysts enough data to consider long-term trends at national, regional, local and institutional levels. FSM is an indicator of a student living in a family with an income deemed to be below the poverty line, and applies to around 13 per cent to 20 per cent of students in England.

One problem of FSM as a measure of SES is that it only divides the population into those living in poverty and all others. But if, as here, the issue is what happens to the poorest in society, then this is not necessarily a limitation. Another problem is that after receiving other welfare benefits, FSM families may not be among the lowest income group (Hobbs & Vignoles 2010); FSM is an indicator of state dependency as well as income. FSM students tend to be markedly different from non-FSM students in terms of the schools they attend, where they live, special needs, ethnicity, first language, their results at school and their subsequent education (Gorard 2012a). FSM is a key indicator for a financial 'pupil premium' in which schools in England taking students eligible for FSM receive advantageous funding per student.

Ethnicity

Ethnicity is a powerful concept that reveals quite large differences in educational outcomes, yet it relies on discrete categories that are mostly inappropriate (Gorard 2001) and either fail to capture the real variation or produce unwieldy schemes and tiny cell sizes (Williams & Husk 2012). Any definition of ethnicity is contentious, confused and liable to change over time, so ethnicity is probably best understood as self-referenced – the definition used by the UK Registrar General. The term is used by others in different and contradictory ways (Salway et al. 2010). It could be based on common ancestry, memories of a shared past or a shared cultural identity that might include kinship, religion, language, shared territory, nationality or physical appearance (Lee 2003). Despite the belief in some quarters that inequalities cannot be overcome without addressing ethnicity, some studies have shown the opposite. If students' own language is respected in assessments then apparent ethnic inequalities can be reduced (Robinson 2010). Similarly, if social class is accounted for then the association of school attainment with ethnic groups falls to almost zero (Strand 2011). To some extent any classification such as ethnicity creates a potential pathology. It is intriguing to note that two countries like England and France have similar patterns of differential attainment (by sex, class and ethnic group, for example) but the concerns differ (Moreau 2010). This might mean that some issues, such as the purported underachievement of boys in England, are only partly grounded in the local reality (Gorard 2004).

SEN

In the UK, students with a learning difficulty are classified as having special educational needs (SEN), and they may have a disability that hinders their progress at school and/or have greater difficulty in learning than most children in their age group. A statement of SEN is given where a statutory assessment is made of the individual need and the necessary number of hours of support as envisaged by the Education Act 1996. The number of children with statements varies with local authority policy, but a statement is usually given when a child cannot be supported within the resources normally available to the school. Therefore, the child is either educated elsewhere or additional resources are provided in a mainstream setting. Around three per cent of students have a statement, and a further 15 per cent to 20 per cent are identified for School Action and School Action Plus. School Action goes beyond what would be considered reasonable for normal personalised learning, and Action Plus begins to involve external specialist teachers or educational psychologists. As may be imagined there is considerable overlap between these four categories – personalisation, Action, Action Plus and statement – and variation over time and between areas.

Existing datasets

Important evidence for this book comes from existing and official datasets. The previous section outlined some of the difficulties in defining and measuring the kinds of variables needed in order to understand how to overcome disadvantage in education. These include difficulties in defining social categories such as ethnicity or measuring outcomes such as attainment. All of the issues mentioned will lead to some level of error and bias in all existing datasets. There are further problems to be considered, of which the most important for any analyst is missing data. These could be entire missing cases from a dataset, due to non-response or dropout, or they could be missing values from existing cases, due to error, lack of knowledge or non-response. Both are serious and neither can be considered random events. The cases missing from a census dataset, for example, are not some random subset of all others. They are much more likely to have certain characteristics than those that responded, on average (Gorard 2013). Non-responders will be more mobile, less prominent, less literate or less likely to speak the language of data collection. Many of the same things are true for cases with missing values. Where a school does not know a child's home address, that child is more likely than average to have moved recently or to attend school less. All of this means that missing data cannot in any way be replaced by technical approaches such as imputing or weighting from the data that is present. The missing data creates a bias in the dataset. Using the data that is present to make up the missing data, as is seen so often in research reports, actually worsens that bias. It also means that none of the techniques derived from random sampling theory, such as significance testing or confidence intervals, can help here either.

ASC

Analysis of the intakes to schools is based on figures from the Annual Schools Census (ASC) for all mainstream state-funded schools in England from 1989 to 2011. This is as long as records have existed that include any individual measures of student disadvantage. The appearance of missing data from mainstream state-funded schools is minimal because it is at school or institution level. The ASC includes the number of full-time equivalent students in each school; the number taking free school meals (FSMt); the number known to be eligible for free school meals (FSMe); the number known to have a statement of special educational needs (SENs), or special needs without a statement (SENn); the number known to have English as a second or additional language (ESL) and the number of each known ethnic origin. The latter is converted here into a binary variable based on the number known not to have reported White UK ethnicity (NW). This aggregation is used because many of the minority ethnic groups are very small. Each of these six indicators is a marker of potential disadvantage in education. The precise operational definition of each has changed slightly over time, and this affects the perceived prevalence of these indicators. Further details are available in Gorard and Cheng (2011).

The relevant intake figures for each school in each year in terms of each indicator were used to calculate the Gorard Segregation Index (GS) and the Dissimilarity Index (D) at a national, regional and local level for primary and secondary schools. GS is the strict proportion of potentially disadvantaged students, using any indicator, who would have to exchange schools with another student for there to be no segregation in the national school system. GS is effectively the same thing as the Hoover Index (Hoover 1941) for looking at residential population concentrations, the delta index proposed by Duncan et al. (1961) as an adaptation of the Hoover index, the Women in Employment index used to measure occupational segregation by the OECD and other bodies, the Robin Hood Index (Maxi-pedia 2012) and the Student Change Index used by Glenn (2011). It is based on the Lorenz curve and closely tied to the Gini Coefficient, and according to some commentators is 'computationally equivalent to the index of dissimilarity' (Long & Nucci 1997, p.431). The formulae for both indices can be found in Gorard (2009a). Both indices are tracked over all of the available years for each available indicator of disadvantage. Their trajectories over time, and changes in the number of schools and students, are correlated using Pearson's r.

NPD

Evidence of the outcomes from schools is largely based on secondary analyses of official datasets in England. The Department for Education Performance Tables website (http://www.education.gov.uk/performancetables/) provides the results and some student intake data for all state-funded schools in England, for every year for which these are available. This includes the number of students per school at the end of their Key Stage 4 (KS4), and the figures for Key Stage 2 (KS2) to KS4 Contextualised Value-Added (CVA). KS2 is the statutory assessment in core subjects usually taken at the age of ten (the last year of primary school). KS4 is the assessment at 16+ labelled 'GCSE and equivalent'. The CVA figures include the 95 per cent confidence interval for each school (upper and lower CVA estimate), and the proportion of the total KS4 students included in the CVA measure. CVA is an estimate of the average progress made by students in each school, taking into account their prior attainment and background characteristics. The way the scores are calculated makes them zero-sum, and 1,000 is added to the result. By design, around half of all schools in England will have scores above 1,000 (positive CVA), and half below (negative). The figures for all mainstream secondary age schools were available from 2006 to 2010. The 2011 Performance Tables also have a value-added measure, but it is not CVA, and so is not directly comparable to previous years. For full details see Gorard et al. (2013).

The Department for Education also maintain a National Pupil Database (NPD), containing longitudinal records for all students in England including their background, SES characteristics, prior attainment, courses taken and qualifications obtained. This database is at least the equivalent of the best such resources in the world. However, like all such databases it has a problem with missing data (Gorard 2010b). Like ASC, it is missing much data on the six per cent of children attending private schools, and those educated at home. In addition, there will be a small number of cases in transition between schools, or otherwise not registered for a school. In some earlier years around ten per cent of the individual student records are unmatched for their characteristics and their attainment scores; a further ten per cent could have records that are unmatched across phases of schooling, caused by students moving between the home countries of the UK, for example. This makes calculation of their CVA impossible. In summary, perhaps 15 to 30 per cent of students will have records missing from the database. Having accounted for these, there could be a further 15 per cent to 30 per cent of students missing data from one or more key variables related to attainment or SES background. As Gorard (2010b) explains, substituting area-based measures such as the index of deprivation (IDACI) to try and overcome these missing data actually makes the problem worse.

In practice, missing cases tend to be ignored, with missing values replaced by a default – such as the modal category. This is deemed necessary in order to retain the cases with any missing values, but it leads to bias. There is plenty of evidence of substantial differences between students with complete and incomplete values in such datasets (Amrein-Beardsley 2008). For example, in the 2007 NPD, 3.3 per cent of state-funded students were recorded with no FSM data. There is a clear aggregate distinction between the examination results of FSM and non-FSM students (Table 2.1). Overall, students from the poorer families achieve lower total points scores in assessments, and lower results per examination entered. This is well-known and part of the reason why FSM is deemed such a powerful indicator of disadvantage in social policy. However, FSM-missing students in state schools have considerably lower scores even than FSM students.

Missing FSM students are therefore a third category of low-achieving students, often not taking traditional qualifications, who are 'mobile' between schools and about whom their schools know less. They are frequently disadvantaged in other

Table 2.1 Means of KS4 attainment scores by each FSM category

	Not FSM eligible	FSM eligible	Missing FSM code
Uncapped GCSE and equivalent points score	385	281	144
Capped GCSE and equivalent points score	304	231	131
Average points score per entry	37	28	27

Source: PLASC 2007

ways as well, and have the appearance of a super-deprived and very low-achieving group. A clear example of the importance of this comes in the calculation of CVA for schools (as outlined previously). At present, students with missing FSM are assumed to be non-FSM (Gorard 2012a). These missing FSM students in the state schools using CVA will be deprived and actually tend to be super-deprived. However, the CVA calculations do not even treat them as FSM eligible. This means that all schools with any of these students will have their CVA scores loaded against them from the start.

HESA

For the European Union (EU), the Bologna commitment involves raising 'the participation of under-represented groups to the point where the higher education population mirrors the overall societal distribution'. This is a tough, but fair, objective. However, it is not just tough to achieve; it is hard to know what it means in real life, because we have less secure knowledge about participation in HE than many people seem to believe. This is so for many reasons. One such reason, as discussed previously, is the continuing problem of defining and collecting measures of participation. In addition, all datasets on student participation have missing cases and missing data from existing cases. The scale and importance of this missing data varies. Recent Eurostudent survey response rates in each country range from two per cent to 88 per cent (Orr et al. 2011). A dataset with a response rate of two per cent or anything like it is completely useless. In addition, the response rate for some countries is not known or is not published. These data are also useless. Even the most complete data have 12 per cent of cases known to be missing, and this 12 per cent is considerably larger than many sub-groups of students who are claimed to be under-represented. Again, such data are largely useless for tracking small changes in minority sub-groups over time.

For this book, data on applications and admissions to university in the UK, broken down by subject, sex and year, come from the Higher Education Student Agency (HESA) Individualised Student Records (ISRs). Even with this census data, the most common occupational background recorded for students is 'unknown' (unclassified). In 2002/2003, 45 per cent of first year undergraduates were unclassifiable in terms of occupational background according to HESA figures (Gorard et al. 2007). This makes small changes in the occupational background of the student body hard to judge, especially as there is a marked growth in non-response to this item over time, and non-response and SES may be strongly related. One cannot say if apparent changes in student SES are due to changes in participation patterns, or are simply differences in patterns of responding to census items. Similarly, after 'White UK', the second largest ethnic origin group in UK HE is also 'unknown'. This group is so large that it is bigger than all of the other ethnic minority groups combined. Again, this makes judging apparent shifts in the much smaller figures for ethnic minority participation very hard. There is no technical or logical solution to any of the problems mentioned, and others like them. The problems cannot be dealt with by sampling theory derivatives such as confidence intervals or imputation. All analyses need to be clear about the assumptions they make, the definitions they use and the data that are missing.

A further problem for what we know about rates of participation, and their causes, lies in who the relevant evidence is obtained from. This leads to considerable potential for being misled. A clear majority of research in this field is conducted with existing students. Almost every issue of a relevant journal carries papers about the barriers to participating in education based on studies of those who have overcome these barriers (at least to the extent that they have become students). Bizarrely, non-participants are largely excluded from education research as well as from education itself, even where that research claims to be trying to find out why they are excluded. There are perhaps three useful categories to distinguish here. First, there are the people who participate in HE. Second, there are those who are marginal – the 'usual suspects' – who might otherwise have gone to university or who are very like those who did go to university. When places at university are expanded, this is the group who will gain most. Third, there are the genuine non-participants. These are very different from those who may make a reasoned choice not to attend HE. For a start, most non-participants in HE do not have suitable entry qualifications. Participation looks very different for this last group, making any evidence based solely on existing or recent participants potentially very misleading indeed.

Error propagation

Missing data and measurement error of the kind described so far nearly always lead to a bias in the measurements involved. It is not random. People who do not respond to questions accurately (or at all) cannot be assumed to be similar to those who do. Children for whom a school has no prior attainment data, or no knowledge of eligibility for free schools, cannot be assumed to be the same as everyone else. Even human error has been shown to be non-random, in such apparently neutral tasks as entering data into a computer. For a single measure, knowledge and reporting of the likely sources and scale of any bias is part of what it means to analyse it. However, as soon as any computation is done with that measure or whenever it is combined in a calculation with another measure then the initial bias begins to 'propagate'.

Consider measuring the height of a child once and then again two weeks later. Each measurement will be in error to some extent, but the error relative to the height of the child will be small (1cm in 1m perhaps). This level of error is useable for everyday purposes (if the child's height had to be written on an official document or used to buy clothes in their absence). However, if the two measurements are used to calculate how much the child has grown over two weeks, then this involves subtracting one height from a very similar height, so that the child's actual height is all but eliminated in the answer. The maximum errors are also added in each measurement (since it is not known if the error is positive or negative in each measurement). This means that the maximum error in the result is larger in absolute terms than in either initial measurement, and this new larger error applies to a number (the apparent difference in heights) that is also much smaller than either initial measurement. The error relative to the height 'residual' will therefore have grown enormously. Imagine that the child was measured as 1m tall on the first occasion but we accept that this might represent a true height of 1m plus or minus 1cm (99cm to 101cm). Imagine that on the second occasion, the child was measured as 1.01m, which might represent a true height of 1.01m plus or minus 1cm (1m to 1.02m). The child appears to have grown 1cm but the true picture may actually be anything from losing around 1cm (100cm–101cm) in height to gaining 3cm (102cm–99cm). Using these data alone, an analyst can genuinely have no idea whether the child has grown, shrunk or stayed the same. A one per cent error in each initial measurement has propagated to a 200 per cent maximum relative error in the result (200 per cent since the true value could be twice as far from the apparent answer of 1cm as the size of the answer itself). This is so even though heights are quite easy to measure (certainly in comparison to the kinds of measures dealt with in this chapter). The initial measurement error has 'propagated' to such an extent that the answer will be misleading in practice. This is a simple example of what goes on all of the time in calculations, usually unconsidered and therefore undetected.

Conclusion

This chapter has described the major sources of existing data used in this book, and the kinds of variables and concepts these involve. Perhaps more importantly, it has outlined some of the unavoidable but serious limitations of any analysis using these data. Unless the analytical compromises necessary are clearly reported, there is a danger that debates about what is happening in overcoming disadvantage will be misinterpreted by commentators as being about issues of substance, whereas they are, in reality, merely about differences in making analytical decisions. Awareness of error propagation is a good example of why this book justifiably yields different answers to some commentators, even where they may be using the same datasets.

Chapter 3

The quality of available evidence

Introduction

This is the second of the two chapters that outline the evidence base for the remainder of this book. This chapter explains why the findings are original and different to what other commentators often merely assume to be true. The first part of the chapter concerns several systematic reviews of prior evidence that form the basis for much of the subsequent chapters. It outlines how material was sought, assessed and synthesised. In general, previous work has been classified in terms of the four components of the causal model (Chapter 1). Only work that does not address one of these components was excluded from consideration. This multi-method and multi-scale approach does lead to a few problems however, especially where authors have over-claimed or not provided sufficient description of the evidence for their claims. The second part of this chapter provides a justification, with examples, for excluding some apparently relevant studies from the research syntheses presented in later chapters. The chapter then moves on to the primary and in-depth datasets used in this book, and any specific ways in which such data has been analysed. It is not the purpose of this book to describe the methods involved in detail, and so readers must rely to some extent on the copious references.

Reviews

One of the chief sources for the evidence in this book is a series of rigorous reviews and syntheses of the pre-existing research literature – both published and unpublished. Each review followed a similar approach, differing chiefly in its topic of interest. The reviews concerned:

- the causal link between individual attitudes and educational outcomes such as attainment and participation;
- the causal link between individual behaviour and educational outcomes;
- the causal link between parental attitudes/behaviour and their children's educational outcomes;

- the causal link between teacher qualities or behaviour and their students' educational outcomes;
- interventions to improve parental engagement in their children's education;
- interventions to improve literacy and numeracy for disadvantaged students;
- interventions to improve post-compulsory participation for ethnic minority students;
- how to widen participation in higher education for disadvantaged students.

The hunt for evidence involved electronic searches of the main educational, sociological and psychological databases. These included the ASSIA, Australian Education Index, British Education Index, EPPI-Centre database of education research, ERIC, International Bibliography of the Social Sciences, PsycINFO, Social Policy and Practice, Social Science Citation Index and Sociological Abstracts. Following a substantial scoping review to test the sensitivity of the search terms, a standard and very inclusive statement of search terms was used for each database. This statement of search terms was tested, adjusted and retested iteratively to ensure that as little as possible relevant material was missed. A key purpose of the search was to gather unpublished literature as well, so that the possibility of publication bias was reduced. Results were added from hand searches of new journal issues, and from experts in the field.

An example of the full search 'syntax' of the terms and the logical operators, used when looking for evidence on the causal link between attitudes and educational outcomes, was:

> (attainment OR test score* OR school outcome OR qualification OR exam* OR proficiency OR achiev* OR "British Ability Scales" OR "Key Stage" OR NEET OR "sixth form" OR college OR post-16 OR "post-compulsory" OR "postcompulsory") AND (attitud* OR expectation* OR aspiration* OR behaviour* OR intention* OR motivation OR self-efficacy OR locus of control OR "family background" OR "home background" OR SES OR "socio-economic status" OR "socioeconomic status" OR poverty OR disadvantage OR "low income" OR deprivation) AND (child* OR school) AND (caus* OR effect* OR determinant* OR "regression discontinuity" OR "instrumental variables" OR experiment* OR longitudinal OR randomised control* OR controlled trial* OR cohort stud* OR meta-analysis OR "systematic review")

Inevitably, each search initially yielded tens or even hundreds of thousands of separate research reports. These were screened for relevance and duplication by title, and the remaining reports were then double-screened by abstract. To be included in the subsequent synthesis the report had to be comprehensible, relevant to the topic and describe the methods and evidence in reasonable detail. In general, the reviews included only material published in English, from 1997 until early 2012. Some studies prior to this were included where they were deemed well-cited pieces or were directly relevant pioneering work validated by the What Works Clearinghouse. The quality of any research as evidenced by its full report was used to judge how much weight to place on its evidence. The reviewers then synthesised all reports according to the four causal criteria (Chapter 1). This inclusive approach, supported by others such as (Lykins 2012), is based on our earlier reviews, which have found that the major problem with poor quality research lies in its unwarranted conclusions rather than necessarily with the evidence or kind of evidence it presents.

However, it was soon noticeable that it is possible to devise a plausible explanatory mechanism for the effect of almost anything, even where there is no empirical evidence of effect, or even where there is good evidence of no effect. This suggests that the theorised mechanism is the least important part of any causal model, and so this is given less emphasis in the following chapters. If it is clear that altering students' attitudes works to improve attainment with no damaging unintended consequences and at reasonable cost, then it matters less if the mechanism is not understood. On the other hand, even the most convincing explanation is of little consequence if student attitude has no discernible or beneficial effect on educational outcomes. Evidence for all three of the other elements – association, sequence and intervention – must be present in order to be confident that any relationship is causal. Very few studies reported effect sizes, making meta-analysis and consideration of cost-effectiveness impossible (Fritz & Morris 2012).

For each review there will be studies that have been missed by the search. These only matter if their inclusion would have substantially altered the conclusions based on the hundreds of thousands of studies that were used. A more concerning issue is that there may be studies or commercial evaluations of learning artefacts missed because they have no publicly available or online reports. These are perhaps less likely to be positive evaluations than negative or neutral ones. There are also well-known problems such as the so-called 'Hawthorne' effect, and higher effect sizes encountered in research with training, expertise, resource and enthusiasm than in roll out of the same interventions. Given these, readers should assume that each review paints a somewhat more optimistic picture than full disclosure would reveal. For further details of each review see Gorard et al. (2012a), Gorard and See (2012) and See et al. (2012).

Problems with prior studies

Conducting wide-ranging reviews of the evidence from prior research involves reading and rating the quality of a very large number of research reports, books, papers, theses and chapters. On each occasion, and whatever the topic, the same initial observations arise. A large proportion of such reports are not really research at all. Occasionally they offer welcome and original thoughts or present an innovative approach to studying an area, but mostly they serve no real purpose other than to fill the journals. Of the remainder, a large proportion of those that seem to present research are actually incomprehensible. It is always astonishing that so many people seem to want to make their research public through publication but cannot explain to others what the research is. Common problems include having no research questions, no description of methods, no presentation of the evidence and no reference to where any of these could be found. There is often no sense at all that the author wants a wide readership. In synthesising evidence it is not safe to do so solely on the basis of what authors claim. Like the first category of non-research, all incomprehensible work has to be ignored. It is, therefore, a waste of money for those who funded it, and a waste of time for those who wrote, published or read it.

Only a minority of reports actually describe research, and in such a way that the reader can begin to make judgements of quality and rigour. Even of this remaining fraction, the majority can clearly be seen as flawed. This means that research that makes a genuine and transparent attempt to answer a clear question must be treasured rather more than it is at present. Such work will not be perfect and is bound to have to make compromises in the real-life world of empirical data gathering and analysis. However, it is often recognisable because it explains its limitations rather than ignoring them or obfuscating. Several such studies are reported in the following chapters of this book. In this chapter, however, the focus is on studies in the previous category; these are among the best because they are relatively clear but they are worse than useless because where they have had impact they have misled their readers.

One of the most noticeable themes from conducting a series of research syntheses is how frequently research reports use strong causal terms to describe their findings, without any apparent justification. Abbot (1998, p.149) complained that 'an unthinking causalism today pervades our journals', because correlation, pattern or even opinion was too often described in strong causal terms. In fact, it seems that causal claims are increasing in research reports, even as the number of studies designed to uncover causes is declining (Robinson et al. 2007). A major problem is authors mis-describing correlations as causal, through forgetting that statistical modelling, including multi-level modelling, structural equation modelling and path analyses merely find sophisticated correlations. They are not a test of causation (Shadish et al. 2002). Yet, it is quite common for studies to present coefficients in regression models as effects and the explanatory variables as straightforward causes. A regression coefficient may be a clue to a cause, but could only be definitively declared a cause if the other elements of a causal model were also present, or in the unrealistic situation of a Granger 'universe of information'. There will always be possible confounds and missing variables. Perhaps because of the traditions of different relevant disciplines such as psychology and sociology, a lot of research considers variables in isolation rather than in concert (Newton 2010).

The red herring of sampling theory

The majority of datasets in studies uncovered by the reviews, and all of the datasets used in this book, are not based on random sampling. Population data, or incomplete, convenience or targeted samples are not random in nature. Therefore, the techniques derived from random sampling theory, such as significance tests and confidence intervals, are irrelevant to them. To use such techniques in error can be very misleading, and usually means that the far more important issues of bias, measurement error and missing data are ignored by analysts (Gorard 2013). This is what the reviews showed again. They encountered significance tests with birth cohort studies and other population data, with non-random samples and with samples designed to be random but in fact not so because of very poor response rates or high dropout. Almost all studies then further misused the sampling theory derivatives in the sense that they presented the significance test outcomes as though they could handle measurement error and the other issues above. In fact, of course, such tests only address sampling variation. If sampling variation is ruled out as an explanation of the difference in scores between two groups, the analyst still has to consider all of the other possible explanations before deciding that the result is substantively important. This is a widespread problem, appearing in all areas including the social mobility studies and the self-efficacy studies described below.

Even when used 'correctly', sampling theory derivatives do not provide the analytical answer that most writers falsely believe they do. The procedure for a significance test (or a confidence interval) generates a conditional probability for the measure or difference achieved. This p-value tells us, under strict conditions and assumptions, how often random samples would generate a result at least as extreme as the one being considered. A key assumption for the calculation is that the score is actually no different from zero (so that the divergence from zero is the result of random sampling variation alone). Of course, this conditional probability of the data given the hypothesis is useless in real life and is not what the analysts want (Gorard 2010c). For example, a question facing analysts is whether a difference between two (or more) sets of scores in their sample(s) would also be found in the population from which the sample was taken. Mathematically this is like drawing six red and four blue balls from a bag of 1,000 red and blue balls, and trying to decide from this sample of ten how many red and how many blue balls there are in the bag. This is clearly impossible to judge. A much easier question is – if there were in fact 500 red and 500 blue balls in the bag, how likely is it to draw six red balls in a sample of ten? Here, the number of balls of each colour is known initially, and the calculation is a relatively trivial probability exercise. This kind of calculation is what statisticians actually do with significance tests. If they assume that there is in fact no difference in the population between two sets of scores, it is a simple matter of calculation to work out how likely it is that they will encounter a difference at least as large as the one they found in any random sample, of a given size, from that population. This is fine, if it is known that the scores do not actually differ.

The problem with significance testing arises because analysts do not know the actual distribution for the population, and do not actually want to know the probability they have calculated. They are using the second kind of calculation (about the sample) incorrectly as though it could answer the first kind of question (about the population). Simple logic shows that this is incorrect. A low probability of the difference observed in the sample, given no difference in the population, does not mean that there is a high probability of a difference in the population. In fact, these two things are contradictions of each other. The two probabilities in isolation are not calculable from each other. A low probability for the sample can be associated with a high, middling or low probability for the population, and therefore says almost nothing in isolation.

Statistical modelling, based on regression, factor analysis and ANOVAs, is also usually treated by the analysts encountered in these reviews as a form of extended significance testing. Therefore, these models have the same serious problems as significance tests. They are often used with inappropriate datasets (such as populations), and the result of the test does not warrant what the analyst uses it for. In terms of intrinsic design, analyses such as structural equation modelling, loglinear modelling, multi-level modelling and path analysis are complex forms of correlation or association. They are not tests of causation.

Issues of research design

The reviews also reveal serious deficiencies in the design of much research. A full causal model of any process should consist of a proposed explanatory mechanism, evidence of an association (such as a correlation), evidence of the events being in the correct sequence (such as in a cohort study) and evidence that altering the proposed cause under controlled conditions will yield a change in the proposed effect (via a randomised controlled trial or similar). The latter element is nearly always missing in evidence of purported causation (despite practical alternatives such as regression discontinuity designs) and so most studies are presenting their evidence as causal without justification. In truth, we know very little about what actually causes differential outcomes for sub-groups of the population. Without randomisation, discontinuity or similar, which will handle any unmeasured variation, if one group has a different outcome to another, we cannot know if subsequent differences were already inherent between the groups. Few researchers are seriously trying to find out.

An extended example

All three problems – causalism, misuse of p-values, and inappropriate design – are present in an example of an influential study of the social cognitive theory of academic self-motivation (Zimmerman et al. 1992). The paper makes strong causal claims from the outset:

> The *causal* role of students' self-efficacy beliefs ... in self-motivated academic attainment was studied ... 'Students' beliefs in their efficacy for self-regulated learning *affected* their perceived self-efficacy for academic achievement, which in turn *influenced* the academic goals they set for themselves and their final academic achievement.
>
> (p.663, emphasis added)

The study used five teachers in two US high schools, and selected one class from each, for a total of 102 students (with 12 per cent refusal). It is clear that the randomisation only occurred at the class level, which is therefore the only level at which it makes sense to conduct sampling theory-based calculations of probability. Five cases are not sufficient to generalise from. When Zimmerman et al. (1992) quote p-values and significance levels based on calculations for individual students they have made a serious error. The students completed self-efficacy scales for self-regulated learning and academic achievement. Parents, teachers and students also provided data on student grades.

The design is a snapshot cross-section with no comparator group, no intervention and no pre-established sub-groups. All of the analysis that follows in their paper is based merely on correlations. This is not a design for testing causation, and there is no justification for the authors' strong causal claims. The authors mis-represent the difference between correlations and causal tests. They are not alone in either error (concerning p-values and correlations), and the paper is discussed here precisely because it is among the best of its kind, and because the concept of self-efficacy developed by the authors has had considerable and wide impact. These problems do not make the study itself worthless. If the authors had described their findings correctly as associations, then speculated about a causal structure and had not used significance as a criterion for any judgement, then the paper would have been ignored here.

The correlation between student grade goals and their final grades was 0.52 (Zimmerman et al. 1992, p.670). This is not evidence of a causal link moving from expectation to realisation since the link could be the reverse (interim grades giving a reasonable clue as to what to expect) or both could be linked by a third factor. The correlation between prior and final grades was 0.23, which is remarkably small for a grade in the same subject over one year. This low correlation may reveal something about the idiosyncrasy of assessments in social studies, which could then undermine the whole thesis of the paper. The low correlation is rather convenient for the researchers' own theory because if little variance is 'explained' by prior attainment there is a larger residual to be attributed to measures of self-efficacy and grade goals. It would have been interesting to compare the findings for a subject such as maths with a far higher prior/post correlation. Small correlations of the kind presented in this paper are easy to achieve even with meaningless data (Gorard 2008b).

It is hard to envisage how this unpromising material could be converted into evidence that students' 'beliefs in their efficacy for self-regulated learning influenced ... their final academic achievement' (p.663). The main culprit is apparently path analysis – a technique for modelling directed dependencies between variables and so describing possible causal links. Path analysis is widely mistaken for a test of causation. It is not. It is simply a presentation, if a causal model is assumed, of the strengths of the links between variables. It is correlation again. Zimmerman et al. (1992, p.670) say:

> Nor was the direct path between prior grade and final grade in social studies significant when the impact of self-motivation factors was controlled statistically.

What this means is that in the model presented in their paper, they simply assumed that the grade goals and self-efficacy measures have to be controlled for. Unsurprisingly, they find that when they make that assumption it weakens the link between prior and final grades. However, this could be true of any measure that can take up the slack. What Zimmerman et al. (1992) have done here is to assume in their model from the outset precisely that which a skim reader might imagine from the abstract that they set out to test – whether self-efficacy is actually an intermediary that needs to be controlled for.

This was a highly-cited paper in a top-ranked peer-reviewed journal by well-known and successful authors from some of the top universities in the world. Some time and space has been devoted to this example, explaining a range of common errors – such as misuse of sampling theory and significance, confusion between association and causation and the mistaken belief that correlation methods such as path analysis can somehow compensate for research design when testing for causation. This is done to show readers that these errors are commonplace.

The crisis account

Unfortunately for rational analysis, the distressing and unfair situation outlined in Chapter 1 is made confusing by some, perhaps well-meaning, commentators who exaggerate the problem to such an extent that they refuse to acknowledge when things get better. Such a stance is absurd because it does not discriminate between policies and practices that might work to reduce the poverty gradient and those that clearly fail or even make it worse. It also means money that could be used to help is being wasted by researchers and research users trying to understand why some things are getting worse when they are not. Such a stance is therefore unethical and unhelpful to those who need help.

Such erroneous accounts are best exemplified by the huge national impact in the UK of a study reported by Blanden et al. (2005). The study purportedly shows that social mobility in Britain is poor and worsening over time, making mobility increasingly difficult for people from poorer backgrounds. The study forms the basis for OECD accounts of social mobility in the UK, and underlies election policy for all parties (Interim Report 2012). This non-existent problem has been a priority for successive administrations. Policy-makers are focusing on solving this worsening social mobility issue when there is no such issue to solve. They have misunderstood the ideas and the evidence (Payne 2012). The crisis has even been accepted as valid by the ESRC – the chief funding body for social science research in the UK. The 2012 ESRC Evidence Briefing on Social Mobility and Education repeats the high intergenerational correlation for UK in terms of education, income and class. It even suggests solutions such as converting community schools to academies to create 'a significant improvement in their student intake and a significant improvement in student performance', and that aspirations, attitudes and behaviours of parents and children 'have an important part to play in explaining why poor children typically do worse at school'. As this book shows, both of these claims are unjustified, as are the claims of the study at the heart of this crisis account.

The Blanden et al. (2005) study was wrong in both of its major claims (Gorard 2008c). Their data, used properly, actually show a high level of income mobility in Britain, about the same for equivalent years in Norway and other Scandinavian countries. The study showed that when considering the earned income of sons, and so ignoring all females and anyone on benefits, around nine people, or 0.004 per cent of the total cohort of 17,000 neonates born in 1958, were more mobile than their peers born in 1970. However, nine out of 17,000 cases is probably not even worth mentioning, and surely not enough to base national policy on. I can see no reason why anyone who actually looks at the evidence would be persuaded by Blanden et al. (2005). Yet all main political parties, and some uninformed commentators, now accept this poor worsening mobility as fact, and use that fact to justify expensive public policies. This is typical of the crisis approach to stratification research. It is, apparently, much more appealing to imagine that things are getting worse.

Elsewhere, there have been claims that the attainment gap between girls and boys, or between ethnic groups, has worsened (Speed 1998, Gillborn & Youdell 2000). This has not happened (Gorard et al. 2001). Some of these authors are even on record as saying that if they have evidence of anything getting better they will suppress it. They prefer bad news, even if it is incorrect. Much of the work in these areas, which includes some of the most prominent, is flawed but so prevalent that it is usually un-remarked upon by peers. Examples include claims about changes over time using only a snapshot of data, other comparative claims made without appropriate comparators, simple misreading of data and misrepresentation of proportions. The invalid conclusions about trends then endanger explanatory work, and the policies and practices intended to help the situation. If we really care about justice in education then we must do better in our education research intended to diagnose problems or to identify plausible solutions. We need to recognise when things are improving, and where there is no evidence or no promise, rather than clinging to cherished or popular beliefs. Otherwise there is no point in having publicly-funded social science.

As shown in Chapter 1 and illustrated in succeeding chapters, educational outcomes are stratified by disadvantage, sometimes to an alarming extent. Recognising where things are getting better in no way denies the existence of this stratification or its importance. Nevertheless, if we take a wider and longer-term view of most educational datasets, the slow and patchy trend in developed countries is towards equity over time (Gorard 2006a). Some reports suggest that students are doing better (more are reaching expected levels) over time in England and Wales, with more gains for schools with high levels of disadvantage (Mattei 2012) and SES differences and achievement gaps equivalent to other countries (Jerrim 2012). Even social mobility in the UK is about average for Europe (Breen 2004), and the majority of people are upwardly mobile and end up in a different class to their origins (Goldthorpe & Jackson 2007). In fact, class inequality in the attainment of qualifications and in post-compulsory participation has been declining in all developed countries for some decades (Ichou & Vallet 2011). These gradual improvements are more likely to be a consequence of wider social and economic changes in the population than a result of changes in education itself (Sullivan et al. 2011). There are, generally, no sudden sustained changes due to policy or practice, of the kind we would expect if investment, legislative changes, new curricula and so on actually made a difference. Education mostly appears to reflect society. It is currently more an epiphenomenon than a determinant of societal justice. Is education condemned to be just a spectator, or can it play a larger role in speeding up progress?

Primary data

A third valuable source of evidence for this book comes from a series of studies conducted by the authors that involved the collection and consideration of new evidence. As with all primary evidence, its disadvantage compared to rigorous reviews and secondary data is that it is based on samples with the possibility of sampling variation, bias and non-response. However, such evidence can provide greater depth, and it allows students and teachers themselves to express opinions and report experiences relevant to overcoming disadvantage in education. This section also provides an outline of the analyses involved in handling such datasets described, and where these analyses are unusual or not obvious from the context. None of the datasets are based on random samples, and so the issue of using significance tests, confidence intervals and the like does not even arise (as outlined previously). In general, numeric data is presented descriptively using graphs or tables, and in-depth data is combined via standard coding methods, using themes as illustrated in the text.

One key source of information for this book, including evidence on students' views of their teachers' competence, is a large-scale national study for the

Qualifications and Curriculum Authority (QCA) intended to establish a baseline picture for the 14–19 curriculum reforms in England (Gorard & See 2011). This involved a systematic sample of 52 educational settings catering for 14 to 19-year-olds in England, selected to represent all regions of England, the diversity of institutions and provision and the range of size and performance. Each case (or school) provided organisational strategic plans, achievement, retention and progression data, prospectus, policies and information on advice and guidance, staff numbers/structure and curriculum range. There was a survey of all Year 11 (2,700) and any Year 12 (2,200) students in each centre and all full-time staff, plus interviews with the management, governors, parents, local employers, a partner organisation, young people disengaged from education or with learning difficulties and Year 11 learners. In total there were 798 student and 295 adult interviews.

The analysis focuses on a survey variable based on whether or not students agree that they 'enjoy school'. This is treated as the dependent variable in a binary logistic regression analysis. Potential explanatory variables are entered in stages: first the individual student background characteristics such as sex, then the school-level characteristics such as curriculum offer and staff responses, and finally the individual student responses to other survey items. This represents a kind of biographical order from birth to current experiences at school. The base level for the outcome simply reflects the proportion of positive responses. It is from the base level that the explanatory variables can be used to create a better explanation of student outcomes. Thus, the variation explained at each stage is:

(Percentage predicted correctly-(100-base))/(100-base)

At each stage, new variables are entered into the model, and then removed in backward stepwise fashion according to their 'effect' size. Thus, some variables are not used in the model, as they contribute nothing to the outcome. Each explanatory variable that is retained has a calculated coefficient that gives an idea of its relative importance to the model. The coefficient is like an odds for one category compared to another (so that 0.5 for sex might mean that males were only half as likely *ceteris paribus* to have the specified outcome). Alternatively, the coefficient for a real number variable is a multiplier (so that 0.9 for school-level FSM might mean that the specified outcome is only 0.9 times as likely for every percentage of the school intake eligible for free school meals). The precise figures are not important here, but their relative importance and direction are important clues to the determinants of student enjoyment at school.

A large study on the wider outcomes of schooling and the importance of student–teacher interactions comes from a series of projects in six EU countries plus Japan, funded by the EU Socrates Programme. This included a survey of nearly 20,000 students across all countries, based on a systematic sample of schools (Gorard & Smith 2010). Some young people, especially in institutions for students educated 'otherwise', were given an abbreviated version of the questionnaire to complete, some had questions read and their answers written for them and some took part as though it were a structured interview. These differences were necessary to allow all volunteers to participate as fully as possible. The instrument addressed the 'amount' and type of injustice students reported experiencing since the beginning of the school year, and the perpetrators of any injustice. It presented vignettes on hypothetical situations in school, providing the possibility of comparing students' actual experiences of fairness with their ideal model of a fair school. It looked at the potential outcomes of school experience, such as aspirations, and at external factors such as the students' home background, parental occupation and education, treatment by parents and wider political and societal views. The full instrument is available via EGREES (2008).

For this international dataset, logistic regression analysis was used, with dependent variables such as whether respondents were willing for another student with difficulties to receive extra help at their expense or not. As above, each regression model used 'independent' variables to predict which category a student would have chosen, increasing the accuracy from near 50 per cent to perhaps 70 per cent or more (so explaining 40 per cent of the residual variation). Independent variables were entered in four blocks representing student background (such as parental occupation), aggregated background (school-level summaries of parental occupation), parental support (such as whether parents talked to children about schooling) and experience of justice at school (such as whether students were bullied). The stages represent a rough biographical order, and so protect the analysis from the invalid influence of later proxies. As with all such models, they do not represent any kind of definitive test but are a way of filtering the results to see potential patterns, and the possible impact of background, parents, schools, teachers and other students.

The book also uses findings from a series of process evaluations, such as a formative evaluation of a summer school programme in 2012, funded by the Educational Endowment Foundation (Gorard et al. 2012a), and from a number of large randomised controlled trials to assess the effectiveness of several of the literacy catch-up schemes described in Chapter 9 (see also Khan & Gorard 2012).

Conclusion

These two chapters have given some idea of the sources of evidence used in the rest of the book. This evidence is large-scale as well as in-depth. Much of it, including all of the reviews and the study of wider school outcomes, is international in nature. The rest, including the existing official datasets, come from the home countries of the UK, especially England. These datasets are among the best and most complete in the world. There is no reason to imagine that the equivalent datasets in other countries, where they exist, will be any better than those discussed here. The evidence is sifted and presented sceptically, and causal claims are made on the basis of the four-criteria model. The range of evidence marshalled here is remarkable. Each dataset used is good if its limitations are understood and respected. Problems arise only when the data is squeezed too hard, the wrong techniques are used (such as sampling theory with population data) or where analyses propagate errors to such an extent that the results are meaningless. However, as illustrated previously, much prior work in this area is very poor in quality in just these ways. All of these factors are reasons why the findings in this book and the conclusions drawn might be surprising to some readers. It is important to recall that making a genuine attempt to overcome disadvantage in education depends on the quality of evidence. Anyone objecting to rigour or clarity is, in effect, saying that they do not care.

Chapter 4

The role of school intakes

Introduction

Having used the first few chapters to illustrate the strengths and limitations of the evidence available on overcoming disadvantage in education, the book moves on to substantive areas. Each substantive chapter has in its introduction a reminder of the sources of evidence used and a few key references where readers can find further results, and more about methods of data collection and analysis. This book is mostly about interventions and possible interventions that could improve educational outcomes for the most disadvantaged families in any society. State-provided compulsory school for children and young adults is itself, of course, such an intervention. Yet, we really know very little about what good it does.

The next chapter begins to look at educational outcomes such as attainment. This chapter looks at who goes to school with whom. In particular, it considers the extent to which school intakes represent society, and to which children with certain characteristics are clustered in schools with others like themselves. Such clustering is termed 'segregation' here to denote the degree of separation of potentially disadvantaged children from others – whether intentional or not. This is an issue of worldwide interest, based on a range of possible indicators of disadvantage such as parental income and recent immigrant status. Such segregation is relevant to discussions of school choice, the diversity of school provision, how school places are allocated, appeals against placement, the school mix effect, targeting of welfare provision, housing policy and a host of other public policy areas as well as simple social justice. As the next section shows, there is considerable evidence of an association between social segregation and damage to society and individuals. The rest of the chapter presents a selection of findings on social segregation in England over the last 22 years, followed by a discussion of the most feasible causes of segregation. The chapter ends by summarising what could be done, easily, to overcome the problem and the damage it is linked to.

Previous work has tended to focus on only one kind of clustering at a time. In the USA, for example, Black–White segregation of students has been the key issue. Early work in the UK concerned the segregation of students by poverty (Gorard & Fitz 1998a), and this tradition has continued ever since (Coldron et al. 2010), even where researchers use alternative and proxy variables to look at the same issue (Croxford & Paterson 2006). Across Europe, the focus has also often been on social background, especially on the segregation of students living in poverty. In Spain and elsewhere, the mixing of recent immigrants is a concern (Bonal 2012). In the Netherlands, tracking by ability and academic/vocational choices have been identified as key determinants of stratification by family background (Tieben & Wolbers 2010). Gorard et al. (2003) looked at figures for other student characteristics such as special educational needs, first language and ethnic origin. However, the government had only recently started collecting these figures at that stage (first language was only part of the annual school census in England from 2000 onward, for example). In Brazil, Black–White segregation has been considered alongside parental education (Bruel & Bartholo 2012). In the US, more recent work has also considered poverty and linguistic minorities (Jacobs 2013) and separation by attainment (Harris, R. 2012). Poverty adds another dimension to racial segregation (Quillian 2012). Gorard and Cheng (2011) have now proposed, on the basis of differing patterns of change over time for different indicators of disadvantage in England, that these patterns must have different causes. Instead of there being one process of clustering students into specific schools, there are several processes. One seems to affect segregation by poverty, another is related to ethnicity and language and another the distribution of students with special needs (and of course there may be others not covered by this dataset).

Sources of evidence

This chapter is based on an analysis of the official records for all schools in England from 1989 to 2011, considering school intakes in terms of indicators of potential disadvantage (such as living in poverty or having English as a second language). The distribution of these indicators is summarised using indices of segregation (or clustering) and the results are compared to local, regional and national data on the economy, the population and the nature of schools. The approach is described in more detail in Chapter 2.

Why does clustering matter?

This section reminds readers of some of the reasons why it matters who goes to school with whom. The clustering of similar students between schools is an important phenomenon (Logan et al. 2012). It is something that policy-makers should be aware of when planning changes to the system of allocating school places, and something that social scientists need to understand if they are to offer evidence-based advice on how to deal with it. Of course, for someone trying to administer an ameliorative package, having all disadvantaged students in a group could be an advantage (Simpson 2004). It might mean that people had fewer chances for comparison and so reduce resentment of disadvantage by reducing self-awareness (Gordon & Monastiriotis 2006). More feasibly, there may be a minority of students in any system who have severe learning or physical difficulties, and require specialist help and facilities. However, the numbers are relatively small, and it is not clear that such facilities have to be provided in separate special schools, as opposed to being nested within mainstream settings. It is generally accepted that any supposed benefits from the segregation of disadvantaged students are more than outweighed by the problems it leads to.

Damage to attainment

Some studies claim that there is a school mix effect on achievement and participation, and that clustering students with similar backgrounds in schools tends to strengthen social reproduction over generations. This is because students in segregated schools receive poorer instruction, less-qualified teachers, substandard resources/facilities and generally poorer local services than elewhere. Their schools are more likely to be in poor inner city settings (Massey & Fischer 2006) and also tend to have more marginalised students or 'difficult' to teach children. These disadvantages feed on each other and perpetuate the problems. Thus, it seems reasonable to envisage a tiered system of schools emerging, with the already advantaged students tending to benefit from their clustering in specific schools.

However, there is little evidence internationally that the overall levels of attainment of a school have much to do with having students with similar characteristics being clustered within it (Gorard 2006b). Some have argued that students in selective schools (or tracks) may achieve higher levels of academic attainment than those in non-selective schools. They may even do better together than separately (Proud 2010). There are normative models showing how peers apparently become more alike, and 'frog pond' models where some students benefit from having a higher profile than their peers. Others have argued that the net effects of these influences are small or even non-existent (Goldsmith 2011). The system as a whole is no better than zero sum, because these divergent effects largely cancel out (Felouzis & Charmillot 2012). Overall, there is no evidence that selective systems are better (Boliver & Swift 2011). Segregation makes no difference to attainment, but will tend to depress the scores of the already disadvantaged, and so increase the poverty gap in attainment.

The influence of family background or SES on the performance of children within the school is similar in the US, England and Sweden (Burstein et al. 1980), but it differs for children between school systems. This is perhaps due to cross-national differences in the social policies governing education (EGREES 2005). Comprehensive, centralised and equitably funded school systems tend to produce both better outcomes overall and also smaller attainment gaps between rich and poor children. In Finland, for example, there is deemed to be higher equality of educational opportunity than in Germany, where the influence of family SES on test performance in scientific, mathematical and reading literacy is noticeably greater (Domovic & Godler 2005). There is further evidence from international studies such as TIMSS, PISA and PIRLS that countries with lower segregation between schools, more egalitarian systems and low achievement gaps tend to have higher average attainment and also the highest percentage of very skilled students (Alegre & Ferrer 2010, Condron 2011). Quality and equality go together.

The influence of a child's background/SES can be countered by a more integrated and egalitarian school system. An integrated school system tends to lead to a more desirable outcome as students' achievement depends less on their social and cultural background (Schutz et al. 2008). For example, for children who do not speak the language of instruction at school, mixing with and exposure to native speakers is perhaps an effective way to successful learning (Lee & Madyun 2008). An egalitarian school system can help to delay the segregation of students by attainment for as long as possible. Such systems can be seen as fairer in reducing the association between background and outcome (Dupriez & Dumray 2006). A number of large-scale international studies have suggested that equality between schools, rather than segregation and tracking, can narrow the achievement gaps in learning outcomes without reducing overall attainment (Haahr et al. 2005).

Damage to wider society

Beyond issues of attainment, who attends school with whom is strongly linked to longer term and wider societal outcomes. The school mix can be important in helping to enhance a sense of what is just and appropriate for students, and seems to influence how students are treated within each school. Children in disadvantaged schools are more likely to be 'diagnosed' with behavioural difficulties, whereas similar children in other schools may be labelled as having learning disabilities (McCoy et al. 2012). Classes in socially disadvantaged areas offer different patterns of teacher–student interaction, similar to younger classes in more affluent areas. Perhaps quality of interaction is part of the explanation for any differences in outcomes (Harris & Williams 2012), and of the achievement gap between advantaged and disadvantaged (Knowles & Evans 2012).

Students may experience the school system working against them, and feel hopeless or that they have to rely on luck. Those in lower track vocational schools have a higher sense of such futility (Van Houtte & Stevens 2010b). For those below average attainment, attending selective schools appears to negatively affect their academic self-concept, and this is a reasonably long-lasting effect (Marsh et al. 2007). Focusing disadvantage into areas or particular schools may also polarise information about future opportunities, and remove role models, so influencing longer-term outcomes such as levels of aspiration (Burgess et al. 2005, Richardson 2012). Segregation is strongly linked to wider social ills, such as ill-health and delinquency (Clotfelter 2001). People growing up in segregated settings may be less prepared for the academic challenges of subsequent education (Gorard & Rees 2002).

Citizenship education has been introduced in many countries to reduce intolerance towards elements of society deemed different, and to prepare students to be part of a fair and democratic society (DfES 2002). Schools promoting healthy eating cannot be effective unless they integrate healthy eating into meals for students and staff. In the same way, citizenship needs to be adopted as school-wide practice if it is to be taken seriously. Merely having teaching programmes about general principles such as anti-racism or overcoming sectarianism will be quickly seen as hypocritical, if these principles are not evident in the makeup of the school. A segregated intake to a school could matter because it provides a context for creating students' awareness of fairness. In divided societies, seen recently in Central Europe and in Northern Ireland, citizenship education alone can actually generate worse results (Print & Coleman 2003, Smith 2003).

More positively, having majority ethnic group friends is linked to increasing the chances of following academic trajectories that end with university attendance. More comprehensive school systems may protect against the negative effects of segregation for second-generation immigrant students (Baysu & de Valk 2012). School ethnic mix is related to self-esteem (Agirdag et al. 2012). Immigrant students in secondary schools in Flanders with more native students are more likely to plan to finish high school and continue to HE, largely due to differences in SES. In fact, students at schools with high numbers of immigrants may be slightly more aspirational once SES is accounted for (Van Houtte & Stevens 2010b). Mainstream schooling for students with learning difficulties has a positive effect on their aspirations (Casey et al. 2006). Inclusive school systems are generally more socially and racially tolerant.

The level of ethnic, and other, segregation in schools can affect racial attitudes, subsequent social and economic outcomes and patterns of residential segregation (the Belfast model – see Gorard et al. 2003). In general, attitudes to school, and a feeling of belonging to society, are somewhat worse in countries with school systems in which students tend to go to school with others like them (rather than a social mix). International studies suggest that such socially-segregated school systems endanger students' sense of belonging, and give no clear gain in exam scores. Putting disadvantaged students together in selected schools does not work. Equity and excellence are completely compatible, while segregation by race or social class, for example, generally gains nothing for a society and could be considered an affront (Massey & Denton 1998).

Patterns of clustering

The previous section illustrated some of the problems in having a substantial level of social segregation between schools. What do natural levels of, presumably unintended, segregation look like? In England, around one third of children from families living in poverty would have to exchange schools with other students for there to be no clustering by poverty. During the period 1989 to 2011, this proportion started at nearer 40 per cent, declined to just below 30 per cent, rose again to over 35 per cent and is now declining again (Figure 4.1). This is true whether eligibility for or take-up of free school meals is used, and whether the segregation index (G) or dissimilarity index (D) is used (Chapter 2). A number of possible explanations have been proposed for these levels and the changes over time, and these are dealt with in the next section. An unexpected finding is that this pattern of between-school segregation over time is the same for both the primary and secondary school sectors. There is no time lag, such that secondary schools subsequently reflect the school mixes of the primary schools that feed them with new students. Whatever it is that determines the level of between-school segregation in each year, and whatever determines the pattern of change over time, it applies to schools for both age groups of students at the same time. When school intakes become more mixed, as they did in 2011, for example, it happens to approximately the same extent in both sectors. The same applies when school intakes become less mixed by poverty, as they did in 1998.

Turning to another indicator, the pattern of segregation by special educational needs (SEN) is clearly different to that for poverty. In 1989, around 50 per cent of children with a statement of SEN in a mainstream school would have had to exchange schools with other students for there to be no clustering by SEN. Like FSM, segregation by SEN declined substantially, but unlike FSM it continued to decline and then plateaued at around 30 per cent from 2006 onwards (Figure 4.2). This suggests that whatever is causing segregation by SEN is different in some way to what is causing segregation by FSM. Although the levels of

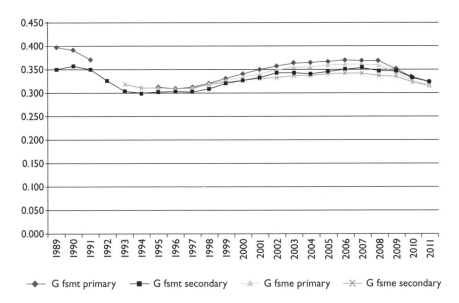

Figure 4.1 Segregation indices for free school meals, all schools, England, 1989–2011.

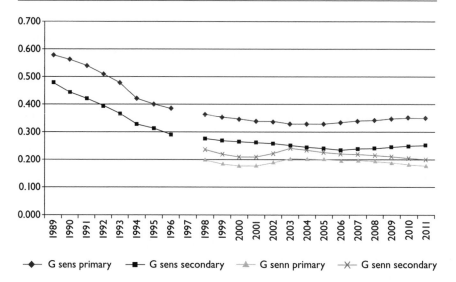

Figure 4.2 Segregation indices for SEN students, all schools, England, 1989–2011.

segregation by SEN are different in primary and secondary schools, the changes over time are remarkably similar. Again, the determinants of the changes over time cannot be sector specific. The figures for special educational needs without statements (SENn) have only been collected nationally since 1998 and show the same patterns over time for primary and secondary, but a slightly different pattern to SENs and of course to FSM as shown in Figure 4.1.

The next two possible indicators of disadvantage in the ASC are ethnicity and language. The between-school segregation of young people for whom English is a second or additional language (ESL) has declined substantially since figures were first collected in 2000 – from 65 per cent to just above 50 per cent. This is a much higher level of segregation than for any other indicator, and it has declined consistently year on year (Figure 4.3). This suggests that whatever is causing it is somewhat different to whatever is causing segregation by FSM and SEN. Like the other indicators discussed so far, the pattern is the same for primary and secondary schools. Figure 4.3 also shows the trend for segregation by non-White (NW) UK ethnic origin. This is the only indicator that shows a different pattern over time plus a completely different level between the two school sectors. There has been a decline of ethnic segregation (for this indicator) in both primary and secondary school sectors since 1997, such that schools show a more mixed ethnic intake overall than they did in the recent past. However, the decline has been much steeper and took place earlier in secondary schools than in primary schools. This delay is not a time lag because it took place among the older school students first. Again, this distinctive pattern needs to be taken into account in any satisfactory causal explanation.

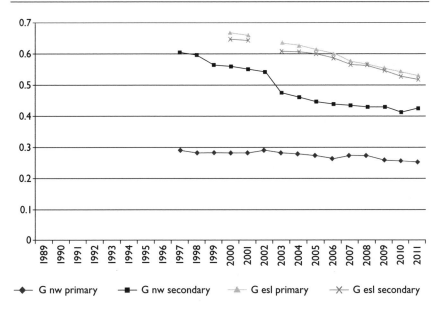

Figure 4.3 Segregation indices for ethnicity and language, all schools, England, 1989–2011.

There at least two kinds of segregation here. The first is for FSM, which shows a different level to ethnicity and language and a completely different trajectory of change over time to all others, including SEN. The other three indicators show a decline over time. However, there could be at least three kinds of segregation, because the pattern for ethnicity is distinctive over time and between school sectors.

Table 4.1 shows the squared correlation coefficients for the six national measures of segregation over time, using the GS index. The same pattern appears with either the GS or D index (Gorard & Cheng 2011). Assuming that the six figures for segregation are linearly related to each other, this R-squared value gives an indication of their variation in common. On this basis, the trend for SENn is not strongly related to any other indicator, not even to SENs. The two estimates of poverty – FSMt and FSMe – are very closely related and are assumed from here on to be equivalent measurements. FSM is also quite strongly related to SENs and segregation by non-White ethnicity, but for both of these the relationship is inverted. The trend in SENs, for example, is apparently nearly the reverse of that by FSM. As might be expected, segregation by ethnicity is quite closely related to English as a second language, but less obviously it is even more strongly related to SENs.

From Table 4.1, the best and most parsimonious estimate might be that there are at least three processes of segregation going on. One is separate for poverty, another for special needs without statements and the other for ethnicity, first language and special needs with statements all together. In fact, this is what principal components analysis also suggests (Gorard & Cheng 2011).

Table 4.1 Percentage variation in common (R-squared) between trends in all six measures of segregation, secondary schools in England

	FSMt	FSMe	SENs	SENn	Non-White	ESL
FSMt	1	94	90	26	79	67
FSMe	94	1	94	30	79	37
SENs	90	94	1	29	94	67
SENn	26	30	29	1	0	0
Non-White	79	79	94	0	1	85
ESL	67	37	67	0	85	1

Determinants

The reason it matters what the patterns of segregation are and how many there are is because this can help to uncover the causes of segregation. Given the damage caused to the educationally-disadvantaged by high levels of segregation, knowing what produces segregation is important in overcoming it. A range of possible causes for segregation have been proposed in the policy and research literature, and this section starts by examining each type in the context of the evidence above. In England currently, between 25 per cent and 50 per cent of students would have to exchange schools for there to be no clustering of similar students. The level varies from students with special needs not statemented – the lowest – to students having English as a second language – the highest. There are a number of reasons why this clustering exists (Gorard et al. 2003). Under Meehl's (1967) conjecture, we should not expect perfect distribution of student characteristics across a real-life school system even where there is no systematic bias. This is partly because students are indivisible. For example, a system with only one minority characteristic student is constrained to have only one school with any students having that characteristic. However, it is important to note that this natural level of segregation is not necessarily random in nature, and that it appears equally in primary schools that are generally quite small and in secondary schools that are much larger. Therefore, commentators such as Leckie et al. (2012) who want to treat the underlying segregation as a random sampling issue exacerbated by the volatility of small numbers are wrong on two counts. We do not need the complexity of analysis that they propose.

School types

The existing research literature suggests diversity of school types as one of the chief causes of socio-economic segregation between schools (Lindborn 2010). It has been claimed that the existence of an independent or private sector in schooling increases segregation, even in state-funded schools. In most developed countries, the need to pay for private schooling means that the intake to these schools is heavily stratified by income. However, private schools in many countries take only a minority of students – such as one to two per cent in Scotland and Wales. This, coupled with the fact that most private school users will not be eligible for benefits such as free school meals, means that the existence of a private sector alone cannot explain the levels of segregation in the state sector. In England, for example, around six per cent of the school population are in fee-paying schools. This figure changed little in the period 1989 to 2011 and showed no correlation at all with the levels of segregation portrayed in Figures 4.1 to 4.3.

It is more usually diversity of schooling within the state-funded sector that is identified as a cause of segregation therein. For example, where schools are selective by ability or attainment, then the system tends also to be segregated by SES, because of the correlation between SES and attainment. Dutch education is tracked at secondary school level, with children allocated to academic and vocational tracks on the basis of prior attainment at a relatively early age. This means that the system is then stratified by family background (Tieben & Wolbers 2010). Students can change tracks later depending upon results. Low-achieving high-status students also tend to prefer grade retention (waiting a year) to choosing a lower prestige track, such as vocational (Kloosterman & de Graaf 2010). This will all tend to worsen stratification. Wherever there is selection by ability, the same is true – whether tracking in Austria or Germany (Schneider & Tieben 2011), or the remaining grammar schools in England (Harris, R. 2012). In the UK, regions and local areas that retain selection to grammar schools have higher levels of student segregation by poverty than areas using non-selective systems.

Religious schools have much the same association, perhaps because religious parents tend to be better educated and have higher incomes than the average for their neighbourhoods (Allen & West 2011). Thus, the student intake to faith-based schools has a higher social background. Church schools in England tend to have a greater proportion of middle class students than present in the local population (Shepherd & Rogers 2012). Faith schools may also encourage racial or ethnic segregation, again because of the correlation between some faiths and ethnic origin. In fact, any alternative type of school can influence the level of segregation. The Magnet schools in the US can have the same racial composition as local regular public schools (Davis 2012), but the Charter schools may be intensifying the isolation of disadvantaged students in other schools serving areas of high disadvantage (Ni 2011). This is a key point. Any new type of school can affect not only its own intake but the nature of the intake to schools around it.

Having a partly 'selective' secondary system in England can help explain why there is social segregation between schools, but it does not explain any of the longer-term trends such as those in Figures 4.1 to 4.3 for England. During the period covered, a small number of LEAs retained grammar schools, which are selective. This division by purported ability also tends to divide students in other ways, such as by poverty and special educational needs. However, the number of such LEAs and grammar schools has not changed significantly, and anyway, these are only secondary schools. Similarly, the introduction of new school types, such as Academies or Specialist Schools in England, or the extension of faith schools beyond Anglican, Catholic and Jewish, does not fit as an explanation for changes over time. This is because the numbers involved are still relatively small, and the changes are too recent for some of the abrupt annual differences in segregation. Most tellingly, until very recently these changes took place almost exclusively in the secondary sector. They cannot be the reason why the primary sector segregation changed in the same way at the same time.

Another possible culprit is differences between schools in terms of their age ranges. Most notably, schools catering for 11 to 16-year-olds are generally associated with lower levels of post-16 participation by their students than schools catering for those aged 11 to 18, even though both types of schools are often in the same authorities. However, while an important point for patterns of later participation (Chapter 8), this post-secondary phenomenon cannot explain segregation in primary schools for the same reasons as those just discussed.

Admission regulations

Countries with selective school systems, whether by academic ability, ability to pay or religious belief, have the most clustered schools in terms of test scores and various measures of socio-economic status including parental qualification, parental education and occupation. For example, countries such as Germany with a system of allocating school places by ability have much higher segregation of rich and poor students between schools than countries such as Finland, which have no such selection by ability. Overall, the Scandinavian countries of Sweden, Finland and Denmark show less clustering on most indicators of student disadvantage, while Germany, Greece and Belgium show the most. Unsurprisingly, policies for allocating school places seem to make a difference to school intakes (Eurydice 2007). Comprehensive systems of schools based on parental preference rather than selection or geographical criteria such as zoning tend to produce narrower social differences in both intake and outcomes. Countries such as New Zealand that have experimented with allocating places at popular schools via a lottery have experienced sudden drops in social segregation (Gorard & Fitz 1998b). Therefore, there are some indications that how places are allocated at schools can influence levels of social segregation.

In England, the unintended 'natural' low level of segregation will be exacerbated by the existence of bureaucratic boundaries making it harder for students to be educated in adjacent local education authority (LEA) schools. This segregation will be further worsened by any policy that links strict area of residence to rules for allocating school places. A key element of school place allocation is the order in which schools or local authorities apply over-subscription criteria to parental choices. If distances to school or catchment areas are used to decide the most contested places then schools will more closely represent the cost and quality of local housing, and in turn the cost of housing will be affected by the perceived popularity of the schools.

However, a sharp change in segregation, such as occurred in 2003 for non-White UK students, really needs an explanation relying on another change in society, that is one-off in nature. In England there have been two important kinds of change over the period covered by Figures 4.1 to 4.3. The rules for allocating school places have been made fairer, and the methods for enforcing adherence to the law have been made clearer and stronger. Places are now allocated in all schools at the same time, some processes such as interviews with parents about their religiosity have gone and there is an Office of the Schools Adjudicator, which exists to sort out disputes and complaints. These changes to the School Admission Code in 2003 and 2007 were well meaning, and may have had some beneficial impacts (Allen et al. 2012). Local authorities appear to be becoming more uniform and transparent in their admissions processes (Rudd et al. 2010). However, the second change has been a rapid increase in the number of schools that are independent of local authority control, and act as their own admissions authorities (West et al. 2011). Some of these schools use selective admissions criteria, including a small growth in selection by aptitude. More problematically, some schools request information on their supplementary admissions forms that is prohibited and unrelated to the admissions criteria – such as parental background, birth place and criminal convictions. One media report suggested that 70 per cent of new Academies fail to follow their own rules on admission procedures (Exley 2011).

Plausible as this sounds as a determinant of changes in school intakes, it is noticeable that there is no consistent, abrupt or delayed change in the patterns of segregation following changes in the legislation on school admissions in 2003 and in 2007 (Figures 4.1 to 4.3). Whatever difference these changes in policy made, they seem marginal in comparison to the other determinants of segregation. This may be because the new procedures were implemented slowly with some schools still apparently not quite following the new rules. Alternatively, it may be because such changes in policy generally make little discernible difference (Gorard 2006a).

Another explanation is provided by the number of schools. In general, as the number of secondary schools in England increases, the segregation by poverty increases as well (correlation of +0.86). This confirms the pattern from a previous decade (Gorard et al. 2003). At that stage, schools were being closed overall and this appeared to re-distribute existing students between the remaining schools more fairly (perhaps because schools with intakes that had high levels of poverty were more likely to close). There is some evidence that a similar situation is happening again. There has been a big rise in school closures from 2007 to 2009 (Barker 2010), with more than 1,300 primary and secondary schools closed in England since 1999. In the last two years, segregation by poverty has reversed and started to fall again. This is a more plausible explanation than those above, because if the cause is economic in nature it is capable of hitting both primary and secondary schools at the same time. However, if it is due to changes in expected numbers of pupils, then this explanation would not work, because planning in primary schools would have to precede that in secondary schools.

Inclusion

There is also an on-going policy of integrating children with special educational needs in mainstream schooling in England, and a parallel increase in the number of children diagnosed as having a special educational need of any kind (Tomlinson 2012). The latter is partly a consequence of an increased range of identified needs and actions (Chapter 2), and partly a consequence of more families seeking recognition of disabilities. The biggest growth has been in non-visible disabilities such as dyslexia (Gorard et al. 2007). For example, in 1996, 394,146 students (13 per cent) were reported to have a special educational need. By 2006, 9.1 per cent of all students were classified as SEN without statements and a further eight per cent had statements. By 2009, 13.5 per cent had SEN without statements and 10.8 per cent with (Maddern 2010).

Inclusion has involved closing special schools and seeking to integrate children with more serious and perhaps more visible disabilities in mainstream school settings. This on-going inclusion of students with statements of special needs in mainstream schools coupled with greater sensitivity in spotting special educational needs has increased the number of SENs students in many schools. It appears also to have had the effect of spreading them more evenly between schools. The correlation between the number of SENs students in the system and their level of segregation in any year is –0.94. This is capable of explaining, by itself, the vast majority of change over time for this indicator. The equivalent correlation for SENn students is also substantial, at –0.90. To a great extent, we need look no further for an explanation (if the correlation has a causal link it cannot be in the reverse direction). The picture in Figure 4.2 is of growth of SEN students in mainstream schooling leading to their more even spread between schools. This deals with the changes over time. Of course, underlying segregation is still running at somewhere between 20 per cent and 35 per cent, and this needs explaining and reducing further.

In fact, the changes in segregation for any indicator of potential disadvantage are quite strongly correlated to changes in the level of that indicator in the state-funded school system as a whole. This is because, generally, the indicators have grown in frequency while their dispersal across schools has also grown (creating lower levels of calculated segregation). The different trends in segregation can be largely explained by different trends in the prevalence of each indicator of disadvantage. This is not an issue of compositional variance in the index involved because the unique advantage of GS is its strong compositional invariance (Gorard & Taylor 2002), and anyway, the same pattern appears also with the Dissimilarity Index (Gorard 2009a).

The same kind of explanation certainly holds for changes in segregation for students reported as being non-White UK in origin. As their number has increased in England over time, they are more evenly spread between schools. The correlation is –0.97 between changes in segregation and the percentage of students reporting non-White ethnicity. This may be partly a historical increase in in-migration, but it may also be due to increased sensitivity in the census about the definitions of ethnic minority categories (with many more sub-categories appearing over time, especially for those students originally deemed 'White'). It could be a growth in reporting as well as a growth in 'reality'. The same applies to students with English as a second language. The percentage of ESL students and their segregation between schools correlates at –0.99. As their number has grown, for both reasons, from 259,947 (eight per cent) in 2001 to 386,575 (12 per cent) in 2009 they have become more evenly spread across the system as a whole. Again, we need look no further for an explanation of most of the changes over time for either of these indicators. However, we still need to understand why there is a stubborn underlying level of 25 per cent segregation or more.

Parental preferences

Some writers claim that allowing parents to express a preference for their child's school is a major determinant of the level of SES segregation, and most claim that segregation rises as such rights are passed to parents. Some commentators have argued that increased segregation is an inevitable outcome of parental choice, and some have argued the opposite, or even that the problem lies in the ability of schools to turn away applicants once a planned admission number is reached. When schools are over-subscribed they might use selection by ability or aptitude, proximity of residence, evidence of relevant faith, special educational need or even a lottery to decide on places. Jacobs (2011) reports that market forces produce segregated intakes, even when factors such as free transport, choice advisers and induction programmes are set up to prevent them. Smithers and Robinson (2010) claim that a preference system leads to schools that are more socially selective than grammar schools with explicit selection. In reality, however, the evidence on the link between parental preference and segregation is not clear. The picture is confounded by economic, demographic and other policy changes, and by the many real-life constraints on choice (Harris, R. 2010). In England and Wales, segregation by poverty fell quite dramatically after the strengthening of school choice via the 1998 Education Reform Act (Gorard et al. 2003). Once selection and residential segregation are accounted for, there is no good evidence that parental preferences worsen the situation. The existence of school choice as such cannot explain the variability over time and between indicators shown for England in Figures 4.1 to 4.3. Once changes linked to the prevalence of any indicator have been accounted for, there is very little of the variation to be explained by other possible factors such as parental choice. Despite successive rounds of legislation and case law in the UK, parental choice has mostly been limited by access to schools and by the widespread use of distance or residential catchment criteria to decide on contested places at over-subscribed schools. As far as it is possible to tell, parental choice in itself has not worsened segregation, and may even have reduced it. Either way, the effects are limited and short-term, and dwarfed by structural, economic and geographical factors.

Economy

The situation for FSM is complex, because segregation here has gone in cycles of decline, stasis, growth and then decline again. Nevertheless, at least part of the explanation surely lies in changes in the indicator itself. As the number and percentage of FSM students rose in the period 1996 to 2009, so the extent to which they were clustered in specific schools declined, and vice versa (correlation −0.93). For example, eligibility for free school meals declined from 554,061 in 1996 to 409,389 in 2008, before rising to 438,855 again in 2009. Over the same period, segregation by FSM tended to rise until the last few years. The level of segregation for FSM take-up is correlated with the percentage of FSMt students at −0.80. In order to assess the amount of variation common to both variables it is necessary to square the correlation coefficient (R) to yield an effect size (R^2). Doing so clarifies the situation. The R for FSMt prevalence and segregation is −0.80, giving an R^2 of 0.64 or 64 per cent. This leaves 36 per cent unexplained. As previously reported, this is then partly linked to the economic cycle as measured by GDP (Cheng & Gorard 2010). When the economy is good, segregation tends to be higher, partly perhaps because fewer families live in poverty. When the economy falters, there is more 'equality of poverty' and levels of FSM students, especially those taking the free meals, tend to rise (Gorard et al. 2003).

Figure 4.4 illustrates the long-term trend of segregation (GS on the right-hand axis) against GDP (on the left-hand axis). There is no overall pattern, and this is reflected in a low Pearson R correlation (−0.22) showing a small, if it were linear, relationship between economic growth and lower segregation. However, any pattern could be in three non-linear parts. Segregation tracks GDP at the outset, and is then strongly but inversely related 1992 to 1998, before tracking GDP again from 1999 to 2008.

It is possible to imagine that segregation usually tracks economic conditions (perhaps with a lag of a year or two) such that an increase in poverty, with students becoming eligible for FSM when not so before, leads to a more even spread of FSM students between schools, but not necessarily any actual exchange of students. If so, then the exception is the period 1992 to 1998, in which segregation by poverty reached historically low levels despite a reasonably buoyant economy. This reduction could have been the result of increased school choice, reined in somewhat in the late 1990s, and largely without the ensuing diversification of schools associated with higher levels of segregation since. This potential explanation requires a minimum of two distinct patterns – one based on the economy and one

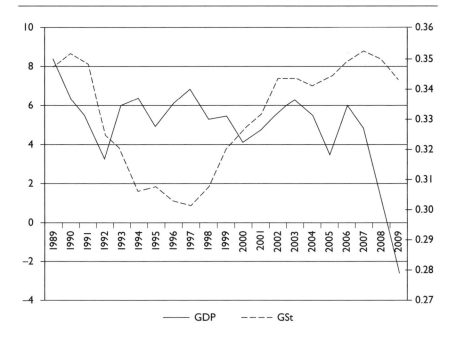

Figure 4.4 Gross Domestic Product UK, and segregation by FSM, 1989–2009

Note: GDP based on current prices seasonally adjusted can be found at http://www.statistics.gov.uk/hub/economy/index.html, accessed 3 March 2010

on education policy changes. It is not as simple as the other explanations offered, and so segregation by FSM seems to have a different set of determinants to segregation by other indicators. The economic explanation has the key advantage that it can affect primary and secondary schools at exactly the same time.

Geography

As demonstrated in Gorard et al. (2003), local levels of segregation are related to the geography of the area. Most obviously perhaps, the nature of the local population has a strong influence on the nature of student intakes to schools. Authorities face pressures due to birth rates, immigration and local development. Some have reported having enough school places but not in the right neighbourhoods (Rudd et al. 2010). This is less of a problem in areas of high population density, which also tend to have better public transport. The limitations of travel mean that where the population differs in different regions of the country, this will also be reflected in the local school intakes. The situation is exacerbated where admissions authorities use catchment areas or residential proximity to decide contested places at popular schools.

Conclusion

The data here are trends and associations, with plausible explanations, but lacking so far the controlled intervention studies usually necessary to establish a full causal model. However, much of the segregation described in this chapter, and evident in other countries often to a greater extent, is intrinsically wrong. In the US since the civil rights movement, or in South Africa since apartheid, it is anathema that Black and White students are segregated between schools (even if inadvertently). Since even those who believe in one of the revealed religions must logically admit that all other religions are wrong, having different faith-based schools funded by the state yet teaching young people these wrong things is both hypocritical and anti-educational. Social, ethnic and economic segregation between schools matters, but not primarily for the sake of test results. For the students at school this is their life. Anything that can be done to reduce institutional isolation by ability, religion, geography, housing quality, isolation or curricular specialisation is also likely to help create higher and fairer levels of post-school participation. Schools, in their structure and organisation, can represent to young people the kind of society that we wish to have, rather than reflecting the inequalities of the society we actually have. Schools can provide 12 years or so of something better, which may then blossom into something even more wonderful when young people leave and expect the same outside schools.

Annual changes in segregation are not caused by anything that could be specific to, or differentiated by, the age range of the schools involved. For example, the changes over time are unlikely to have been caused by the introduction of new types of schools. The new Free Schools in England, set up by local parents and other interested bodies and based on the Swedish model and US Charter schools, were introduced in 2010 and are just getting going. This is too early. Academies, which are similar to both Free and Charter schools but were set up initially as a national intervention to deal with 'failing' schools, have been around since 2002 (Chapter 5). Therefore, Academies could be involved in more recent changes to segregation; however, until very recently they only affected the secondary school sector. There is no conceivable way that their onset could have created an instantaneous and equivalent change in the primary sector.

The annual changes in FSMe or FSMt do not match those for SENs, which in turn are different to those for SENn. This means either that the determinants of between-school segregation are specific to each indicator (i.e. there are at least three processes of segregation in play) or that the same determinant(s) is/are producing a different effect for each indicator. Either characterisation leads to the elimination of further candidates for determinants that would be plausible otherwise. For example, it is unlikely that market forces, as represented by parental preferences for schools, could lead to these very different trajectories for different indicators but the same trajectories for both sectors.

The single biggest factor linked to changes in levels of segregation over time is change in the prevalence of each indicator of disadvantage. Since the changes have had different trajectories, this is reflected in their clustering in school intakes. Indicators such as SEN, NW and EAL have all increased consistently since records began, and their segregation between schools has declined in an almost equal manner. The reason for these changes may be different. SENs has increased in mainstream schools partly as a direct result of inclusion, and less as a result of increased sensitivity in reporting. SENs has simply increased through pressure and diagnosis. NW and EAL have increased, again partly due to increased sensitivity and reporting but mostly due to recent patterns of immigration. FSM portrays a different pattern linked partly to the economy, which helps fix how prevalent FSM is, partly to the tightening up of the regulations for eligibility, and to the patterns for the other indicators since FSM is correlated with SEN and so on. There is even a possibility that in the early period, the decline in FSM segregation was due to freeing up of school choice.

Unfortunately, many of these explanations for annual changes do not include suitably malleable factors that policy-makers and practitioners can act on. Immigration and the health of the economy, for example, are not exactly 'fixed' determinants but they are also not completely under the control of national governments and certainly not of education systems alone. To suggest that policy-makers should seek to ensure the health of the economy would be vacuous. Perhaps just as obviously, including more young people with special needs in mainstream settings rather than special schools reduces their segregation. However, deliberate separation is still the norm in some developed and many developing countries, so the scale of these results should give them a reason for change or at least reconsideration.

For most indicators of disadvantage the fluctuations in segregation over this period are at a smaller scale than the more permanent underlying levels of segregation. There must be somewhat different reasons why the segregation index for any student characteristic is not zero, or even close to zero. Even those indicators with sharp declines are levelling off at around 25 per cent to 30 per cent segregation. To understand more on this requires a consideration of variation in levels of segregation in different regions, authorities and types of schools. To a great extent, the determinants of segregation appear similar now to those reported on the basis of a mixture of large-scale and in-depth evidence presented by Gorard et al. (2003). The factors that have not changed much over the past 22 years in England include the existence of limited overt selection by ability in some areas, and the reasonably high level of faith-based schools. They include patterns of residential segregation, compounded by travel limitations and policies such as catchments and feeder schools. The student body in most schools tends to reflect the nature and cost of local housing more than anything else, and this leads to segregation and ghettos.

The key issue for this book is how to reduce the potential damage caused by socio-economic segregation between schools. Controlling the school mix could be one of the most important educational tasks facing central and local government, even though they probably do not realise this. Partly this is beyond their control, since a key driver of change over time appears to be the number of potentially disadvantaged students identified, which in turn is caused by better diagnosis and record-keeping, inclusion and the economic cycle. Of course, a government can act to encourage or control immigration, and it should act to reduce levels of and numbers in poverty. But to cut into the existing underlying permanent levels of segregation requires more than this. It requires the more radical step of dismantling the apparatus that creates the underlying segregation in the first place. Given that techniques such as changing the way in which school places are allocated have no obvious financial cost, and would have a zero-sum effect on attainment at worst (Chapter 5), there is no reason not to proceed as follows.

A society that wishes to gain all of the proposed advantages of mixed school intakes needs to do more than offer choice. A national school system, intended to have mixed intakes, should be comprehensive in nature, and without curricular specialisation, religious identity and financial or academic selection. The same admissions criteria should apply to every school. Schools should not select by attainment or aptitude. They should not select by student background, or by faith. Government could offer free travel (for those entitled) to any feasible school, not simply to the nearest available. In the short term it could offer incentives to schools taking students from disadvantaged backgrounds (the pupil premium in England), ensure via banding or similar that school intakes represent the variation in the local population and it could decide contested places at popular schools by lottery, not by distance or residence. Such measures would reduce social segregation between schools and slowly reduce the purchase premium on houses near desirable schools, creating a backwash on residential segregation and so a virtuous circle of inclusion and integration.

Chapter 5

The role of schools

Introduction

One of the reasons often used to try and justify the selection of student intakes to schools, or to create systems that divide students into discrete tracks from an early age, is that this is necessary to improve overall performance. Since SES and other student characteristics are correlated with attainment from an early age (Chapter 1), this means that selection must lead to higher social segregation between schools. Chapter 4 has shown that opting for higher segregation yields a considerable risk of damage to societal cohesion and to the well-being of students. So whether selection works, in the sense of improving attainment overall, is a key question for overcoming disadvantage. If it does not, then the risk from increased social segregation is being run for no reason. More generally, it is important to know what schools can do to improve attainment, especially for their most disadvantaged students and those least likely to succeed. This chapter considers the model of school effectiveness currently dominant in research, policy and practice internationally. There is no doubt that academic outcomes from schools are heavily stratified by social and economic background, at least as much as school intakes are. These linked patterns of stratification are repeated in every developed country studied, and for every new cohort of students. This is well-established and well-known. What part can schools play in reducing the impact of early disadvantage? Do schools themselves make these patterns better or worse?

Judging school performance could be useful for other reasons as well. In most developed countries, the majority of schools are publicly funded, and so the custodians of public money want to assess how well that money is being used. Policy-makers will be interested in how well this public service is working. Families might want to use a measure of school quality when making educational choices. Heads and teachers might want feedback on what is working well and what is in need of improvement at their own schools. There are also, of course, a number of differing ways of judging school performance. Schools could be evaluated in terms of financial efficiency, student attendance, student enjoyment of education, future student participation in education, student aspiration, preparation for citizenship and so on (see later chapters). The most common indicator of school success lies in the student scores in tests intended to discover how well students have learnt what is taught in the school.

It is clear that attainment is strongly related to social background from early schooling onwards, and presumably pre-existing it; however, it is not then possible to compare raw differences in attainment over phases of education (Gorard 2008b). If 80 per cent of children attain the expected level at Key Stage 1 in England, and only 70 per cent attain the expected level at Key Stage 2, this does not necessarily mean that the gap between the majority and the 'underachievers' has widened. Neither the expected levels at each Key Stage nor the actual levels of attainment achieved by students are moderated in relation to the other Key Stages. The percentage of young people attaining five GCSEs at age 16, for example, is not comparable to the percentage leaving higher education with a first class degree, or the percentage of the population using a home computer to access learning opportunities online. This difficulty in calibrating differences in attainment over the life course means that there is no solid evidence about whether schools improve, worsen or simply have no impact on this stratification (see Chapter 8).

Another way of tackling the question of changes over time is to look at repeated snapshots of the impact of schools on the patterning of qualification outcomes. Over the past 30 years a series of studies have focused on how much difference any school makes compared to all others (Rutter et al. 1979). School 'effectiveness' researchers accept that raw-scores are not a measure of performance, because most of the variation in school outcomes is due to school intake characteristics. However, they assume that any residual variation in raw-scores, unexplained by student intake, is evidence of a differential school effective (Kyriakides 2008). What is interesting is how dominant this version of school effectiveness has become, so that to question it is interpreted by some writers as the same as suggesting that schools make no difference. This chapter outlines how differential school effectiveness works, describes three major flaws in the approach and looks at the evidence relating to differential effects for schools and types of schools. The chapter ends with a consideration of the implications for overcoming poverty.

Sources of evidence

The evidence presented in this chapter is largely from secondary analyses of official datasets in England. These datasets include the Department of Education Performance Tables, the Annual Schools Census and the National Pupil Database. School performance is looked at in terms of statutory assessments (Key Stage results) and related to prior attainment and the nature of school intakes in terms of indicators of potential disadvantage (as described in Chapter 4). The approach is described in more detail in Chapter 2 and in a series of publications including Gorard (2009b, 2010b) and Gorard et al. (2013).

Judging school performance

Ranking any set of schools by their student scores in formal assessments of learning shows that schools at the high and low ends differ in more than their student assessments. Schools in more expensive areas with more expensive housing, or that select their students, will be more prevalent among the high scores. Schools with high student mobility, in inner-cities, taking high proportions of children living in poverty, will be more prevalent among the low scores. This illustrates that raw-score indicators are not a fair test of school performance. The differences in student outcomes between individual schools, and types and sectors of schools, can be almost entirely explained by the SES and prior attainment differences in their student intakes (Coleman et al. 1982, Gorard 2000, Lubienski & Lubienski 2006). The larger the sample, the better the study, and the more reliable the measures involved, the higher the percentage of raw-score difference between schools that can be explained like this. However, the total variation in scores explained by student intakes will never be exactly 100 per cent (Meehl 1967). So the crucial question for policy is whether the small remainder of variation is error and bias, or whether it is evidence of differential school performance.

For a considerable time now, authors such as Goldstein (2001) have argued that this residual variation is meaningful evidence of a 'school effect', and that it can be illustrated through a valued-added (VA) approach. Goldstein and others have also argued for a long time that value-added results should be used by policy-makers and practitioners to judge the performance of schools (and individual teachers – see Chapter 6). In the value-added approach to judging school performance, schools are judged by the progress that their students make during attendance at the school, not on their absolute levels of attainment. Data on all students in the relevant school population is used to predict as accurately as possible how well each student will score in a subsequent test of attainment. Any difference between the predicted and observed test result is then used as a residual. The averaged residuals for each school are termed the school's 'effects', and are intended to represent the amount by which students in that school progress more or less in comparison to equivalent students in other schools. A school with an average residual of zero is estimated to be 'performing' about as well as can be expected, given its intake. A school with an average above zero is doing better than expected. This judgement should be independent of the raw-score figures, making it fairer than assessment of raw scores. Since this 'school effect' is deemed a characteristic of the school, not its students, it should be reasonably consistent over time where the staff, structures, curriculum, leadership and resources of the school remain similar over time.

In England, and elsewhere, this approach took firm hold in policy and practice, and the results are in widespread use. National figures for all schools are published by the Department for Education as 'School Performance Tables'. Individual school results are used in setting targets, development plans, assisting the school inspectorate OFSTED to judge the quality of schools and by some parents to help select a school for their child. They have even been used to close schools down. The results therefore matter, and the assumption has generally been that the method works well enough to form the basis for such life-changing decisions. Is this really so?

The problems with value-added as an approach

This school effectiveness industry is actually rife with problems, such as widespread abuse of statistical techniques of the kind described in Chapter 3. These include, for example, the use of significance tests and multi-level modelling with a non-random sample with only 66 per cent response (Antoniou 2012). But the problems run much deeper than this.

Dependence on raw scores

Perhaps the biggest single problem with a value-added approach is that it could never do what it was designed for – to be independent of the raw-score results. Because the VA score is based on the difference between prior and subsequent attainment, the variation in VA scores is half derived from the variation in prior attainment scores and half derived from subsequent attainment. This means that the R-squared correlation between prior attainment and the VA for any set of schools will be at least 0.5 (or R of above 0.7). In fact, the observed correlations can be even higher than this (Gorard 2008d, Ready 2012). An example from Gorard (2006c) follows.

Figure 5.1 shows the GCSE results in 2004 for the 124 schools with complete information in York, Leeds, East Riding of Yorkshire and North Yorkshire. The x-axis shows the percentage of students in each school gaining Level 2 (five or more GCSEs or equivalent at grade C or above). The y-axis shows the official Department for Education value-added scores (with 1,000 added so that 1,000 becomes the average score). There is a near-linear relationship, yielding a correlation of +0.96. This means that purported value-added and raw scores are here measuring what is effectively the same thing. Value-added is no more independent of subsequent attainment than prior attainment is (also correlated at +0.96). It is almost entirely predictable from the raw scores. It would, therefore, be much simpler to use the raw-score values than to bother with the computation of 'value-added' figures that tell exactly the same story. However, these raw-score values have already been (rightly) rejected by most commentators as not being a fair indicator of school performance. This means, ironically, that the value-added scores have to be rejected on the same grounds.

Instability over time

A second serious problem with value-added scores is that they are much less stable than raw scores, and schools portray what are apparently dramatic swings

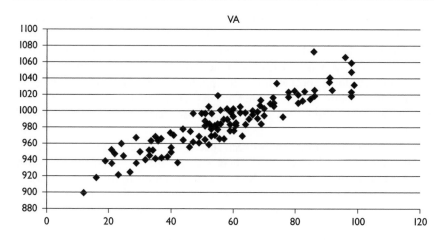

Figure 5.1 The relationship between value-added and absolute attainment, 2004.

Source: DfES School Performance Tables

in effectiveness every year. The fact that these results are not even more unstable may simply be because raw scores are quite stable over time for each school, and VA scores are heavily dependent on these raw-scores.

A number of studies have found VA correlations of only around 0.5 over two successive years for the same schools (Gray et al. 2001, Leckie & Goldstein 2009). All VA is inherently unstable (Kelly & Monczunski 2007). This was confirmed in an analysis of all secondary schools in England over five years by Gorard et al. (2013). Within two years the majority of a school's CVA (Chapter 2) is unrelated to its prior CVA (Table 5.1). Around 75 per cent is attributable to something else. This makes CVA almost entirely useless for practical purposes because it is not a consistent characteristic of schools. CVA could be something that changes in schools very rapidly. In this case, parents cannot rely on using it, when their child is choosing a secondary school at the age of ten, to make predictions about the likely results five or six years hence. Local politicians and others cannot use it to make judgements about the future of schools since the measurement is so ephemeral. Alternatively, and more simply, the CVA scores could be largely not a characteristic of schools at all.

Table 5.1 R-squared for CVA scores over time, England

	2007	*2008*	*2009*	*2010*
2006	0.62	0.26	0.31	0.21

N= 2,897 schools

Note: 1,118 of the total of 4,015 secondary school or college entries on the DfE School Performance website had significant amounts of relevant information missing in at least one year.

Figure 5.2 shows the CVA scores for all 2,897 schools in England with complete CVA information for 2010. It is a cross-plot of CVA score (x-axis) and number of students in the school used to create the CVA score (y-axis). It shows that all of the very large schools have CVA at or near average, and that the most extreme CVA scores are for schools with very few pupils. The correlation between school size and the absolute deviation from average CVA in 2010 is –0.22. This suggests that at least some of the CVA results are a consequence of the volatility of small numbers.

There is a similar correlation between coverage (Chapter 2) and CVA score. In 2010 it was –0.21. This means that there is a tendency for schools with less than 100 per cent of the data for their KS4 students to appear to have more divergent CVA scores. To some extent then low coverage is the same as having fewer students at KS4. Having fewer students leads to volatility, especially towards higher CVA. The schools with the highest reported CVA have data on ten to 20 per cent of their students missing from their coverage. Coverage was as low as 50 per cent in some schools, both in 2006 and 2010. This means that the problem is worse than just having low numbers. If schools only have data on 50 per cent of their students, there is a real danger of considerable selection bias. Most schools could improve their relative position in CVA enormously by omitting the least flattering 50 per cent of their student scores. This may have happened inadvertently if the students who are hardest to trace, most likely to drop out or be excluded, or who take the least traditional qualifications are also likely to be the least flattering for the school CVA score.

An important step in dealing with these issues in the data is to reduce the apparent variation caused by the volatility of small numbers, and by low coverage in some schools. To deal with the coverage problem, and gain an estimate of its likely impact on CVA estimates, the calculation below omitted all schools with less than 95 per cent coverage. This is a fairly tolerant approach, because almost any school could look good in CVA if they could omit their least favourable five per cent of students. The DfE present 95 per cent confidence bounds. The larger the school and/or the larger the deviation in CVA from 1,000, the more likely it is that the CVA measure and both the upper and lower confidence intervals will deviate from 1,000 in the same direction. The DfE are incorrect in using confidence intervals in this way, because there has been no random sampling of schools and so no sampling variation to estimate. Nevertheless, the confidence intervals do take both factors of scale into account. They are presented by DfE, and are used by schools and authorities as a way of judging whether the CVA deviation from 1,000 is 'significant' rather than a result of uncertainty and small numbers. Therefore, the analysis that follows considers only those schools whose entire 95 per cent confidence interval is either above or below 1,000.

The assumptions made here are not strict, and the assessment is based only on the direction of CVA. There is no school that has exactly the same VA score even across two years. The precise model used for VA calculations is always modified using the existing results to make it fit best. This means that the regression

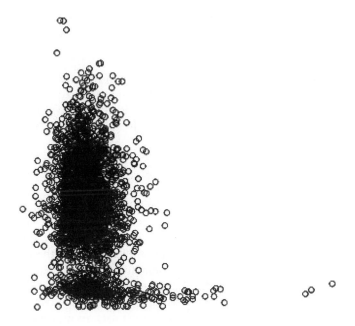

Figure 5.2 Crossplot of CVA measures and the number of students in each school, England, 2010.

coefficient used to adjust for student poverty varies from year to year. This is strange. If prior attainment and student background characteristics make a difference to subsequent attainment, as they appear to, why is this difference not the same every year? In other areas of science, formulae are not adjusted to suit the precise results of each experiment – that would be the cart pulling the horse. Yet, only 203 schools had complete CVA measures for five years, with CVA in any year that was clearly above or below 1,000, and 95 per cent coverage or better in all years. Of these 203, there were exactly 100 schools with CVA above 1,000 for all five years, and 73 below.

If, for the sake of illustration, the CVA measures of the original 2,897 schools meant nothing about school performance then almost exactly half of all schools would have positive CVA each year, because that is how CVA is calculated. If the CVA measure was not really a consistent measure of the school to which it is attached, then in each succeeding year almost exactly half of those with positive scores the previous year would have a positive score again. After two years, around 25 per cent of schools will have had two positive scores, 25 per cent will have had one positive followed by one negative, and so on. Thus, after the five years 2006 to 2010, 1 in 32 schools would be expected to have consistently positive scores each year. This would be 91 out of 2,897. The same number would be expected to have five successive negative CVA scores, yielding a national total of 182 schools with a consistent direction of CVA, even if CVA was not actually a measurement of any school characteristic at all. This is very close to the figure of 173 that was found in practice. Since the use of confidence intervals has not eliminated the very small but high CVA schools, because 95 per cent coverage is not very stringent and because we cannot include in the calculation any school that has no data in any years, this figure of 173 suggests that CVA does indeed mean nothing. There is no evidence that the published CVA scores are a measure of anything securely to do with school themselves at all. How else could these scores arise?

Largely the result of error

All value-added analysis involves finding the difference for all students between their predicted and actual attainment. The difference between any predicted and actual attainment will tend to be insubstantial because the model will be best fit, and the predicted and actual attainment scores will always be of the same order of magnitude. This means that the figure computed for the student value-added score is usually very small, perhaps even negligible, in comparison to the attainment scores from which it is calculated. The results are also heavily dependent on the quality and completeness of the data. As explained above, and in Chapter 2, there will be errors and missing data in every real life VA calculation. This creates a substantial initial source of inaccuracy for any VA calculation, and there is no way of adjusting for this statistically since the data just does not exist. It would be wrong to assume that the missing data was somehow a random subset of the data that does exist.

The VA system used in England from 2006 to 2010 factored student background characteristics into the calculations. This was done in order to improve the quality of the predictions and reduce the size of the residuals for disadvantaged groups of students. This Contextualised Value-Added sounds a sensible and fair innovation. However, it means that more data is needed on each student and this adds considerably to the level of missing data. At least ten per cent of students are missing data every year on each key variable such as whether they are eligible for free school meals, living in care, their ethnicity or additional educational needs. All of these initial errors are compounded by the VA calculation itself to generate a far higher level of error in the residuals that result. The residuals tend to be very small, in comparison to the actual scores; however, because the errors in the actual scores can be negative or positive, when the residuals are created their maximum initial errors are added. The outcome is a larger error component in a much smaller result. The maximum error can, and usually does, dwarf the residual by several orders of magnitude (Gorard 2010b). This makes the estimated result just about meaningless. This is what the figure of 173 above demonstrates.

Summary

There is growing evidence that the value-added method, for all of its appeal, just does not work (Hoyle & Robinson 2003). The sample sizes, especially in primary, are too small to allow analysis of single school performance data (Ridgway & Ridgway 2011). Value-added is presented by advocates as being fair and neutral, but it can have an erroneous impact on the reputations of schools and lives of individuals. It has the potential to damage teacher expectations of some students, and by building in the student context may encourage them to treat inequalities as fixed rather than to help to overcome them (Bradbury 2011). This means that school improvement based on purported school effects does not work either. Again, the research in this area is often very poor, cherry-picking results, ignoring design, lacking comparators. As Coe (2010) ironically points out – it is easy to 'improve' any group of schools. Start with an exceptionally poor year of results (that provides the stimulus for improvement but also encourages regression towards the mean); take on any initiative and put money into it (encouraging a Hawthorne effect); use this initiative to change the student intake towards those individuals likely to score higher anyway; use soft measures such as perceptions and ratings as far as possible; choose the areas of improvement after the initiative so that it is easier to pick ones that show promise and above all avoid a fair test in the form of random allocation or similar comparator (rely solely on before and after, or in extreme cases, just after). Such school improvement work is common, and is generally the epitome of all that is wrong with education research.

Types of schools

A good example with many of these characteristics is the official evaluation of the Academies programme in England. Since there is no evidence that individual schools are differentially effective, in terms of test outcomes at least, it follows that there is no evidence that types of schools are differentially effective. Again the key issue concerns the standard achieved or progress made by equivalent students. Academically or socially selective schools, overtly or unintentionally, will tend to have better raw-score results than comprehensive schools or those schools taking students who have failed the selection. However, this result is caused by the students themselves, not the schools. The same thing applies to all types of schools. Despite this, policy-makers worldwide keep creating new kinds of schools that are very similar to every other kind (i.e. there is no dismantling or radical re-engineering of the concept of schools), claiming success for electoral or other reasons, and then not allowing these schools to be evaluated properly. Several studies based in the US have reported evidence that attainment can be affected by the type of school attended, such as the Promise Academy charter middle school (Dobbie & Fryer 2009), Knowledge is Power Program (KIPP) middle schools (Woodworth et al. 2008, Tuttle et al. 2010) and more general Charter schools (Gleason et al. 2010). A recent example in England is the Academies programme, started by one government in 2000, continued by the next government from 2010 and extended to include 'Free' schools.

The original programme of academies involved schools running at-risk, in special-measures or with particularly poor examination results. Academies were intended to replace schools in areas of high socio-economic disadvantage, with falling intakes, spurned by those local parents able to find an alternative school for their child. The new schools are mostly re-launched versions of one or two existing secondary schools with new buildings, state-of-the-art facilities and changes in leadership. They are independent of local government control, have voluntary or private sector sponsors, are allowed to have a specialist curriculum, have start-up and extra recurrent finance and can select ten per cent of their intake by aptitude. The first three opened in 2002.

The government and the school sponsors reported almost immediate success for these new schools, claiming that they had improved GCSE results dramatically for the first students to take exams since the schools became Academies (BBC 2004). But even superficial consideration of the figures showed that this was false (Gorard 2005). The results were sometimes worse than for the predecessor schools, and the intake to the schools had changed, presumably as a result of their re-badging. Each school now took fewer FSM-eligible children. The transcript of Parliament (in Hansard) records that when the Minister responsible was presented with this simple re-analysis he rejected any short-term indicators of failure even though they had been happy to accept short-term indicators of success. Academy sponsors, the Department for Education in England and government ministers suddenly began to demand that people wait until a whole cohort of students had been through the Academy system.

The Academies that were up and running by 2005/06 took a considerably higher proportion (36 per cent) of children eligible for free school meals (FSM) than the remaining educational institutions in England (13 per cent). This is not surprising, given that they were meant to have been selected as some of the most challenged schools in the most deprived areas. It also goes some way towards explaining the generally lower level of raw-score results in Academies for students aged 16. Over the long term, national school-level results at KS4 and the percentage of students eligible for FSM correlate at around –0.5 (Pearson's r). Schools with more FSM students tend to have a considerably lower percentage of students reaching Level 2 at KS4 (five good GCSEs at grade A* to C, or equivalent, often needed for entry to sixth form).

The 2007 results were the first for the students in the age 15 cohort who almost all joined the three original schools while they were Academies, as opposed to previous cohorts who had the school(s) change around them. The first three Academies opening in 2002 did not at first have higher raw-score results than the schools that they replaced. However, they had reduced their FSM intake, and increased their rate of student exclusions. Given the strong correlation between deprivation of intakes and examination outcomes, these changes in intakes over time and the annual national increase in GCSE scores across the board, we would expect examination outcomes to rise in Academies even if the re-launch had made no difference at all. What all three schools have done, both in absolute terms and relative to their surrounding schools, is to substantially reduce the percentage of students eligible for FSM since becoming Academies (Tables 5.2 to 5.4). Given the objectives of the programme, this was and is a kind of success in stemming one part of the apparent spiral of decline. It does mean, however, that the schools cannot also claim exam success with equivalent students.

As can be seen for all three schools, there were years after becoming Academies in which students achieved worse Level 2 scores than had been seen in the schools they replaced. For example, the score for the predecessor to Unity was 17 per cent in 2001, but 16 per cent in 2005, three years after becoming an Academy. The final column in Tables 5.2 to 5.4 shows that where the figures overlap the situation was worse, if Level 2 requires a C grade or better in both maths and English. This suggests that the shift in the more general Level 2 figures, above and beyond what might be expected by the reduction in FSM, is due to changes in exam entry policy. In order to boost their apparent league table position, many schools at this time began entering students for dual and triple award qualifications (such as IT), deemed to be equivalent to GCSEs, but apparently considerably easier to pass. Academies did this as well as other schools, but were more secretive about their use of 'pseudo' courses, leading to calls for the Freedom of Information

Table 5.2 Intake and outcomes for the Bexley Business Academy, 1997–2011

Year	FSM	Level 2	Level 2 including English and Maths
1997	53	13	–
1998	49	24	–
1999	52	14	–
2000	50	10	–
2001	49	17	–
2002	46	–	–
2003	42	21	15
2004	37	34	13
2005	38	29	15
2006	39	32	17
2007	39	31	19
2008	–	–	29
2009	–	–	40
2010	–	–	42
2011	31	–	52

Table 5.3 Intake and outcomes for the Greig City Academy, 1997–2011

Year	FSM	Level 2	Level 2 including English and Maths
1997	48	14	–
1998	56	11	–
1999	42	15	–
2000	43	25	–
2001	31	30	–
2002	39	–	–
2003	43	35	19
2004	47	26	10
2005	44	54	10
2006	38	59	15
2007	39	65	21
2008	–	–	30
2009	–	–	40
2010	–	–	30
2011	–	–	37

Table 5.4 Intake and outcomes for the Unity Academy, 1997–2011

Year	FSM	Level 2	Level 2 including English and Maths
1997	60	13	–
1998	62	2	–
1999	51	13	–
2000	46	4	–
2001	57	17	–
2002	47	–	–
2003	49	16	7
2004	50	17	7
2005	49	16	6
2006	44	34	14
2007	45	45	12
2008	–	–	18
2009	–	–	23
2010	–	–	28
2011	–	–	25

Act to be extended to force them to answer questions about their exam entry policies (Stewart 2010). Figures such as 65 per cent Level 2 for Greig City Academy in 2007 are likely to be based on these alternative qualifications because there is no equivalent growth of students gaining maths and English. Subsequently, using the new official Level 2 indicator including maths and English, neither Greig City nor Unity seem to have improved much despite a national growth in Level 2 from 48 per cent in 2008 to 59 per cent in 2011. Bexley has done better than them, but not necessarily better than the national trend, and has anyway continued to decrease its FSM intake. Overall, there is no clear evidence from these, or from the newer Academies, that Academies have performed better than the schools they replaced would have done (Gorard 2009b). For what it is worth, it is interesting to note that the 2011 value-added scores for the first three Academies are 991, 996 and 998. All are officially deemed to be performing at (or indeed just below) national average, by the same Department for Education that also claims that these schools are more successful than most others.

To say that struggling Academies are doing no better than their non-Academy peers or predecessors is not to denigrate them, but it does demonstrate that the programme is a waste of time and energy at least in terms of this rather narrow measure of outcomes. Of course, one can argue that the schools have been a success in maintaining numbers and reducing the proportion of disadvantaged students. This is certainly true for two of the first three Academies, which were selected as among the most deprived schools in England. However, the programme now includes Academies that had been private or selective schools and among the least deprived in their areas, so this is no longer a sensible way of assessing success for the programme. There are also opportunity costs. The money involved since 2002 could have been used differently – spent on refurbishing the most deprived schools or used to follow the most deprived students to whichever school they attended. The same is true for all recent new school schemes in England, such as the Specialist schools, and will almost certainly be true for as yet untested schemes such as Free schools and their equivalents worldwide.

Conclusion

The results in this chapter mean that VA models cannot be used as an ethical basis for policy or practice decisions. All of those schools negatively affected by their VA results may have been treated unfairly. Parents should not have been encouraged to choose, nor inspectors to judge, schools on this basis. Whatever it is that VA is scoring, it is so volatile that it would be absurd to encourage parents to use purported 'school effects' to help select a secondary school for an 11 year old.

However, it is important to recall that the evidence does not suggest schools make no difference. Going to school is an important formative experience for young people, for good and ill. The evidence does not even mean that some schools are not more effective than others, with equivalent students. They may be. It merely suggests that traditional school effectiveness approaches based on VA, involving a central zero-sum calculation, are ineffective in picking this difference up. What VA models are mostly picking up instead is at least partly due to variation in the raw-scores (Gorard 2006c), partly due to factors such as low coverage and small numbers (Gorard et al. 2013) and partly a very large propagated error component (Gorard 2010b). Even in England with a centrally-collected annual school census and attainment dataset for all students that is probably unsurpassed in quality in Europe (EGREES 2008), at least 30 per cent of cases are missing, unmatched across linked datasets or erroneous. This level of error in the data is hugely magnified when the value-added analyses focus on the inevitably small differences between predicted and subsequent attainment for each individual. The relative error in the figures propagates from something of the order of 30 per cent to 1,000 per cent or more, making the eventual results completely meaningless. Other countries may have bigger residuals but these will probably have emerged from worse data, with even greater relative errors. Current school effectiveness work is, therefore, as misleading as the crisis of stratification studies discussed in Chapter 3, and in the same way leads to misleading, wasteful and therefore unethical ideas for school improvement.

The school system in England is designed through its funding, its laws about when and how school places are allocated, regulations about teacher development, inspections, national curriculum and standard attainment in key stages, to try and make as little difference between schools as possible. England has built a system of maintained schools that remains loosely comprehensive, and is funded on a per-student basis adjusted for special circumstances. The curriculum is largely similar (the National Curriculum) for ages 5 to 14 at least, taught by nationally-recognised teachers with Qualified Teacher Status, inspected by a national system (OFSTED) and assessed by standardised tests up to Key Stage 3. Education is compulsory for all, and free at the point of delivery. In a very real sense it sounds as though it would not matter much which school a student attends, in terms of qualifications as an outcome. This is rightly so, in a democratic, developed country with an education system like that in England designed to promote equality of opportunity. The quality of education available in a national school system should not depend upon where a student lives. Perhaps what this chapter shows is that in this respect the system is working well.

Policy-makers could and should take pride in and protect such a situation. Politicians could disseminate the truth that in terms of traditional school outcomes it makes little difference which school a student attends. This might reduce the allure of specialisms, selection by aptitude or attainment, faith-based and other needlessly divisive elements for a national school system. It could reduce journey times and the premium on housing near to what are currently considered good schools. This would lead to a decline in socio-economic segregation between schools. Reduced segregation by attainment and by student background has many advantages both for schools and for wider society, as well as becoming a repeating cycle, making schools genuinely comprehensive in intake as well as structure. New school types or schemes for only some are not the way forward. The poverty gap will be made smaller by reducing differences between schools, opportunities and treatments, not by celebrating them.

Chapter 6

The role of teachers

Introduction

Chapter 5 demonstrated how hard it is to find good evidence of the differential effectiveness of entire schools or school types. This chapter looks at the evidence for the differential effectiveness of teachers in terms of student outcomes. As may be imagined it is just about impossible to demonstrate that one teacher is more or less effective than any other using the techniques from Chapter 5. This is not necessarily because teachers are not differentially effective, but because the calculations involved are not possible with current methods. Of course, this is not to suggest that teachers in general do not make a difference – only that they are not obviously differentially effective. The evidence from student reports is that there is considerable variation in the skills, even the very basic skills, of teachers. This may be partly the result of variability in the process of admitting and qualifying trainee teachers. This chapter looks at each of these issues in turn, before considering the implications for overcoming disadvantage. The next chapter looks at the more important impact of teachers on the wider outcomes of schooling.

Attracting, retaining and developing teachers of the highest quality are concerns for the education systems of all countries. A common belief among policy-makers and many other commentators is that there is considerable variation in the effectiveness of teachers, and that this differential effectiveness can be measured and so rewarded or penalised. Such effectiveness is almost always conceived in relation to student academic attainment at school. Good teachers are, in this view, those that teach the students who then gain the best possible test results. Large-scale international surveys have found associations between student attainment and their teachers' educational level and years of experience (Wobmann 2003). Influential authors such as Hattie (2009) have suggested that the role of teachers is crucial in the learning of young people. In his analysis of largely passive post hoc studies, teachers appear to be more important than structural issues such as parental choice, class size and financing. 'Good' teachers tend to be passionate, welcome error, proceed through a spiral approach and give meaningful individualised feedback.

Of course, when pressed, such commentators would concede that identifying differentially effective teachers is not easy. Confounding factors include the background, prior experiences and initial talent of the students, the variability between alternative measures of attainment in terms of examining body, year, syllabus, region, mode of examination and subject (Chapter 2) and the inconvenient fact that most students are taught by more than one teacher, perhaps including those outside the school system such as family, peers and tutors. In order to overcome all of this 'noise' and be safely identified, the differential impact of teachers on their students' attainment would have to be very considerable. Yet there are systems in operation around the world that claim to be able to make that identification safely, and teachers are therefore rewarded and punished on that basis. One such example is the long-running Tennessee Value-Added Assessment System (TVAAS) in the US. This chapter suggests that it is not currently possible to identify a differential teacher effect on student attainment or progress in this manner. Successive chapters then look at the more promising evidence concerning the beneficial impact of teachers on a wider set of student outcomes.

Sources of evidence

This chapter is based on several sources of evidence, discussed in greater detail in Chapter 2, and in a series of publications such as those discussed later in this chapter. The evidence relevant to the critique of differential teacher effectiveness is largely drawn from a study conducted for the EU Directorate General for Education and Culture, and an analysis of the National Pupil Database in England (Gorard 2010b). The evidence on students' views of their teachers' competence comes from a large-scale national study for the Qualifications and Curriculum Authority in England, intended to establish a baseline picture for the 14–19 curriculum reforms (Gorard & See 2011). The evidence on wider outcomes of schooling and the importance of student–teacher interactions comes from a series of studies in six EU countries plus Japan, funded by the EU Socrates Programme (Gorard et al. 2012b), and from a review of evidence conducted for Teach First (Gorard & See 2012).

Teacher effectiveness

There are a number of reasons why policy-makers and education leaders might want to be able to evaluate the effectiveness of teachers, including for inspection, improvement, targeted development, incentive payments, promotion and, in extreme cases, dismissal. For each of these reasons, policy-makers and education leaders might wish to specify a different version of teacher effectiveness. Teachers might be considered effective if they worked well together, could control their classrooms or encouraged students to attend school, select the teacher's bespoke courses, raise their occupational aspirations or stay in subsequent educational phases. Such teacher 'effects' might be immediate, as in inhibiting students from smoking at school, or longer-term, such as inhibiting students from smoking in later life. Often, however, a very narrow and immediate definition of teacher effectiveness is used, focusing on what can be deduced about short-term learning from pencil-and-paper testing of students.

It is generally accepted that students are not an entirely blank slate, certainly not by the time of their second and subsequent teachers. Students have some kind of pre-existing propensity to do better or worse in standard tests of attainment at school. This could be called talent and/or motivation, but why it exists, if it does, and whether it matters is not the subject of this book (Chapter 1). Therefore, it is widely recognised as unfair to judge the proficiency of teachers solely on the final results of their students, because some students are intrinsically easier to teach than others. To take an obvious example, it would not be fair to conclude in a selective system of schooling that teachers in the grammar schools were more competent than those in secondary-modern schools simply because students in grammar schools tend to perform better in measures of attainment. The students have been selected at age 11 to attend grammar schools precisely because they appear to be the most likely to do well in similar tests at age 16, for example. The fact that this selection is successful, in its own terms, does not provide any evidence at all about relative teacher competence. What is needed instead is a method of separating the progress made by students that is attributable to their teacher, from their students' overall level of attainment, from the progress attributable to other influences (including, of course, any other teachers) and from any errors in the measurements. This teacher 'value-added' approach sounds challenging, and indeed it is.

To see how problematic this more sophisticated approach is in practice, the TVAAS is used here as an important case study. Since at least 1996, Sanders (2000), Sanders and Rivers (1996) and Sanders and Horn (1998) have claimed to be able to estimate teacher effectiveness from student test scores. TVAAS defines teacher effectiveness in terms of the progress made by their students while at school, as judged by changes in their test scores. The claimed result is that 'Our research work ... clearly indicates that differences in teacher effectiveness is [*sic*] the single largest factor affecting academic growth of populations of students' (Sanders, 2000, p.334). TVAAS has been claimed to be 'an efficient and effective method for determining individual teachers' influence on the rate of academic growth for student populations' (Sanders & Rivers, p.1). The system uses the academic test scores of students, tracked longitudinally, in a complex statistical analysis, to estimate the impact of teachers. There is a plausibility about the logic, just as there is with school effectiveness (Chapter 5), which coupled with a hunger for teacher accountability measures and a faith in technical solutions, has led some commentators to extol this approach. Barber and Mourshed (2007), for example, call the research by Sanders 'seminal' in showing how important effective teachers are, and how damaging poor teachers are, for student learning. They conclude that the quality of instruction in education is paramount in student progress, and therefore that the preparation of teachers is a key determinant of education quality. This McKinsey report, and others following, has been highly influential, and the research 'finding' about the importance of 'good teachers' is now reflected in some important policy documents, including those of the European Commission and the OECD (Coffield 2012).

Yet every step in the argument towards that conclusion is questionable. Even if more or less effective teaching made a difference to student progress this would not necessarily make quality of instruction paramount. Even if quality of instruction were paramount this would not necessarily mean that teacher quality is determined by teacher education, and so on. The key issue is whether the original premise about judging teacher effectiveness is valid. The answer is that Sanders' (and Barber's) assertions about teacher effectiveness have almost no scientific justification. The model of teacher effectiveness makes a number of important assumptions, each of which is considered in turn.

Tests taken by students are an accurate measure of teacher-directed learning

As with purported school effects, much of the variation in gain scores between students will be the result of error and error propagation. As outlined in Chapter 2, even nationally moderated statutory tests involve a high level of measurement error. And as outlined in Chapters 2 and 5, this initial error will propagate exponentially in the specific value-added calculations involved. The problem will be even worse here than for schools because the number of students involved in any calculation for teachers will be much fewer, and so the results will be even more volatile. There may be a small 'residual' of this residual gain score that could be attributed to the impact of teachers (and of course to all other competing explanations such as the continuing effect of student background), but it is hard to see how this might be identified separately, and then quantified in practice.

Not all areas of teaching are routinely subject to statutory testing in Tennessee or elsewhere (Sanders & Horn 1998). Even in England, which has a famously prescriptive programme of statutory testing at ages 7, 11 and 14, the focus is largely on maths, science and English. This means that some teachers cannot be included in any teacher effectiveness system, since their subject contributions are not tested (most obviously perhaps sports and PE staff). It is also very rare for one student to come into contact with only one teacher, even for one subject. Team-teaching, teaching assistants, online and virtual participation and replacement and student teachers, among other factors, will confuse the issue further. Teachers and their styles might vary over time, and might be effective for some students but not others. Their effectiveness might depend on the precise topic taught within any syllabus.

Differences in test scores can be attributed to the impact of teachers

As noted in Chapter 5, early studies of school effectiveness found little difference in the outcomes of schools once their student intake differences had been taken into account. Similarly, the differences in student outcomes between teachers can be largely explained by the differences in their student intakes. Even school and teacher effectiveness researchers accept that most of the variation in school outcomes is due to school intake characteristics, but they have claimed that the residual variation (any difference in raw-scores unexplained by student intake) is evidence of differential teacher or school effectiveness. The TVAAS work follows this line of argument, except that it attributes the residuals to teacher effects alone. The idea that unexplained variation in student progress is attributable to teachers is not tested in any way by the statistical modelling that ensues. It is merely taken on trust from the outset. What are the reasons this assumption might be false?

Perhaps most obviously, the residual variation in student gain scores has long been attributed to other factors, by analysts other than Sanders. These factors include external determinants such as the continuing influence of differential family support, socio-economic trajectories and cultural and ethnic-related determinants. They include school-level factors such as resources, curricula, timetabling and leadership. They also include educational factors beyond the school, such as district and areal policies and funding arrangements. Of course, all such attributions may have no more justification than an attribution of the residual gain scores to the impact of teachers. But they are all in competition to explain the same small amount of variation (once prior attainment is accounted for). In addition, of course, the residual scores also contain a very substantial error component.

Sanders and Horn (1998) explain that they are dealing with 'fractured student records, which are always present in real-world student achievement data' (p.248). What they mean by this is that some student records will be missing or damaged, and some records that are present will contain missing data. They do not explain, in any of their publications, how large a problem this is or what they have done about it. Traditional statistical analysis does not address this issue.

To estimate the problems in Tennessee by comparison, schools in England are annually required by law to provide figures on student characteristics and qualifications for the National Pupil Database (NPD). The database ostensibly has records for all students registered as being at school in England. The NPD is a high quality dataset, much better than any analyst would hope to generate through primary data collection, and yet as explained in this book missing data remains a substantial problem even here. Once all cases that are unmatched or missing a key background variable or an attainment score are deleted from the 2007 NPD, then there are complete records for less than 60 per cent of the school-age population. Statistical analysis cannot make up for this, because the missing values are heavily biased rather than random (Gorard 2013). What is true for the NPD in 2007 and subsequently will also be true for the school records for Tennessee in 1993 and subsequently. Note that in order to judge teacher effects, Sanders had to break down their student figures in terms of the teacher for each subject, and match these records to individual teacher records. This is an unimaginable task with fractured records, and a clear area for the introduction of further errors. A considerable proportion of students will be missing for each teacher, and a considerable proportion of students will have an unknown teacher.

Even some of the information that is present in any schools database, whether NPD or TVAAS, will be incorrect. Assessment via examination, project, coursework or teacher's grading is an imperfect process. Learning is not an easy thing to measure, unlike height or the number of students in a classroom. However well-constructed the assessment system, there will be considerable measurement error, over and above the errors caused by missing data. Then there will be a small number of additional errors stemming from coding, transcription, matching and storage of records. Each of the two attainment scores in any teacher effectiveness model (and of course any other variables used, such as the link between teachers and students) will have the kinds of errors illustrated so far. It would be conservative to imagine that a national or state assessment system was 90 per cent accurate as a whole (or that 90 per cent of students were recorded with the correct mark/grade). It would also be quite conservative to imagine that, overall, only around ten per cent of the cases or variables used in a teacher effectiveness calculation were missing (or incorrectly replaced by defaults). This means that each attainment score is liable to be no more than 80 per cent accurate – or put another way, the relative error is at least 20 per cent in each set of figures used in any effectiveness calculation.

Such errors are said to 'propagate' through calculations, meaning that everything done with these scores is also done with their measurement errors. Since we do not know whether the error in either score is positive or negative when we subtract, we are effectively adding the maximum error components. This means that the estimated gain score for each student is the difference between the predicted and achieved score (obviously a number that is considerably smaller than either score) plus the sum of the absolute errors in both scores. The error will tend to get larger and the numbers in which the error occurs will get a lot smaller. A realistic 20 per cent relative error in both the predicted and achieved scores for each student could lead to a relative error of 10,000 per cent, and often much more, in the student gain score. This makes the average gain scores per teacher completely unusable in practice.

In summary, a very high proportion of the apparent gain scores for any student will actually be an error component deriving from the propagation of missing data, measurement errors and representational errors. It would be quite unwise to attribute the meaningless differences in these 'scores' to the influence of teachers.

Teacher effectiveness is a relatively static phenomenon

The fact that teacher effectiveness data contain substantial initial errors, and that these propagate through the calculation, does not mean that we should expect the results for all teachers/schools to be the same, once prior attainment is accounted for. The bigger the deviations between predicted and attained results, of the kind that researchers claim as evidence of effectiveness, the more this could also be evidence of the error component. We would expect the results to be volatile and inconsistent over years and between key stages in the same schools. This is what we generally find. There is huge year-on-year variation in purported school effects (Chapter 5). School effectiveness work involves analysing results for an entire cohort, and treating all subject areas as equivalent for analytic purposes. This means that the average number of cases per school might be 100 or more. In teacher effectiveness on the other hand, which attempts to measure progress in terms of individual school subjects and teachers, the largest number of cases involved is likely to be a teaching group of around 30 students or fewer. Irrespective of all other factors, this will make teacher effectiveness scores even more volatile than purported school effects, because of the small numbers involved. In this context, it is intriguing to note the observation by Glass (2004) that one school directly on a county line was inadvertently attributed to both counties in the TVAAS, and so two VA measures were calculated. These two VA measures for the same teachers were completely different – presumably because like VA measures for schools, they did not really mean anything at all.

If teacher effectiveness is such a volatile phenomenon, altering easily across years, classes, students and even arbitrary county lines, then it would not be appropriate to use the past performance of students to judge the present, and perhaps future, effectiveness of teachers. Our lack of ability to calibrate the results of teacher effectiveness models against anything except themselves is therefore a problem. In everyday measurements of time, length, temperature and so on we get a sense of the accuracy of our measuring scales by comparing the measurements with the qualities being measured (Gorard 2010a). There is no equivalent for teacher effectiveness. Advocates claim that effectiveness figures represent fair performance measures, but they can provide nothing except the purported plausibility of the calculation to justify that.

The irrelevance of technical solutions again

It is worth pointing out at this stage that any analysis using real data with some combination of inevitable measurement errors will be biased, and so will lead to an incorrect result. Of course, the more accurate the measures are the closer to the ideal correct answer we can be. However, there is no reason to believe that any of these sources of error lead to random measurement error (of the kind that might come from random sampling variation, for example). Those students without test scores, who refuse to take part in a survey, are not registered at school or are unwilling to reveal their family income or benefit (for free school meal eligibility purposes) cannot be imagined as some kind of random sub-set of the school population. There is no kind of statistical treatment based on probability theory that can help overcome these and other limitations. Whether as simple as confidence intervals or as complex as multi-level modelling, such techniques are all irrelevant.

Unfortunately, the field of teacher effectiveness research works on the invalid assumption that errors in the data are random in nature and so can be estimated and corrected, based on techniques based on random sampling theory. When working with population figures such as the NPD, these techniques mean nothing. There is no sampling variation to estimate when working with population data (whether for a nation, region, education authority, school, year, class or social group). There are missing cases and values, and there is measurement error, but these are not generated by random sampling, and so sampling theory cannot estimate them, adjust for them or help us decide how substantial they are. Sanders and Rivers (1996) state quite clearly that they are working with the 'entire grade 2–8 student population' for Tennessee' (p.1). Yet their reported analysis cites statistical significance, p-values and F-statistics calculated for this population. These are clearly statisticians who do not understand basic statistical principles. This kind of work has been described as Voodoo science (Park 2000), wherein adherents prefer to claim they are dealing with random events, making it easier to explain away the uncertainty and unpredictability of their results.

The progress score for each student is independent of level of attainment

Sanders and Horn (1998, p.254) claim that 'African American students and White students with the same level of prior achievement make comparable academic progress when they are assigned to teachers of comparable effectiveness'. What does this mean? What could it mean? The teacher effectiveness is calculated on the basis of the progress made by students, so this claim by Sanders and Horn is tautological. It is only possible to judge 'comparable effectiveness' by the level of progress made by students, and so by definition the students will make comparable progress. In fact, the whole argument by Sanders and all others about the importance and impact of teachers is completely circular. Effective teachers are defined as those with students making good progress, so obviously, but by definition only, students make good progress with effective teachers. Empirically, this means nothing.

Teacher quality and learner enjoyment

It is not possible to identify differentially effective teachers because of the confounding factors and errors in the measures of student progress. What does this mean for the strong intuition that some teachers are better than others? After all, absence of evidence is not evidence of absence. There may be a teacher effect on student learning but it may be too small in comparison to the noise in the measuring system. It is clear that students themselves report considerable variation in the quality of teaching, as they experience it (Gorard & See 2011). In our QCA dataset (Chapter 3), a majority of students nearing the end of their compulsory schooling did not enjoy education. In fact, only 44 per cent of students in Year 11 enjoy being at their school. One of the reasons for this is clear; only 38 per cent say that most of their lessons are interesting. These figures are slightly lower than those reported by OFSTED (2007), which included primary and early-age secondary children as well. Internationally, enjoyment of learning tends to decline with age (Hagenauer & Hascher 2010). OFSTED (2007) also found that the most popular suggestion as to how to improve school (79 per cent) was to have more interesting lessons. According to reports of school inspections conducted by OFSTED, much teaching in England is boring – the basis of the most complaints – and fails to inspire students in thousands of schools (Marley 2009).

The enjoyment of education by students has been a long-standing area of interest for some commentators and many practitioners (Harris & Haydn 2006). Yet it is relatively recently in the UK and elsewhere that declared policy has so clearly turned towards enjoyment of learning as a key objective (Welsh Assembly Government 2009, LTS Scotland 2009). Even here, as elsewhere in the literature, enjoyment of learning is promoted largely as a step towards school improvement (Dugdale 2009). But enjoyment is about a lot more than improving attainment; it would probably also impact on young peoples' lives outside and beyond school (Pugh & Bergin 2005). It could enhance attendance and inclusion at school and lead to higher participation in education and training following school, but like health it is also important in its own right. According to students, it would be relatively easy to increase overall levels of enjoyment.

Table 6.1 shows the result of a logistic regression model using a number of possible explanatory variables to represent the difference between those students finding their school enjoyable and the rest. Students' personal and family background explains some of the outstanding variation (ten per cent). Very little

Table 6.1 Cumulative percentage of variation in responses to 'I enjoy school' explained by each stage of analysis

Individual student background variables	10
School-level variables	3
Individual experiences of education	33

Note: In this table, the figures show the percentage of remaining variation in student responses that can be explained by each group of variables. The student reports of experiences at school explain 33 per cent of the variation in responses, over and above ten per cent explained by student background, and three per cent explained by institutional-level factors.

of the variation in responses is explicable by school-level factors. Most of the differences between those who enjoy school and those who do not are related to their individual experiences of education (33 per cent).

Enhancing enjoyment of school and interest in lessons should be easy, because the patterning and stratification of school opportunities and outcomes that hinder traditional school improvement work do not appear very strongly here. There is little difference in the survey according to student family background (such as eligibility for free school meals), prior attainment, the kind of school attended, its intake and geographical location, its academic standing, its curriculum offer and the staff priorities as reported by teachers. This is a very useful finding, because it means that any attempt to enhance enjoyment for all does not need to face those structural and socio-economic barriers that school improvers usually face. It would also be relatively cheap, since it does not of itself require new buildings, extra teachers or different kinds of schools. Students can be 'objectively' disadvantaged, in terms of challenges to their learning or a deprived economic background, and still enjoy learning. Indeed, providing shelter from the impact of disadvantage is one of the main reasons for having and supporting a state-funded education system.

Some of the experiences of students at school that are related to enjoyment appear with their coefficients in Table 6.2. Restrictions on choice at age 14 caused by school pressure and timetable blocking constraints reportedly reduce the likelihood that students enjoy their school and lessons. Conversely, enjoyment of school is strongly enhanced by student sense of autonomy – including being allowed to work at their own pace, discuss issues with staff and other students and being encouraged to make up their own minds about issues raised. These outcomes are also linked to good facilities and resources, in the form of specialist staff, suitable rooms for teaching and small classes. Finally, they are also linked to variation in delivery, including practical work, visits and field trips and contact with students on other programmes.

It is clear that students' reports of enjoyment relate very much to their experiences of school. They find lessons that are varied and innovative in delivery interesting. For example, they enjoy physical activities, practical work, debates,

Table 6.2 Individual background variables in model for 'enjoyed school'

Enough chance to discuss	1.54
Contact with other students on other programmes	1.45
Suitable teaching rooms	1.41
Can work at my own pace	1.39
Encouraged to make up own mind	1.30
Choice of course restricted by school pressure	0.68

Note: In this table the figures are odd ratios. A student reporting being restricted in choice of course is only 0.68 times as likely as a student not so restricted to report enjoying school.

dramatisations and activities that are less conventional and out of the ordinary. Teaching is more than simply disseminating knowledge. It is about engaging pupils in their learning. Students also expect respect and autonomy. These patterns of enjoyment form codes and concepts used to analyse the interview data, a fraction of which is presented below. The generalisability of the examples from interviews stems both from the logistic regression model and from their relative frequency in transcripts. Here the focus is on factors that recur in different ways in different stories.

Students gave many examples of lessons that they had enjoyed and will always remember. These are inspirational:

> I had one teacher who would do, like, to show Women's Liberation he wore a bra and took it off, and … I just … that … I will never ever forget that. And to do Hippies we walked into the classroom and there were candles everywhere, he had his tie round his head, you know, and it was just so different and so funny that you won't ever forget it, so …

Enjoyment is important to learning. Students are more likely to want to learn if they enjoy the lesson or see the value of the lesson. Enthusiasm in teaching can make learning enjoyable. If teachers enjoy teaching, pupils are more likely to enjoy the lessons. Students appreciate the opportunity to have a say in their own learning, for discussion and learning in small groups. These are associated with good experiences at school. Students also reported enjoying contact with students on other courses or programmes (such as social or pastoral activities, learning off-site or houses and competitions). Where students see schools as supportive, enjoyment is more widespread (Battistich & Hom 1997).

Another aspect of students' school life is their interaction with teachers and other adults in education. Time and again students report positive experiences of school when they have good relationships with teachers. A part of this is the sense of trust and respect they receive from these adults. For some students this is as simple as being allowed to address their teachers by their first names. To them this is like being treated as grown-ups. This was particularly the case for students who learn off-site, away from the school environment. Students sometimes compare their treatment at school quite unfavourably with their treatment in such centres.

> I enjoy it, it's a more comfortable place than being around a school environment, more fun in lessons, teachers are nice, you don't have to call them Mr. and Mrs, it is more first names.

Perceived lack of respect from teachers is often cited by students as justification for their own bad behaviour. Students recounted instances of teacher behaviour that can depress ambition and dampen motivation.

When I actually went for an interview at [agricultural college] and got my place ... I showed my [pastoral teacher] and ... she actually turned round and said that it's a load of rubbish, there's no point doing it, 'cos I ain't going to get nowhere in life 'cos I never come to school ... I might as well just drop all my dreams and just be a bum, basically, live off Social. Which really put me down.

Bad classroom teaching techniques can also frustrate students, spoil their enjoyment of school and affect their learning. These are the most common complaints among students.

I am failing my (subject) because my teacher does not speak up and only talks to the front row.

Students described lessons where there was little attempt at engaging them. For example, there was no eye contact, with teachers talking like a recording and expecting students to listen and copy notes at the same time.

Teachers often go too fast, like you're saying; you don't end up knowing what's going on because you're trying to take notes like as fast as you can, and so you are not listening, so then your notes aren't completely there, so ...

Cos, as soon as the teachers ask a question he doesn't like give anyone else a chance to think about it, he just shoots off. Basically all of you just sit there, you're still thinking about the question and (expletive) gives the answers, so you kinda get the thing that you're not doing anything in the class, you're just sitting there and just going there to listen to someone else talk.

Uninspiring teaching was the basis for most complaints from students. Most of the negative experiences, such as listening for lengthy periods, copying, note taking and having to sit still for a prolonged period, relate to teachers' poor pedagogic skills.

He just stands at the blackboard, or the whiteboard ... and just writing on the board.

Support at school was another aspect that students reported as helping them to enjoy school more. This is particularly so for students who are struggling; they find it frustrating if given no assistance. Students complained of being left without help and given meaningless activities:

We're given a sheet and we're just spoken to and we write down notes and then the sheet is, at the end of the hour, two hour lesson, is lost and never seen again. We don't really learn that way.

Sometimes it is not that teachers do not give the assistance, but that they are not aware that a child needs additional support.

> I don't think there's many teachers in this school that understand that like kids learn in different ways
>
> Like, sometimes, teachers think it's a good idea for you to sit silently in class, and to only listen to them ... but I think it's good to be able to talk between yourselves and ... not, like, obviously about the subject. But to be able to sit there in silence for an hour lesson just looking at a whiteboard, it does give you a headache.

The good news is that many young people reported receiving additional support from their school and teachers. Students appreciate such help, which enables them to enjoy school more. There were instances when the approachability of the teaching staff helped to make school life pleasant:

> Yeah, all that I have to do is just go and speak to my teachers and say I'm struggling with this and the teacher will say come to me at a certain time and we'll see what we can do about it.
>
> 'Cos I get support in them, and I get help with my work sometimes. A person what comes and sits next to me and tells me what to write and helps me read it.

Students also reported that they like being with other people who wanted to learn. Lessons can progress peacefully without constant interruptions from disruptive students. This makes the learning experience more enjoyable. Other things that contribute to enjoyment are working in groups, small classes, being allowed to voice their views and being with students who share their interests.

> I prefer to work in a group, because if you have one on one it's really, really nervous. But if you have a friend with you it's like you've someone else to talk to.

On the other hand, the behaviour of other students can also spoil the learning experience for others. Abusive behaviour such as bullying, violence, theft and social isolation are examples of such negative behaviour (Gorard & Smith 2010). It is not only frustrating for students but teachers as well.

> But there's some teachers that can't control the classes. So, like, all the students will be talking, and doing their own stuff. So that's when we don't learn as much, and the lesson's just wasted.

Despite plentiful students' accounts about enjoyment in school, none of the thousands of teachers in our survey mentioned prioritising enjoyment for students as an objective, even though there was a prompt for this. This is sad because while enjoyment is presumably neither necessary nor sufficient for learning to take place, student reports of enjoyment are an indicator of what has gone well and what has not.

Conclusion

According to students, there is clearly huge variation in the quality of their teachers, and yet we are seemingly unable to measure the difference this makes to student attainment. If there is such variation, how could it arise? One possibility suggested by previous evidence is that some of the better candidates for teacher training in England are being turned away while some others are accepted, because of the institutional nature of the application process (Gorard et al. 2006). Another related possibility is that teacher trainees are being passed in some institutions but would fail in others. This is because a quota of places is awarded to each teacher training institution, and they have the responsibility for accepting trainees. More trainees apply every year than are accepted, but those rejected by some high prestige institutions are actually better qualified than the best-qualified trainees accepted at some lower prestige institutions. Only a more co-ordinated national system of application and selection can prevent this. The problem of such variability in teacher quality may also arise because each training institution is permitted to decide on trainee outcomes. There is no relationship at all between the intake qualifications of trainees and their outcomes. This might be because the institutions with less qualified intakes are genuinely performing better, and so levelling the playing field for their trainees. However, OFSTED inspections also suggest that several of these institutions just do not have the capacity to judge teacher quality for themselves, even though they are responsible for qualifying teachers.

When assessing the impact of teachers on student attainment, the propagation of initial error and the stratified nature of the confounding variables faced are such that no teacher 'effect' can be safely attributed. The teacher effectiveness model does not work as intended, and should not be used for making policy, or promoting or condemning teachers. This is in no way an argument for using raw-scores to assess teacher performance instead. That would be at least as bad. Nor does the evidence suggest that teachers, in general, are not useful and important. It is simply that with our current approaches based on student test outcomes we cannot safely identify any individual teacher who is differentially or consistently effective with equivalent students.

Despite this, the belief persists that some teachers are very different to others, and the reports of their students confirms this. There are accounts of excellent, imaginative and co-operative learning. There are also, at the other extreme, reports of individual teachers whose lack of basic pedagogic social interaction skills is so great that it is hard to envisage how they function as teachers at all. Their existence, if these student voices are accepted as valid, suggests that a lot of work needs to be done in attracting, selecting and developing appropriate teachers (Gorard et al. 2006). Further possible improvements would be to set up in-career development schemes and inspections to remind practicing teachers of the lasting importance of their behaviour when they interact with students. All young people must interact with teachers, and for an extended period. A meta-analysis of over 100 studies found that the student–teacher relationship was the most important factor in effective classroom management and students' engagement in learning (Marzano et al. 2003).

Chapter 7

The wider outcomes of schooling

Introduction

This chapter takes seriously one of the most important results from Chapters 4 to 6, that the most discernible differential impact of schools and teachers may be on student outcomes other than attainment. As explained in Chapter 2, these psychological outcomes are even harder to measure than attainment or learning, and almost impossible to calibrate. On the other hand, they are found to be far less stratified by SES variables and prior attainment, which means that the school and teacher 'effects' could be much greater. Despite almost an obsession in policy circles, there are grave doubts whether 'attainment' as such is what learning in schools should be about (Barnett 2011).

The next chapter looks at the impact of schools and teachers on post-compulsory participation. This chapter looks at how students are treated by and interact with teachers, and the link between this and outcomes such as civic participation, trust and sense of fairness. Young people generally gain skills and qualifications and learn to socialise during their compulsory schooling. They also learn how to assess whether something is fair or not, and apply this knowledge both to schooling and to wider society and later life (EGREES 2008). Whether students are, or feel that they are being, treated fairly might influence their academic outcomes (Molinair et al. 2013). But social justice at school is about much more than outcomes and inputs. It is about life as it is lived (Griffiths 2012). There is reasonable evidence that the quality of student–teacher interaction in schools is linked to students' sense of justice, trust in others and reports of citizenship activity. Perhaps then this is the clearest difference that individual teachers make to the wider outcomes of schooling. It may also turn out to be one of the most important.

Fairness is hard to define in terms of criteria that apply in school just as elsewhere. There are several well-known principles, such as equality of treatment or of outcome, that purport to lay down what is fair, but are actually contradictions. There is no single principle that adheres in all educational situations. Any principle intended to enhance justice will be flawed in the sense that it will tend to lead to injustice in some situations (Themelis 2008). Schools should not be allowed to use more funds to educate boys than girls, or to offer specific curriculum subjects only to different ethnic groups. It might, however, be considered fair for schools to use more funds for students with learning difficulties, or to respect the right of each student to gain a qualification in their first language. In short, any principle needs to be adjusted for use depending upon the setting and actors involved.

Young people in different countries seem to understand this complexity in practice, and there is widespread agreement over what would be fair in any set of circumstances. In education, some resources or outcomes should be distributed equally – including respect by teachers for their students. Some should be open to all – such as extra help when requested. Others can be fairly distributed in proportion to contribution or even talent – including punishment for disruptive behaviour or high grades for good work. Further assets may be deliberately distributed unequally without consideration of contribution, such as greater attention given to disadvantaged students (Riley 2004). All of these allocations can be construed as fair by the same person (Lizzio et al. 2007, Thornberg 2008). One possible over-arching criterion for judging fairness is the source of responsibility, or at least perceived responsibility. A difference or action is only unjust insofar as it could have been avoided by others, or is their responsibility (Roemer 1996, Whitehead 1991). An individual is deemed responsible for their effort, and so a greater reward for some can be deemed fair, for example (Raty et al. 2010). Students struggling because of inherent weakness or a temporary problem are permitted unequal or compensatory treatment by other students, because the strugglers themselves are not to blame.

Given the variation in students' reported experiences of teaching and of their relationships with teachers (Chapter 6), it would be odd to find no evidence of any impact of this on the students. What follows is based on a set of associations rather than a definitive test of influence, but in that it is no different to studies of teacher academic effectiveness, which are also purely correlational. What follows in this chapter differs from traditional studies of school and teacher effectiveness because the 'effect' sizes uncovered are far larger (large enough to overcome noise in the measurements, and less stratified by student background characteristics). Therefore, it is reasonable to conclude that what follows is indicative evidence of the impact of teachers on wider school outcomes, such as whether students learn to trust their teachers and so trust others in wider society, and whether they are willing to forego something in order to help others (Gorard 2011).

Sources of evidence

The evidence presented in this chapter is discussed in more detail in Chapter 2, and a series of publications such as Gorard et al. (2009), Gorard and Smith (2010) and Gorard (2012). The work was largely funded by the QCA in England and by the EU Socrates Programme, and conducted in England, Wales, Belgium, Czech Republic, France, Italy, Japan and Spain.

The experiences of students

Students' reported experiences of interacting with teachers are generally consistent across social, economic and family background groups. In all countries covered by our international dataset, males, females, high and low attainers, those from families with professional educated parents and those with less educated or unemployed parents, recent immigrants and second language speakers, for example, all report pretty much the same experiences. This lack of stratification is rare in education research. In general, the same percentage of each student category agreed that their teachers treated them with respect, explained until they understood, encouraged autonomy in learning, generally treated all students the same, gave extra help where needed, punished students justly and marked work fairly. Of course, the situation is not ideal, since the percentage saying these things about teachers can often be low, but at least different kinds of students are not reporting different levels of agreement. The same lack of variation is also noticeable in some less desirable experiences – such as punishments being used unevenly, teachers getting angry with students and teachers having favourites.

There is also little variation between groups of students in their responses to their treatment by other students. Students who reported being from different family backgrounds, at varying levels of attainment and across all countries, responded equivalently to questions about being left out, bullied, having something stolen, having good friends and having friends who are immigrants or low attainers. As with student–teacher relationships, the most notable finding is how little stratification there is in student–student relationships. Student reports of their relationships with other students are mostly positive. Over 90 per cent of students have good friends, less than ten per cent are left out by others and only around seven per cent feel invisible to their peers; however, the overall figures for negative episodes are still substantial because of what they could represent. School can be a frightening and disagreeable experience. Students with low marks, who have repeated a year or who have moved to the country of the survey after birth, are somewhat more likely to report being left out or bullied. Bullying is intrinsically unfair and unpleasant, but for several students the teachers also bear some responsibility for not dealing with it adequately:

> When I said to a teacher that I was bullied, he did not listen to me. But when his favourite student went to say that he was bullied, the teacher listened to him. (Japan, male)
>
> Somebody was bullying me and hit me when no one watched. The teachers did not respond to this so I pushed the person over. I was the one who got told off. (England, male)

Students are generally concerned about physical intimidation and violence – traditional bullying – whereas teachers claim to be as concerned about indirect bullying (Maunder et al. 2010). Perhaps there is a misunderstanding or a mismatch of priorities.

Young people generally want their teachers to treat other students with equal respect, treat their opinions with care and not humiliate any of them. They want teachers to continue explaining until everyone understands a new topic (a threshold criterion of justice). Students are content for teachers to discriminate on the basis of effort and work quality, and to use praise for those who deserve it (a meritocratic criterion of justice). Being treated differently in this context is not unfair, if it is justified. However, students do not want teachers to treat hard-working students the best in other and irrelevant situations. In these ways, students confirm the ideas of fairness outlined at the start of this chapter. They adapt universal principles to the context and actors involved. Unfortunately, their experiences with teachers do not match these quite minimal requirements. Too many teachers appear to be mis-applying the criteria of justice to the 'wrong' domains. Less than half of students consider their teachers to be interested in students' well-being, using punishments fairly, marking work even-handedly or explaining things in a way that all students can understand. Of course, some of the claims could be wrong or exaggerated, but the students were generally thoughtful and credible informants. So even allowing for some misunderstandings, there is evidence of a widespread problem here that could be summarised as 'favouritism' by teachers. Probably the greatest area of concern among students was about teachers' apparently indiscriminate way of allocating rewards and punishments:

> When I made the same mistake as another student, the teacher shouted at me and struck me, but he did not get angry with another student and he just laughed at him. (Japan, male)
>
> In the history class, I left my book and I got yelled at for five or ten minutes and the teacher hit my head about ten times, also, I was called back after the class. When another student, who was cleverer than I, left his book, he was told only to go home to bring it, but he was neither hit nor called back afterwards. (Japan, male)

The domain-specific nature of the underlying criteria of justice applied by students is made clear by the minimal support across all countries for the idea that hard-working students should be treated better by teachers. Students agree that hard work or effort is important in terms of teachers awarding marks. This is not a contradiction. It seems that hard work should be rewarded in awarding grades – slightly more so than quality of work. But in all other respects, hard-working students should be treated the same as others. According to the students it is teachers who are not observing the domain boundaries, in inequitably generalising their appropriate treatment of talented or hard-working students in the domain of marking to other domains relevant to trust, autonomy and respect. What difference might such inconsistencies by teachers make to student outcomes?

Civic participation

An example of a wider outcome from education, desired by policy-makers and many other commentators, is preparation for citizenship including future civic participation. A number of institutions in England and worldwide use accreditation awards that make civic and community engagement part of the assessed curriculum. More commonly, schools and colleges have introduced various mechanisms for developing students' capacity to express their own views and engage in decision-making, such as student councils, representation on governing bodies and student surveys to inform organisational planning and processes. In the QCA dataset, in which students take part in such activities or vote in school/college elections, is used as an illustration of a more general pattern of citizenship participation, including enthusiasm to vote in national governmental elections. Around 44 per cent of students report voting in school elections. The logistic regression model is around 80 per cent accurate in explaining the difference between these and the other students, in terms of other variables (Table 7.1).

Students from professional families are more likely to report voting in elections. What is of more interest is the lack of association with so many other background variables, such as individual poverty, ethnicity, language, immigration and so on. Schools in cities and with high proportions of FSM students report less citizenship participation (Table 7.2). This suggests a school mix effect, because individual FSM is not related to voting. Students in institutions where staff report prioritising citizenship are less likely to vote in elections. Although the causal sequence is unclear, this is a strong indication that it is not so much what teachers say that matters here (Paterson 2009).

Table 7.1 Accuracy of model for 'voted in school elections'

	Percentage explained
Background	5
School/college	9
Individual responses	21

N=4,900 for this and subsequent tables

Table 7.2 School/college variables in model for 'voted in school elections'

Variable	Odds
Urban location	0.56
FSM institution (%)	0.82
Staff priority to developing citizens (%)	0.61
Staff priority to increase HE (%)	0.63
Staff priority to raising aspirations (%)	1.56

Table 7.3 Individual response variables in model for 'voted in school elections'

Variable	Odds
Learn also in work environment	1.28
Can work at own pace	1.20
Enough individual attention	1.23
Contact with other students	1.32
Employment guidance	1.28

The final stage of the model involves student reports of their school/college experiences. Students are more likely to vote in elections where they receive individual attention from staff, experience autonomy in learning and have contact with students on other programmes or via work experience (Table 7.3).

Citizenship in action, as exemplified in interactions between students and staff, may be as important as formal pedagogy and principles for the development of citizenship behaviour, such as voting and public service. Our student accounts suggest some differences could be based on a feeling of being treated more as a young adult in some institutions:

> Some teachers don't respect you and wonder why you cause so much trouble … The teachers say we want respect from you but they don't normally show it to us. They're the teacher they're always right, we're the kid and we don't know what we are going on about.
>
> Teachers are much, they respect you more, talk to you like, not like you're a little kid, treat you with a bit of respect, give you a bit of leeway if you're like that with them, if you do what they do, they'll be alright with you.

As explained in Chapter 4, where there is dissonance between the kinds of principles, use of initiative, critical questioning and trust taught in schools compared to the way schools are run, then citizenship is bound to fail (Fisher 2011). Strong civic knowledge is not enough (Cosgrove & Gilleece 2012). It may even be counter-productive if it isolates or offends minorities by being taught in a, possibly inadvertently, partisan way (Ortloff 2011). It is probably not an exaggeration to say that civic participation cannot be taught. It can be encouraged and demonstrated, as has apparently happened through democratic practices in specific schools (Maitlies 2011, Hope 2012).

Willingness to help others

Another possible wider outcome of schooling is willingness to help others or for them to be helped at one's own expense. In the international dataset, a number of vignettes or small stories representing conflicting criteria of justice were particularly useful when dealing with some of the most vulnerable students. One scenario asked whether help given in class is fairer when evenly distributed, like respect, or when it is given according to need:

If a student has difficulty reading and finds it hard to keep up in class, do you think it is fair that

1   the teacher spends more time helping this student
2   this student should have to work harder to keep up with the rest of the class
3   the student is taught in a different class.

Students in most countries are divided between requesting that a struggling student makes more effort and a teacher gives more help. In reality of course these approaches are not exclusive. Indeed, support for the teacher giving extra help may be contingent on the student being deserving of help by showing that they are making an effort (according to responsibility theory). This was made clear through another vignette. When a student is badly behaved then there is very little support for the teacher giving the culprit extra attention. Presumably, in this case the attention is neither deserved by the efforts of the student nor required to overcome an inherent disadvantage, again in line with responsibility theory. In England alone, there was little support for extra teacher attention for the struggling learner. Instead, students predominantly supported the struggler being taken out of class for extra support. The comprehensive and inclusive nature of most schools in England is in contrast to the widespread retention of special schools in France, selection in the Czech Republic and so on. This might mean that the issue of help for challenged students is more time-consuming in a typical English classroom. It is easier for students to agree to extra help for others in a heavily selective educational setting, for example, because the cost of enforcing that principle will have been lower for those students. The English students tend to be concerned that their peers who were less academically successful or who misbehaved in class claimed the lion's share of the teacher's attention and praise:

How the naughty children get more attention and get highly praised when they manage to produce the same amount of work as the rest of the class which they should be doing anyway. (England, female)

I had finished some work and asked my teacher to read it and see if I could improve, but she said 'no' because she was dealing with other students who were misbehaving. (England, male)

Overall, 52 per cent of students reported that they were happy for a teacher to give extra help to a student with a specific difficulty (even at their own expense in terms of time). Table 7.4 shows the extent to which these students can be predicted by adding variables representing student background, and school experiences to a logistic regression model. The model explains around 36 per

Table 7.4 Percentage of variation in agreeing to help for others, by batch of variables

	Percentage explained
Student background	19
School level	2
Individual experience	15

Note: the variables representing parental support add nothing of substance to any of these models, and this stage in the analysis is simply omitted in the reporting here.

cent of the otherwise unexplained variation in responses, which is a reasonable 'effect' size.

Individual student background variables increase the accuracy of the model. As suggested above, the biggest single factor here is the country of the questionnaire (England or other countries like Italy). The sex, prior attainment and immigrant status of the student were not related to this criterion of justice. Also unrelated are the occupations, education and country of origin of parents.

A large number of school experience variables are not relevant to increasing the quality of the prediction, including whether a student repeats a year or more. But there is a very clear relationship, once the preceding factors such as student background are accounted for, between students' reports of justice in school and their willingness for a student in difficulty to receive extra help. Being respected by teachers, with teachers not getting angry in front of others, not punishing students unfairly, being concerned for student well-being and prepared to explain until everyone understands, are linked to students reporting being prepared to support help for those with difficulties. This suggests a role for teachers in educating citizens who are tolerant and supportive of the difficulties of others (examples appear in Table 7.5). They do this not only through citizenship pedagogy but through their exemplification of good citizenship in action.

There is similarly a key role for the students. Having friends is important, as is avoidance of being mistreated by other students. Those reporting being hurt, bullied and having things stolen by other students at school are all less likely to support extra help for others. Perhaps this is because, as others have found, students who find school unsafe tend to have poorer relationships with their teachers anyway (Boulton et al. 2009). This is not a school mix effect (where those attending schools with low levels of theft are more supportive anyway).

Table 7.5 Coefficients for student/school experience variables and willingness to help or not

I have good friends in school	1.70
Teachers were interested in my well-being	1.27
Teachers got angry with a student	0.81

Thus, it appears to stem directly from treatment by others. There is a role for teachers here then, in preventing such mistreatment.

Conclusion

The similarities between the determinants of behaviour at school, sense of justice and hope for later life are remarkable. The wider school outcomes discussed in this chapter, and others like them such as learning to trust (Gorard & Smith 2010), feeling prepared for the world of work (Gorard et al. 2009) and aspirations (Chapter 8), are often only rather loosely related to individual student backgrounds and objective disadvantage (Vyverman & Vettenburg 2009). Not only are they little stratified by student origin; there is also no evidence of a school-level 'effect' (Quintelier 2010). This is very different to attainment, where the student background and prior attainment accounts for almost all of the variation that can be explained.

For these kinds of wider outcomes, the noticeably strong association is not what kind of students an individual attends school with, but what happens in interactions with teachers and others when at school. Part of this may be because concepts such as trust or citizenship are even harder to moderate than attainment scores, and reported levels of subjective experiences like enjoyment could anyway be deemed illusory where the young person is in objectively disadvantaged circumstances. But the individual is the best source of information on this, and it is clear overall that the enjoyment and satisfaction with their treatment is even higher among those clearly challenged students taught in separate settings like special schools (Gorard & Smith 2010). Chapters 9 and 10 look at whether these psychological outcomes are linked to attainment and participation, and whether self-reports of intentions are linked to subsequent observed behaviour.

Students' reported experiences of school are related to their perception of trust, respect and fairness at the hands of their teachers and other adults in education. Teachers were not often seen as good role models themselves. Students complained of unfair and inconsistent treatments, such as teachers having favourites and treating certain pupils more or less favourably than others. This has implications for citizenship education in schools. Teachers not only have to set the example, they also have the responsibility to protect children from the kinds of abuses that students report at the hands of other students (ranging from overt bullying to social isolation). The proposed solutions to problems in schools as mini-societies are largely cost-free, and almost as simple to implement in practice as changes to structures (Chapter 4). They do not require new buildings, extra teachers or different kinds of schools.

Interestingly, our study found that the views of students are very similar across different types of school systems and countries. They confirm the ideas of responsibility theory and domain-sensitivity. Students clearly distinguish between the universal aspects of fairness. Students' accounts of unfair treatment by teachers, if accepted, have implications for the preparation and development of teachers. Teachers, as role models, have a responsibility for their students' sense of what is right. So, emphasis needs to be given in initial teacher preparation to the principles of equity, and the common dangers of applying the principles in the wrong domains. These lessons need to be reinforced through the continuing development of good practice. Teachers need to be aware of the distinction between universal principles of justice such as respect and discriminatory ones such as reward and punishment based on talent and effort. One of the most common complaints of students is that teachers actually forget this distinction, treating hard-working students differently from others where such discrimination is not justified. In such cases, the cheap solution is constant vigilance and rehearsal of good practice. This might have greater impact on a range of behaviours from classroom interaction to subsequent participation.

School is a mini-society and students learn about what society is like through their lives at school. There is little point in overtly teaching that people can be trusted if students are not trusted in schools, and teachers themselves do not behave according to students' perception of socially accepted principles of justice. Teachers can model such behaviour in their day-to-day interaction with their pupils by applying such principles in their teaching behaviour. This might also have an effect on post-compulsory participation, which is the subject of the next chapter.

Chapter 8

Post-school outcomes

Introduction

Once compulsory schooling is complete, concern over disadvantaged students tends to focus on patterns of participation and non-participation in post-compulsory episodes rather than attainment. In fact, as this chapter demonstrates, a love of learning and a positive lifelong attitude to education are further possible wider outcomes of schooling. In England and Wales, over a third of the adult population regularly report not having participated in any formal episodes of learning at all since reaching school-leaving age (Selwyn et al. 2006, White & Selwyn 2011). This third is heavily stratified. Individuals living in remote areas, from families with less prestigious occupational backgrounds, with lower incomes, the unemployed or economically inactive, severely disabled people and ex-offenders with lower literacy skills are all less likely than average to participate in any episodes of formal education or training after the age of 16. For as long as we have accurate records it appears that certain groups in the population of the UK have been more likely to be routinely excluded from participation in many forms of post-compulsory education (HEFCE 2005). Those individuals who do participate in post-compulsory education are often heavily patterned by 'pre-adult' social, geographic and historical factors such as socio-economic status, year of birth and type of school attended (White 2012). Similar patterns have been found in all other countries.

Despite problems with the existing datasets (Chapter 3), such patterns are too strong and too widespread to be an artefact. However, the reviews conducted to provide the evidence for this book revealed little solid work on the causal nature of inequities in post-compulsory education. The traditional economic approach to explanation, whether human capital or rational choice theory, has been tested in practice, and does not yield accurate results for individuals. In a sense, both versions have been falsified – perhaps because individuals do not make accurate assessments of outcomes due to their differing beliefs about the value and purpose of academic learning (MacNab 2000), their commitments to future education are based more on ethical principles than these theories can encompass (Carroll 2000) or their outcomes of interest are much wider than employment (Zepke &

Leach 2011). Some students continue with extended education because they report believing that they will gain in the long-term through enhanced earnings (Kay & Sundaraj 2004). Others leave for the same reason, seeing education as a poor alternative to earning money in a job (Ulrich 2004). Policy-makers have realised that economic incentives and legislation enforcement are not sufficient in themselves to change the behaviour of a whole population.

This chapter looks at the evidence on what has been tried and what can be done to ensure that non-participation, where it occurs, is a choice rather than a stratified outcome of compulsory schooling or social disadvantage.

Sources of evidence

This chapter uses evidence from a series of studies of patterns of participation in post-compulsory education, described more fully in Chapter 2. Sources include an ESRC study of UK HE participation and occupational progression, and reviews of existing evidence for the Department of Education in England and the Higher Education Funding Councils for England and for Wales (Gorard et al. 2007, Gorard et al. 2011, Smith & Gorard 2011, See et al. 2011).

Patterns of initial participation

Widening participation (WP) in formal post-compulsory education and training is a common policy agenda in most developed countries. Several key policies relevant to widening participation have been introduced in the UK in the last decade. The legal leaving age from education and training has been raised from 16 years to 17 in 2013, to age 18 by 2015. The government also has a commitment to fair access in higher education by increasing participation from under-represented groups (DfES 2003a).

The proportion of young people participating immediately beyond compulsory education increased from 88 per cent in 1999 to 90 per cent in 2010 for 17 year olds, and from 62 per cent to 68 per cent for 18 year olds (DfE 2011). Therefore, voluntary participation at the age of 17 has already grown, and the growth has been greatest for many disadvantaged or previously under-represented groups. For example, while 38 per cent of White UK students were in full-time education at age 18 in 2009, the figures for minority ethnic groups were higher – 51 per cent for Pakistani, 53 per cent for Bangladeshi, 66 per cent for Black African and 41 per cent for Black Caribbean origin (DfE 2010). These minority groups were also reportedly more likely to be in higher education. As shown below, such comparisons are harder to make than some commentators imagine, and of course, they take no account of the type of institution attended, the qualifications gained and subsequent occupational trajectory. However, there is an indication here that immediate post-compulsory education is relatively un-stratified in terms of who continues and who does not, unlike the later-life learning and other opportunities that were identified as particularly problematic in the introduction.

Despite making the kinds of necessary judgements and compromises about the definitions of participation, populations, mature students and other categories described in Chapter 2, Table 8.1 shows how difficult it still is to decide whether a social group is under-represented in education. In the UK, the social class composition of all undergraduate students has changed little over time. In the example years here, the proportion of students in each category of the Registrar General's scale remains about the same. There is a slight decline in all figures except the category 'unknown'. It is important to note that occupational groups are not evenly divided in the population. The dominance of certain social groups in HE is partly a function of their numerical frequency in the population, which changes over historical time, to an extent that is not always made clear in media and policy reports. If the population is becoming more middle-class over time, students at HE (who tend to be younger than the population as a whole) would quite rightly be more middle-class than the resident population. In itself, this would not be unfair or even disproportionate in relation to the correct figures for the appropriate age-related population.

Even so, in comparison to the national population census 2001, students in HE appear to come disproportionately from managerial, intermediate and semi-routine occupational backgrounds. However, in 2005 as many as 23 per cent of students had no recorded occupational background, and in the 2001 population census 38 per cent of householders had no known occupation. In reality, the kinds of people for whom data is missing in the census may be the same as in the HE data, or they may not be. Perhaps missing data from the population census over-represents the transient and homeless. Perhaps missing data for HE over-represents well-off families concerned that their response might lead to problems with fees or bursaries. This uncertainty makes judgements about under-representation problematic. For example, 62 per cent of the population reported

Table 8.1 Percentage of heads of households by occupational class, UK, 2001 census of population, and of all HE students by occupational class, UK, 2002–05

	Census 2001	HE 2002	HE 2003	HE 2004	HE 2005
Higher managerial	10	19	18	18	17
Lower managerial	17	25	25	25	24
Intermediate	6	13	12	12	12
Small employers	7	6	6	6	6
Lower supervisory	8	4	4	4	4
Semi-routine	7	10	11	11	11
Routine	7	5	5	5	4
Unknown	38	18	20	20	23

Sources: UCAS and National Statistics – http://www.statistics.gov.uk/ accessed 20 February 2013.

Note: Unknown includes never worked, long-term unemployed (and unknown or invalid response)

an occupation in the census, and 17 per cent have a lower managerial occupation. This means that 27 per cent (17 in 62) of the population with known occupations are lower managerial, which is higher than the proportion of HE applicants with the same background. Does this mean that managerial backgrounds are slightly under-represented in HE, the exact opposite of what most accounts suggest? Not knowing means that it is not really possible to say whether managerial occupations are over-represented in HE or not. It is very tricky to decide whether a specific social group is proportionately represented in HE – much trickier than commentators usually suggest.

Widening participation, in the sense of including more disadvantaged students, whether intentionally or not, has been taking place since at least 1940 in the UK as part of a relatively long-term historical and social trend. This trend is largely undisturbed by any specific policies to widen participation. However, the early 1990s saw a dramatic change due to a rapid increase in the number of places available at HE institutions (Mayhew et al. 2004, Raffe et al. 2006). A very similar trend has occurred across Europe, with a growth of participation to 40 per cent of the young population by 2000, and sharp drops in inequality of access to HE by parental education and occupation (Koucky et al. 2010). The 'effect' size (R-squared) of expansion and equity is around 0.2. This suggests the quickest and easiest, and once everything is taken into account perhaps even the cheapest, way to widen participation is simply to increase the number of funded places at universities. The universities will generally find students if there are places to be filled, and the historical evidence is that these new students will be disproportionately from the less represented social groups. By 2000 the proportion of young people with the required entry qualifications at Level 3 (two A-levels or equivalent) and attended university in the UK was above 94 per cent. Therefore, most people who were qualified to go to university did so, and the stratification of occupational backgrounds in HE represented simply the stratification of prior attainment at age 18. The problem, for HE entry in general, is nothing to do with the admissions. Indeed, the student body attending university each year is slightly more representative of the total population than those applying are (Gorard et al. 2007, Anders 2012).

The population as a whole was 92 per cent White UK, according to the 2001 census, but the student body in HE was only 87 per cent White UK in 2000, and this dropped to 84 per cent by 2005 (DfE 2010). Therefore, one could argue that the HE system somewhat over-represents the ethnic minority groups. But the ethnic diversity of the population is greater among younger age cohorts who are more likely to enter HE, so perhaps the general age population is not a good comparator (Chapter 2). Also, after White UK, the second largest category in the census is 'unknown'. In fact, there are more cases with unknown ethnicity than all other ethnic minority groups combined. Around ten per cent of students also do not report ethnicity. The number of cases in each of the ethnic categories is generally small – too small for suitable analysis and much smaller than the number of missing cases. Despite their growth in number, the categories for ethnicity do not do justice to the real diversity of individual origins (Gorard 2001). All of these factors together mean that it is not possible to differentiate robust patterns for specific minority backgrounds from the 'noise' generated. Existing figures provide no reason to assume that ethnic minorities, in general, are under-represented in HE. There is actually a stronger case that the majority White group is under-represented at present.

Another area of concern for WP is the participation of students with some form of disability. In the UK, there has been an increase in the proportion of HE students reporting a disability, with the proportion almost doubling over a decade even while the numbers of students overall was growing. It is not immediately clear whether this increase in students with a reported disability is evidence of a widening of opportunities, or more to do with an increase in reporting (as in Chapter 4). It is clear that the major part of this increase has been for students with a non-visible disability such as dyslexia. In fact, if the figures for dyslexia alone are subtracted from the figures for disability, there has been no overall growth in the proportion of other disabled students since 1995. The numbers involved here are smaller than for many specific ethnic minority groups, making any claim to under-representation even more difficult. Disability is not covered by the population census, and other estimates from National Statistics present sample data in which serious and mild disabilities are aggregated with long-term illnesses such as asthma. Between 15 per cent and 20 per cent of the child population have reported a disability or long-term illness in repeated surveys over the past decade. Of these, the majority (over 40 per cent) suffer from asthma, and others suffer from other illnesses apart from a disability. This means the proportion of children with a reported disability is very similar to the proportion of HE students with a disability (six per cent to seven per cent). The possible under-representation of the less than one per cent of the population with reported 'serious disabilities' is too difficult to determine for the same reason as for specific minority ethnic groups.

Barriers to participation

The potential explanation for low participation rates among certain groups is often believed to be related to their characteristics. Tackling these characteristics head-on forms an attractive, simple package for policy-makers (National Audit Office 2002, Council of the European Union 2010). For example, if low-income families are under-represented in HE, the cost of HE may be a barrier to participation. The solution would be bursaries, free places, reform of benefit rules and so on (Metcalf 2005).

One study claimed that the Education Maintenance Allowance (EMA), a monetary incentive awarded to students from low-income families, was successful in encouraging young people to stay on in full-time education (Middleton et al. 2005). In this study a quarter of the students who received the allowance stated that the EMA was 'very important' in their decisions to stay in full-time education, but 73 per cent of those who said the EMA was 'very important' also said they would 'probably' or 'definitely' have stayed on without it. Also, contrary to popular belief, finance is not the main reason given for non-participation (Selwyn et al. 2006). Few students report dropping out of education because of finance alone. If cost is the barrier to participation by low-income groups then removal or reduction of the cost should lead to increased participation from lower-income groups. Financial incentives such as grants, fees remission and means-tested bursaries would help increase participation. This, however, does not happen in reality. There is little direct evidence that these approaches are effective in increasing participation by low-income groups (Chapman & Ryan 2002, Taylor & Gorard 2005). The introduction of tuition fees in Wales 1999/2000, for example, made no difference to overall levels of participation or participation by poorer candidates (Gorard & Taylor 2001). In the UK as a whole, more students from low-income families have attended HE in the era since grants and free places were removed than they did when attendance was entirely state-sponsored (HEFCE 2005). Participation did not decrease in the recent economic downturn as many saw extended education as an alternative to work. Overall, finance may not be an important factor in stratifying access to HE (Dearden et al. 2004).

Other purported barriers such as time, travel and institutional behaviour also show no evidence that they actually stratify access (Gorard et al. 2007). Attractive as the idea of barriers to learning may be, both as an explanation of the differences in participation and as the basis for their reduction, the evidence base is weak. No attempts have been made to evaluate interventions to overcome barriers in a controlled manner using appropriate designs for causal models. One of the main reasons for this is that young people leaving school at 16 with no qualifications are unlikely to be concerned about issues such as fees, travel, or adjustment to the HE culture. They will generally not consider HE as a possible future, for the simple reason that they did not meet the entry requirements. The stratification of HE does not really occur at acceptance, at application or any time near these. It occurs much earlier in the life course.

A life course approach

To understand the patterns of post-16 participation one needs to look at each individual's biography and their learning 'trajectories' over the longer-term. Some people leave formal education at the earliest opportunity, some return to formal learning later in life while others continue into extended initial education and end their formal learning there. Which of these 'trajectories' an individual takes can be accurately predicted by characteristics already known by the time they reach school-leaving age. Biography-based analyses, conducted in several different regions totalling 10,000 adults across the UK, have shown that the same determinants of post-compulsory participation appear each time. Similar results were replicated in other countries (Antikainen & Huusko 2008). For example, Gorard and Rees (2002) entered variables measuring five groups of determinants – time, place, sex, family and initial schooling – into a logistic regression model in chronological order as they occur in real life. It was found that early characteristics, such as age, sex and family background, predict later learning trajectories with 75 per cent accuracy. Adding the variables representing initial schooling increases the accuracy of prediction to 90 per cent. Beyond this, other measurable variables of adult life can add little to the predictions. Almost all the variation is accounted for once background and early schooling is taken into account. There is not enough variation left for barriers to make any difference to participation. This suggests that subsequent life events do not make much difference because an individual's 'learner identity' is already set.

What these findings mean is that early experiences in initial schooling could be an important factor in shaping an individual's long-term orientations towards learning, and thus their success or otherwise in education and access to further and higher education. Success and failure in school form part of students' experiences of school, and these are important determinants of their subsequent attitude to learning and participation. Those who failed are less likely to see the relevance of post-compulsory education, and believe that such education is not for them. Where schools systems are highly selective and where course selection rather than institutions are stratified, similar impacts are seen (Thomas and Webber 2009).

Early experiences of school are therefore important for future participation in education and learning. Negative experiences of school, such as inadequate attention, unfair treatment, experience of exclusion, inappropriate curriculum and poor quality teaching can all be seen as barriers to academic success (Strand 2007). This is especially so for some Black Caribbean students. There were aspects of Black Caribbean students' experience of school that led them to believe that higher education was not something they could aspire to (Bowl 2001). Some studies cited negative peer pressure as a critical demotivating factor among African Caribbean and Black Caribbean students (Education Commission 2004). Strand and Winston (2008) calculated that students with disaffected or negative peers were three times less likely to continue in education. Positive peer influence, on the other hand, can encourage participation. For example, students explained that they wanted to go to university because many of their friends were doing so (Joseph Rowntree Foundation 2006). A positive school experience, high quality staff support, a positive attitude towards school and high academic expectations can reportedly improve students' aspirations and hence post-16 participation (Clayden & Stein 2002). These issues are considered further in Chapter 10.

Family background is influential in many ways, most obviously in material terms, but also in terms of what is understood to be the 'natural' form of participation. For many people who participate actively in post-school learning, such participation is the prescribed norm within the family. The community and even the individual seem to be less influential. Families are universally acknowledged as a key determinant of educational performance in primary and secondary schooling and, by extension, in higher education too. Minority ethnic groups with a high rate of post-16 participation tend to be from families that place a high value on education. In our review we found many studies testifying to this. For example, Dale et al. (2000) found that among young Pakistani and Bangladeshi students, the ability to remain in post-16 education depended heavily on parental support. Gayle et al. (2002) found that after controlling for educational attainment, parental occupational social class was still linked to participation in HE. Among Indian and Pakistani students, family issues were often given as reasons for not continuing post-16 education (Middleton et al. 2005). These suggest that the family socio-economic background may be a key determinant of young people's potential to continue in education. There were also reports of Asian mothers, particularly those who are less educated, discouraging their daughters from going to university, for fear of not being able to find suitable husbands. These issues are considered further in Chapter 11.

This does not imply that people do not have choices, or that barriers have no impact at all, but rather that choices occur within a framework of opportunities and expectations determined by the resources people derive from their background and upbringing. Of course, there may be important variables as yet unmeasured to explain these findings. One possible interpretation is that family poverty, lack of role models and a sense of 'not for us', coupled with poor experiences of initial schooling, can conspire to create a kind of lifelong attitude to formal learning – a negative learner identity. In this case, the obvious barriers such as cost, time and travel are largely irrelevant, and major changes in external factors such as economic recession may not lead to noticeable changes in trajectory (Edwards & Weller 2010). In the family, social or economic situation for any individual, the choice not to participate can be completely rational. We need to revise any complacency that the existing set up for learning is appropriate for all, and that the reluctant learner need only be lured back 'on track'.

The determinants of intention to participate

In the QCA dataset, only just over half of students (55 per cent) reported that school so far has encouraged them to want to learn more, and that they plan to continue in formal education after compulsory school. A similar picture emerged from the study by OFSTED (2007). Table 8.2 shows the result of a logistic regression model using a number of possible explanatory variables to try and explain the difference between students planning to continue in education after 16, and the rest. The student personal and family background explains the bulk of the variation that can be explained, meaning that intention to study after compulsory schooling is stratified. In particular, students from families living in poverty are less likely to report wanting to stay on in education after age 16. Girls and students speaking a language other than English at home are much more likely to continue to post-compulsory education (there was no direct measure of ethnicity or immigrant status).

Table 8.2 Percentage of variation in responses to 'I plan to continue in education after age 16', explained by each stage of analysis

Individual student background variables	14
School-level variables	2
Individual experiences of education	9

The variables measured or available at school level are largely unrelated once this individual student background has been accounted for. The staff attitudes, approaches and reported priorities, overall school results at Key Stage 4, ethnic mix of students, geographical location, curriculum offer, school type (such as faith-based or single sex) and the management organisation of each school are all unrelated to patterns of reported participation plans.

The final stage in the model, using individual student responses to their experiences of schooling so far, is almost as influential as student background. Indeed, experiences of school so far are the major malleable determinants here. Participation relevant outcomes are positively influenced by the provision of good information and guidance for the future, a feeling of being in control, advice from immediate family and contact with students doing other courses (perhaps offering insights into alternatives, or even things to avoid). So the overall impression is that students want help from various sources, but to feel that the choice remains theirs (Table 8.3). These outcomes are also enhanced by being in small classes with appropriately specialist teachers, indicating that the quality of the learning environment also plays a role. The determinants are very similar to those in Chapter 7. The next section looks at what can be done to improve the situation. Chapter 10 examines the evidence as to whether intentions to stay on are good predictors of actual behaviour.

Table 8.3 Individual response variables in model for planning to continue in education

Choice influenced by family	1.37
Contact with students on other programmes	1.30
Teachers for specialist subjects	1.30
Choice influenced by school pressure	0.56
Learning also at work	0.53
Learning also in college	0.42

Interventions

There have been even fewer rigorously evaluated interventions to try and increase post-compulsory participation for disadvantaged groups than there have to increase attainment at school. Few researchers or funders seem to care enough to find out what works. Some evidence suggests that mentoring, provided by faculty members, may have positive effects on the educational outcomes of ethnic minority students. However, the overall evidence is far from convincing, and the most positive results tend to come from the smallest or weakest studies.

Our study uncovered a number of intervention programmes aimed at increasing post-compulsory education. These include the use of mentors (such as the Achievement Mentoring Program (AMP), the Undergraduate Research Opportunity Program (UROP)), enhancing motivation (for example, the Advancement via Individual Determination (AVID) programme) and detracking. Of the three mentoring programmes, one found positive effects, one had no effects and one showed mixed effects.

Holt et al. (2008) and Clarke (2009) evaluated the same programme (AMP) involving matching students to teachers as mentors. The study Holt et al. found no differences between mentees and controls in terms of grade point averages, absences and the number of discipline referrals. Clarke undertook a similar study but extended it to 18 months, and reported positive results on grades in language and maths but not in social science. This suggests that a longer time period may be necessary for the effects of the Achievement Mentoring intervention to be seen.

In a randomised controlled trial involving 1,280 university students to prevent drop out of ethnic minority students in university, faculty mentoring was reported to be effective in lowering the drop-out rate of intervention students compared to a control group (Nagda et al. 1998). Although no significant differences were found, the authors reported that the programme benefited African American students whose academic performance was below the median for the ethnic group. Positive trends were also reported for Hispanic and White students who participated in UROP. A similar study matching traditionally under-represented minority students at university with demographically similar faculty members also reported positive effects (Campbell & Campbell 1997). This is a cohort study involving 678 students. The results showed a higher Grade Point Average for mentored students than control students (2.45 vs 2.29), more units completed per semester (9.33 vs 8.49) and a lower dropout rate (14.5 per cent vs. 26.3 per cent). The pattern of differences continued and appeared to be cumulative.

It is important to note that mentoring strategies are effective only when they involve teachers or faculty members. Peer group mentoring did not achieve similar positive effects. For example, Thomas (2006) found no differences in college adjustment, GPA and retention between those on the programme and those in the control group, suggesting that student mentoring may not be effective for African American university students. However, it has to be noted that this was a small study involving only 80 students (50 in intervention and 30 in control).

Another programme combining school engagement and monitoring strategies, known as 'Check and Connect', to support students with emotional and behavioural difficulties reported positive effects (Sinclair et al. 2005). Treatment students were more likely than those in the control group to be engaged in school, complete their assignments, earn credits in their first year of high school and be on track to graduate in five years. The same people extended the study to include a larger sample (n=147) and found that at the end of the four-year follow up 31 per cent of the 74 intervention students and 14 per cent of control students were still enrolled in school but had not yet graduated. However, there was no difference in on-time school completion. Another study involving 1,762 ethnic minority high school students evaluated the efficacy of a supportive and personalised learning environment on students' academic outcomes (Kemple & Snipes 2000). Results were inconclusive. The programme appeared to increase school attendance slightly but had no impact on graduation rates.

Other studies have found that de-segregation in the form of detracking or heterogeneous streaming improved the likelihood of disadvantaged students gaining a higher-status diploma (Burris et al. 2008). The researchers tracked six cohorts of students from ninth through to twelfth grade. Three cohorts before the detracking and introduction of universal acceleration in maths were used as controls. Their performance was compared with another three cohorts of students who had been accelerated and heterogeneously grouped in maths and experienced some detracking in ninth grade. The study found that detracking increased the odds of obtaining an IB diploma by 70 per cent and even more for gaining a Regents Diploma, ranging from a three-fold increase for White and Asian students, a five-fold increase for African American and Latino students eligible for free or reduced price lunch (FRPL) to a 26-fold increase for African American or Latino students not eligible for FRPL.

Another attempt to increase participation involved intervening in improving students' motivation and attitude towards school. Black et al. (2008) examined the (AVID) programme, which involved a combination of motivational and academic skills training. Their study found that AVID students had higher enrolment in eighth-grade algebra than comparison students, and fewer days of self-reported school absences. They also scored significantly higher on college plans and spent more time on homework (self-reported). However, there were no differences between groups in terms of standardised test scores and self-reported grades.

There are also studies that combined a number of intervention strategies, hoping that one would work. One such study is by Padgett and Reid (2002). The intervention, known as Student Diversity Program (SDP), combined close monitoring with peer and faculty mentoring, motivational and academic skills training and academic and social support (Padgett & Reid, 2002). The aim of the intervention was to increase the retention rates of Black student athletes and other students considered at risk of failure in one US university. This was a case control study, which compared the graduation rates and final GPAs of 39 SDP students with those of 434 matched students who were not in the programme. SDP students graduated at twice the rate of comparable students matched on sex, ethnicity, age, transfer status, entering GPA and date of enrolment. However, there was no difference between the two groups in terms of the average final GPA.

Conclusions

The standard account of post-compulsory participation is that it is explicable by human capital theory, but that current inequities need to be sorted out. The most popular approach to making participation easier for under-represented disadvantaged groups is to remove barriers. As this chapter portrays, this will not necessarily be sufficient, and it will inevitably change the nature of whatever it is that people are meant to participate in. If the format, culture or language of post-compulsory and higher education is changed to suit marginal participants then the current evidence of the advantages and payoffs from education are no longer valid. In addition, removing obstacles and discriminatory practices in later phases ignores imbalances in participation that result from prior societal and educational inequity such as that at school.

Overcoming the traditional barriers can and will only attract the usual suspects (i.e. those most like those already participating, such as students with just an A-level grade lower). Many individuals are already on a pathway or trajectory leading to HE or not long before application and admission, and it would require a longer term and more radical solution than overcoming barriers to influence this. But, while long term, the idea of influencing aspirations and intentions directly is probably not radical enough. What people at age 11 say they might do at 16 or 18 is neither accurate nor reliable enough to be worth investing more in (Chapter 10). The education system in England and Wales has compulsory schooling for all, based loosely on a comprehensive and egalitarian model, until age 16. A greater element of selection is introduced for continuation post-16, such that prior attainment begins to influence how, and even whether, an individual continues in formal education and training. This is despite growing pressure for everyone to continue formal education in some way. Some individuals leave formal learning at, or even before, 16 and never return. On one reading of the evidence, this is a key target group for the widening participation agenda – those least likely to participate again. But, of course, those least likely to participate again are largely ignored as poor bets in practice, in favour of those more like the usual suspects for HE.

There are few other ways forward at present. There is a pressing need for positive interventions to improve participation, but these are just not happening at present (Gorard et al. 2011). The only one identified here is that adult mentoring is an effective measure for improving outcomes for students in higher education. There is evidence of positive effects of having non-parental adults (in particular staff or faculty members) as mentors on student behaviour, academic performance, drop-out rates and retention. However, other studies have shown that the effects of mentoring take time to be realised.

Currently, there are two alternative generic approaches to widening participation in HE. The first approach involves adjusting entry requirements, allowing students from disadvantaged backgrounds the benefit of an A-level grade or similar. However, if we continue to use prior qualifications as a key criterion for

HE entry on the assumption that qualifications are a fair indication of talent, then even dabbling would not fundamentally change the nature of each annual HE intake because qualifications are so strongly linked to social and economic origin.

The alternative is to take a life course and society-wide view of the underlying inequality that produces the socio-economic stratification of HE participation. The strong correlation between school-level qualification and later educational success (Schofield & Dismore 2010), and between educational outcomes and success in employment, is something quite artificial. It is the product of our own regulations. For example, only those students with 'good' GCSEs are qualified to stay on at school, only those with 'good' Level 3 qualifications are likely to be accepted at university and more likely to be offered a 'good' job if they have a 'good' degree from a 'good' university, and so on. Since early attainment, personal background and personal characteristics are good predictors of qualifications, taking a life course view may reduce the apparent influence of qualifications, if qualifications are simply a substitute measure of an individual's prior social and economic determinants of 'success' at school and beyond.

The second approach would therefore be to reject prior qualifications as a criterion of entry, and promote open access to further and higher education as in some European countries such as Finland. This could mean changing our focus to equality of outcomes rather than equality of conditions. Accepting or denying admission to higher education based on some artificial criterion is a form of indirect discrimination in favour of those whose previous life experience provides social and cultural advantage (Tannock 2008). In England educational institutions select students on the basis of educational attainment. It is considered unfair and illegal to select students based on sex, SES, ethnicity or age. However, if attainment is stratified by these same variables, then it would be equally unfair and unethical to select students using attainment (Walford 2004).

Both approaches would be courageous, but once we have eliminated overcoming barriers and promoting intentions as unworkable there is little choice; they are definitely alternatives. Morally we cannot continue to use qualifications while working to overcome initial inequality to promote fairer outcomes, since we are admitting that qualifications are heavily biased and so currently not merited (although there remain other, more sound, reasons for overcoming initial inequality). If we accept qualifications as currently awarded on merit then it would be equally immoral to try and change their distribution to one that was less merited.

Chapter 9

Targeted approaches

Introduction

Given that we cannot easily identify the characteristics of a differentially effective school (Chapter 5) or teacher (Chapter 6), at least in terms of improving student attainment, reducing the poverty gap in attainment or extending post-compulsory participation, this chapter highlights more focused interventions and teaching approaches. The chapter continues from the last section of Chapter 8. It presents the findings from a series of reviews, evaluations and randomised controlled trials looking at literacy interventions, catch-up programmes, summer schools and the use of IT to reduce the poverty gradient during compulsory schooling. What it reveals again is how little secure knowledge there is about what works to overcome educational disadvantage, or to assist those students in danger of falling behind.

Reading is a fundamental skill for later life and forms the basis for any child's subsequent learning at school. In the UK, 20 per cent of children in their first year of secondary school were found not to be able to read at a level suitable for their age (National Literacy Trust 2010). The situation may be as bad, and as stratified, in other countries. Many of the proposed interventions in this chapter are therefore about literacy and the almost equally important issue of numeracy. Many of these focus on the end of primary or the start of secondary school – the transition period – when problems have become clear and some kind of 'catch-up' is proposed. Students who were already struggling with basic literacy and numeracy at primary level may be particularly sensitive to this transitional phase.

Sources of evidence

This chapter is based on a number of recent studies, including a review of evidence on interventions to improve literacy for disadvantaged students in England during their transition to secondary school (See et al. 2012), a number of randomised controlled literacy interventions (Khan & Gorard 2012) and a formative evaluation of a summer school programme (Gorard et al. 2012b). The methods are described further in Chapter 2.

Summer schools and catch-up programmes

The first proposed intervention is the use of the long summer vacation to provide catch-up programmes. There are reports of effective summer literacy supplementary activity (Borman & Dowling 2006), and better teaching or supplementary programmes for students lacking effective reading and comprehension skills (Reidel et al. 2003, Somers et al. 2010). However, this evidence is not always clear. See et al. (2012) conducted a review of the evidence on the transition from Year 6 to Year 7 worldwide, and the possibility of students catching up in literacy. They came across several further studies concerning the impact of summer school programmes. One study of around 2,000 students in transition from primary to secondary school divided them non-randomly into two groups. It found no differential impact on literacy gain scores between the groups who attended a 50-hour summer literacy school compared to a control. Both groups demonstrated an equivalent decline in scores from pre- to post-test – the so-called summer learning loss (Sainsbury et al. 1998). Therefore, it seems that the reason for any decline over that crucial summer is not to do with whether literacy practice and teaching takes place. It could be due to anxiety about changing school, a change in school routine or a different curriculum emphasis. A smaller, more recent study from the US involved 331 students from first to fifth grade in one school (Kim 2006). Using stratification in terms of pre-test reading ability, students were randomly allocated to a treatment or delayed treatment in a waiting-list design. The treatment involved receiving ten free books to read during the summer vacation, including postcards and letters to stimulate reading. Using self-report, the treatment group read three more books, on average, than the control. However, this did not convert to any difference in the literacy scores between the groups after the vacation. The number of students is quite small in the preferred age range (fifth grade) and 52 students moved away during the summer (proportionately for each group and stratum). Nevertheless, this study again shows little promise from summer programmes.

Chaplin and Capizzano (2006) reported a purportedly randomised evaluation of the BELL summer programme (http://www.experiencebell.org/) in Boston and New York. However, they present data relating to only 44 per cent of the original applicants to the programme, meaning that their use of statistical significance is totally incorrect. The summer programme involved both maths and reading, but the results are only presented for reading. The difference in test scores between treatment and control groups were negligible, and provided no evidence of a beneficial impact. The report claims that this is because the control group had 16 more days in school before the post-test than the treatment group did. This flaw in the original design may indeed be the reason for the lack of a more positive result, but the study does not demonstrate a positive result, and it looks like dredging to try and account for this afterwards (Gorard 2013). The overall effect size of this summer programme on reading, not calculated in the report, was only around 0.02, and the performance of the control group in vocabulary was actually better than the treatment. This report therefore provides very far from convincing evidence of effect, and was generated by authors with a potential conflict of interest. Harvard Family Research Project (2006), clearly also with a link to BELL and so a potential conflict of interest, presented a number of evaluations of the BELL summer schools and accelerated learning programme. These were little better. The gains observed were generally higher in both maths and reading for the six-week programme than the four-week one, although low income children had lower gains and in several years actually lost ground. Higher gains were generally reported for the younger year groups.

Put another way, what these studies may show is not that summer interventions cannot work, but that it is not just about doing something well-meaning and plausible over the summer. For example, it is necessary to have some further input rather than just providing books. On the other hand, the other studies suggest that simply having more 'school' over summer does not help either. As far as we can tell from the evidence here, summer school programmes have not been shown to be effective in improving literacy for students in transition.

Given that there is little robust evidence on the efficacy of the BELL approach, one organisation ran a pilot summer school in England in 2012, based loosely on the BELL approach. If feasible and successful, this intervention was to be improved and then scaled up for wider trial. The four-week programme was intended to reverse summer learning loss, develop children's skills and confidence and increase parental engagement in the learning of their children. It provided targeted small-group academic tuition focusing on literacy and numeracy and a diverse programme of enrichment activities, at an estimated cost per student of £1,100. The children involved in this pilot were in Years 5 and 6 in the summer of 2012. It took place in a fairly deprived area of north-east London. Gorard et al. (2012b) carried out an evaluation, the purpose of which was to assist in the formative development of the intervention for a subsequent larger evaluation. The pilot summative evaluation was based on student educational outcomes as assessed by their test scores leading up to, including and following Key Stage 2 for numeracy and literacy. An effect size of the gain in scores based on those attending and not attending the summer school was estimated, to assess the impact of the programme. Evaluators also observed staff training and implementation of the programme in practice. The fieldwork included interviews with the organisers, trainers, staff, parents and students, plus participant observation of activities and lessons.

As a concept, the summer school 2012 can be considered a success. It recruited and trained staff in a relatively short time, and met its target of students. Staff, students and parents supported the programme and were generally appreciative of the opportunity. Health and safety, provision of food and access to water and general care were seen to be good. The correct number of sessions was staffed at the planned staff–student ratios. A range of activities was undertaken, culminating in a plenary graduation event. Some afternoon enrichment activities were more popular than others, such as the graduation and white water rafting, while games during breaks were very much appreciated. Therefore, summer provision for struggling students in a relatively disadvantaged area seems feasible.

This pilot summer school was intended to recruit 160 students who were coming to the end of Years 5 and 6 in their primary schools. In the event, 152 were enrolled, which suggests that, given the short lead-in time, recruitment should not be an issue. There is demand for such schools in relatively deprived urban areas, and some children and families will clearly agree to attend. However, of those for whom there are records, attendance by some young people was as low as five per cent. It was clear from discussion with parents and students that some did not understand that the summer school was a four-week commitment, and several had arranged family holidays that clashed, despite agreeing to attend. There is no clear evidence that the summer school children were initially especially disadvantaged or low-achieving compared to those not attending. In fact, Year 6 summer school children were already ahead in maths and Year 5 students in reading – compared to other students from the same primary schools.

Transport was provided for students from their home area to the summer school. This was to assist parents and ensure a prompt start. A substantial breakfast was provided on site to encourage healthy eating and as a kind of incentive. Students were briefly registered, and announcements and arrangements for the day were made. Then all students were divided into eight teaching groups of between 16 and 20, with a trained teacher and one or more mentors or peer mentors. The morning consisted of literacy and numeracy development using a mixture of activities, presentation and team work. In general, the impression from the lessons was that the atmosphere was often very like a traditional primary school classroom. Teaching was quite formal, and was observed to be very variable in quality. There were quite basic pedagogical and factual errors in some classes (just as described in Chapter 6). PowerPoint displays were too small to be read by the class, writing was too faint or too poor to be read and teachers often stood in front of their displays anyway. The result of these errors and others like them was that young people often did not appear to understand the ensuing activities. There was sometimes an apparent lack of interest by teachers, never dealing with specific individuals or tables for example. There were many examples of broken promises to students, such as offers of prizes and rewards that never materialised.

The evaluators conducted interviews with students over the four weeks, including with some key informants who were interviewed repeatedly, and found generally positive views:

> Teachers are kind here. In main school teachers are not kind. If someone does something wrong then teachers will start shouting. Here they just give warnings.
>
> I like the dance. There are two mentors. They are showing us dance and we are preparing for the street dance performance. I am enjoying a lot.

However, a minority of students also complained of fighting and bullying going on, and many more mentioned feeling let down by the lack of trips and activities that they felt they had been offered.

The evaluators spoke to parents on several occasions, who were generally very supportive and appreciative of the summer school. Of course, since these informal interviews took place on site these responses are limited to parents (almost entirely mothers) who turned up to events or to collect their children. Nevertheless, the level of enthusiasm is clear:

> My son is so excited that he wakes up early at seven and gets ready himself to come. He said that it was fabulous. First day he was a bit reluctant to come but second day he was already out of bed to come.
>   I have two kids and keeping them occupied requires a lot of money … So it's good for my daughter to get out and do stuff. Plus they keep their brain going in the morning. A bit of maths and a bit of literacy. And she does not seem to be complaining which is a good thing.

The most common complaints were that the activities did not live up to billing, and that more, and more varied, activities should have been provided. This gap between what is promised, or thought to have been promised, and what happens needs to be addressed. Several parents wrote about 'false promises' or 'a lot of broken promises', and this is an issue that the evaluation team also noted more widely.

Table 9.1 presents the summary results for all Year 6 students for whom there is at least one pair of pre- and post-results for reading. Surprisingly, the pre-summer KS2 fine points score in maths and the raw-score in reading is lower on average for those students not attending the summer school than the other students from the same schools used as a comparison. This initial difference is not large, but it does raise the question of whether some of the most disadvantaged students did not take part in the summer school, either through selection or self-selection. Both groups show gains over the summer period (i.e. there is no discernible summer loss, even for those who did not attend the summer school). The gain scores for both groups when converted into a standardised 'effect' size show very little difference between the groups. The attendees at the summer school are slightly ahead in maths and slightly behind in reading, but the differences are small. Given the small size of the summer school group, and the scale of missing data, the most appropriate conclusion to be drawn is that there is no evidence of a beneficial impact from the summer school for Year 6 students on the basis of this comparison. The results for Year 5 students were even lower.

Overall, there is little evidence of enhanced student progress in attainment in the term following attendance at the summer programme. Matched pair comparisons and analysis by level of attendance in summer school confirmed this, and suggested that summer school attendance created no benefit in numeracy

Table 9.1 Estimated impact of Summer School Programme on Year 6 reading

Treatment group	N	KS2 raw-score	September raw-score	Gain	Standard deviation	'Effect' size
Summer School	34	33.4	34.9	+1.53	5.64	−0.02
Comparison	53	32.5	34.2	+1.74	9.70	−

and literacy test scores for either year group. There is little promise here. Even with successful enrichment and motivational activities, simply using four weeks of holiday for more schooling does not seem to help. The pilot has been successful in demonstrating that the concept is feasible, but it has not demonstrated that it is effective in improving the educational outcomes of disadvantaged children. Coupled with the prior studies (discussed earlier) there is no basis for rolling out this kind of intervention more widely.

Use of technology and software

Another popular measure to improve learning is the use of technology in the classroom. The appeal is obvious. Students can work at their own pace, and teachers are freed up to some extent to focus their attention on those who are struggling. Access to technology in schools in England has grown exponentially since the 1980s. It is now routine for most schools to use technology-based products such as software packages and websites in teaching and learning – both in literacy and other core subject skills. Part of the reason for this scale is enhanced government funding for technology-based purchases and for staff development in the use of IT. Spending on IT continues to rise, and the government in England has long recommended using technology solutions in all school subjects (DfES 2003b).

However, the evidence on the educational benefits of these various technology products is not particularly clear. IT is used in the classroom, and independently and less formally by individual learners. IT can be used in the classroom in isolation or as part of a blended learning approach. It may be used for different tasks over different lengths of time, even within one school. The beneficial outcomes sought could be enjoyment, autonomy of learning, future participation, personalisation, freeing up teachers to deal with other issues, cost effectiveness or simply enhanced learning outcomes. It is, therefore, hard to say whether and to what extent technology-based instruction 'works'. In addition, many of the studies directly addressing the efficacy of IT in literacy education have been descriptive in nature, relying on the impressions of participants. These studies often find an apparently positive impact on the acquisition of student literacy skills (Cox et al. 2003, Pittard et al. 2003, OFSTED 2004). However, others have argued that the small sample sizes, the lack of comparators and of research design and the passive retrospective nature of some of this work combine to offer a potentially misleading picture (Waxman et al. 2003).

In this light, it is interesting that experimental studies of the effectiveness of software packages in improving literacy skills tend to show rather different results. Rigorous intervention studies with suitable controls often find little or no positive impact from the use of technology-based instruction compared to standard or traditional practice. A number of studies and systematic reviews have found that software packages had no effect on reading achievement (Lei & Zhao 2005, Dynarski et al. 2007, Borman et al. 2009). Brooks et al. (2006) report a trial of 155 Year 7 students in one school, which may have led to some diffusion of the process, and around 25 students dropped out of the study before analysis. Students were randomised either to a treatment group receiving one hour per day for ten days of literacy development via computer, or to standard treatment (with a waiting-list design). There was no statistically significant gain for the treatment group in spelling. The control group had significantly higher gain scores for reading than the treatment. So, again, software by itself does not work, at least not after ten hours, and may actually harm progress in literacy.

Khan and Gorard (2012) randomised 23 initial Year 7 literacy classes involving 672 students either to standard treatment or use of a piece of widely-used commercial software that claimed to improve literacy levels in six weeks. The process evaluation suggested that staff, students and even parents were enthusiastic about the software approach that was used in all literacy lessons for a full term. Both groups improved their literacy scores, but the standard treatment group made much more progress. As Table 9.2 illustrates, the control group exposed to standard practice in literacy lessons, no routine access to computers and no access to the treatment software, also improved their standardised mean score substantially. There is no prima facie case here that the improvement for the treatment group was due to the software used. In fact, it would be easier to mount an argument that students using the software were disadvantaged (effect size of −0.43). Far from helping, the use of software may have hindered. This is an important conclusion, with wider implications than might be imagined at first sight.

The producers of the software tested by Khan and Gorard (2012) had apparent evidence that their product worked, based on before-and-after data. This demonstrated that students using the software for a long period improved their literacy on average. This claim is valid. What the trial showed was that the control group improved even more. This is why before and after designs without a true counterfactual are misleading (Gorard 2013). One such study is that reported by

Table 9.2 Effect size of ICT intervention

Treatment group	N	Pre-test mean	Post-test mean	Gain	Standard deviation	'Effect' size
ICT	319	823	863	+40	71	−0.43
Standard	346	817	886	+70	71	−

Johnson and Howard (2003). It looked at the impact of using a specific software package on the reading achievement and vocabulary development of 755 third, fourth and fifth graders from low socio-economic backgrounds in the US. There was no control and so no randomisation. Their paper does not present the improvement scores, but does claim that 'high' users of the software showed greater gains than 'low' users. Without a real comparator this is meaningless, as the usage might be the cause or the effect of literacy gains, or of something else such as motivation. This is no better than the evidence presented by the software manufacturers. Similarly, Meyer et al. (2010) conducted a study to evaluate the effects of a web-based tutoring system on reading comprehension for fifth and seventh grade. Two key design features were the type of feedback offered by the system (elaborated or simple) and the degree of choice students had in practice lessons (choice or no choice). They explored the effects of these on different measures of reading comprehension and the extent to which gains were maintained across the summer break, giving them 12 treatment and control conditions, and students were allocated by stratified randomisation to each. This all sounds perfectly plausible, except that the study involved only 111 students in both grades combined, giving an average of four students per grade and treatment arm.

The evidence is that the use of software, in itself, does not work and is not a solution to the poverty gradient. The vehicle of delivery, as with the issue of timing of summer schools, is not the active ingredient. The results may depend on the precise activities undertaken. This is especially clear where a technology-based approach is compared directly to another form of literacy learning (unlike the summer schools, which were generally compared with no treatment at all).

Individual studies with no obvious promise

Some specific interventions for improving literacy for struggling students, especially during the transition, have apparently only been evaluated once, and many of these show no promise at this stage. Sometimes this was because the work itself was very weak. For example, Lingard (2005) pursued Literacy Acceleration, an intervention developed by the author for students identified as having literacy difficulties in the first two years of UK secondary education. The study only reported on 38 students involved in the scheme, all in the same school, and compared to the other students in their classes who had much higher levels of literacy at the outset. There was no randomisation, yet the author cited significance levels as though they meant something in this context. Rider (2010) involved 52 eighth-grade students in a district-adopted, developmental reading course to improve the reading achievement of struggling middle school readers. The students improved their reading comprehension over time. However, no comparison group is reported, and it is not clear how the participants were selected and assigned, so the results are largely meaningless.

Guthrie et al. (2009) conducted a pre- and post-test quasi-experimental design to examine the effects of Concept-Oriented Reading Instruction (CORI) compared with traditional instruction on the reading performance of low-achieving readers in fifth grade. The intervention lasted 12 weeks. Outcome measures were compared using the Gates-MacGinitie Reading Test. Results showed that intervention students scored higher on word recognition speed and reading comprehension than control students. Unfortunately, CORI (two schools) and control students (one school) were drawn from different schools and CORI students had higher grades at the outset. Also, among the low achievers only seven per cent in the CORI group were identified as requiring special education, whereas in the control group 22 per cent were so designated.

Sometimes an evaluation, while far from ideal, tended to show that the intervention was of no benefit. This is more useful knowledge, unlike the weaker research above. For example, Puma et al. (2007) evaluated a structured writing programme, 'Writing Wings', for disadvantaged students in US third to fifth grade. The study involved 152 classroom teachers randomly allocated to treatment or control, of which results were available for only about 80 per cent. There was no difference in the writing ability or teacher ratings between the groups. De Corte et al. (2001) used an experimental design to evaluate a research-based and practically applicable learning environment for enhancing text comprehension strategies for fifth-grade students in Belgium. Participants were students in four experimental classes (79) and eight control classes (149). Schools were 'contacted' at random (and it is not clear what this means). The experimental group outperformed the control group in the use of strategy and application during text reading (process measures). There was no clear difference in the reading comprehension test outcome scores. The suggestion is that a powerful learning environment may encourage students to use and transfer reading comprehension strategies, but this does not necessarily result in improvement in reading comprehension performance. Wheldall (2000) reported on an Australian study to determine the effect of using the Rainbow Repeated Reading (RRP) programme to complement a MULTILIT (Making Up for Lost Time in Literacy) curriculum for low-progress readers – already deemed successful by the author. The progamme was added to a randomly allocated sample of half of 40 low-progress readers from Years 2 to 7 enrolling onto the original MULTILIT programme. The RRP group did no better.

Programmes with weak or mixed results

READ180

One intervention that has been more extensively tested, but without a consistent picture emerging, is READ180 (WWC 2009). This is a reading programme designed for students in both elementary and high school whose reading achievement is considered below the proficient level. The programme is a combination of computer software to track and respond to individuals' progress, literature and direct instruction in reading skills. A large number of studies have investigated the impact of this intervention. WWC (2009) lists 111, but most of these did not meet basic WWC standards for evidence and design, and are not considered here. Of the remainder, all are based in the US and used an experimental or quasi-experimental design. Several found no clear impact from READ180 on comprehension for students in fifth or sixth grade. Interactive Inc. (2002) reported mixed results, but a re-analysis by WWC found no clear differences. Assignment to groups was violated as a number of schools included in the treatment group students whom they thought would most benefit from the intervention, and parents/caregivers and students were allowed to request inclusion or exclusion, while students with a reading score lower than grade 1.5 were not allowed to take part at all. The average effect of READ180 across the three grades as calculated by WWC also suggests that the effect was not large enough to be considered important. The same is true for Kim et al. (2010) in a study of 294 struggling readers across fourth to sixth grade, although here the intervention was adapted to last 60 minutes per session rather than 90.

Two studies did find apparently significant gains in comprehension, but these only involved older students in ninth grade (White et al. 2006, Lang et al. 2008). Even here there was no gain for students at 'high risk' from poor literacy. Caggiano (2007) found a difference between the treatment and comparison group after READ180, using the Scholastic Inventory Reading comprehension assessment (designed by the developer of the programme) for the sixth grade only. There were no differences in other grades, and no differences in any grade from sixth to eighth in terms of standard reading assessments. White et al. (2005) evaluated the READ180 program in 16 public schools in the US, with 617 students identified as below their grade level in fourth to eighth grade. Outcome measures were compared with a control group of 4,619 unmatched students from the same schools who did not receive the intervention. The treatment group showed higher gains in reading scores than the control, but this could simply be regression to the mean if the other group were not also below grade level to start with. The study made a very common mistake in this literature, in using significance testing with a sample that was neither randomly drawn nor randomly allocated to groups.

Sprague et al. (2010) present what were in effect separate evaluations of READ180 in five sites across the US. One site in Ohio involved only youth detention centres, and is ignored here. Otherwise, students ranged from sixth to tenth grade, mostly in Title 1 funded schools, and defined as struggling readers below their grade level. In the first year 5,551 students were randomly assigned to treatment or control groups. However, only 4,443 students were included in the study. There was a high attrition rate in one site (Portland) where only 45 per cent of initial students were included in the final analysis. Some sites used the State Assessment tests, and some used the Scholastic Reading Inventory as pre-tests. Eligible students were randomly assigned to one of two supplemental programmes – READ180 or Xtreme Reading – or to 'business-as-usual' where they received regular instruction. Only one site showed significant intervention effects, and then only for middle school (not high school). However, this site was Portland with 55 per cent dropout from the study, which the multi-level modelling and other complex analyses presented by the authors simply do not address. In fact, 'significance' does not mean anything here. Woods (2007) examined the impact of READ180 on levels of reading achievement involving 384 students assessed as below grade-level readers, by teachers sixth to eighth grade in a middle school in Virginia, over a three-year period. There were reported implementation problems in the first year, and no difference was found in progress between those assigned to the intervention or control after one year. However, the gains for the treatment group were significantly higher in the second and third years following treatment. The report does not describe how the cases were assigned, and therefore whether 'significance' is relevant.

The only study with a reportedly unequivocal finding was conducted by the same organisation that created and markets the intervention itself, and therefore there is a conflict of interest. Scholastic Research (2008) reported significantly different results in general literacy for 285 students across sixth, seventh and ninth grade after one year of READ180, compared to 285 matched (not randomised) students. All were considered to be struggling as readers, and a majority had English as a second language.

Taken overall, the evidence presented here is almost that we know READ180 does not work. It did not work with standardised assessments rather than those created by the programme's producers. It did not work in the few randomised control trials presented. It did not work for those most at risk, or those in fifth or sixth grade. Reading intervention has been found to be less effective for older children. Yet there is some more positive evidence as well, presented by the programme's producers, in studies without randomisation or where there is high dropout. The fact that results were mixed across sites and year groups and for different components of literacy suggests that there may be an issue with the consistency with which the programme has been implemented. Even so, there must be better approaches. In real-life rollout of any intervention, such inconsistency of delivery is to be expected.

Project CRISS

Project CRISS – Creating Independence through Student-owned Strategies – is a programme aimed at improving reading, writing and learning for third to twelfth-grade students. It requires teachers to adopt purportedly new teaching styles that include monitoring learning, integrating new information with prior knowledge, and which encourage active learning through discussion, writing, organising information and analysing structure of text to improve comprehension. Teachers are given training in the form of workshops, to become CRISS-certified trainers. Like READ180, this programme has been the basis of extensive research

(WWC 2010). However, only two studies out of 31 met WWC minimal evidence standards.

James-Burdumy et al. (2009) report on a randomised controlled trial that examined the impact of Project CRISS and three other reading comprehension curricula (Read About, Read for Real, and Reading for Knowledge). The study involved 6,350 fifth-grade students in 89 schools not already implementing any of the four curricula. Schools were randomly assigned to one of the four interventions or to control groups. This review only considers the effect of Project CRISS and those students and schools that were evaluated by WWC. So, only 1,155 students attending 17 Project CRISS schools and 1,183 students in control schools were included in the analysis reported here. The programme lasted nine months. The study found no positive effects for Project CRISS on the passage comprehension subtest of GRADE, nor the science or social studies reading comprehension assessments. In fact, the fourth curriculum, Reading for Knowledge, had a statistically-significant negative impact on fifth-grade reading comprehension. When all four intervention groups were combined, intervention group students scored lower than control group students on both outcomes. Horsfall and Santa (1994) conducted a randomised controlled trial of Project CRISS in 16 fourth, sixth, eighth and eleventh-grade classrooms in three schools. Around four or five students dropped out from each class, in a programme lasting 18 weeks. Project CRISS was judged to have a positive effect on comprehension, after nine months, measured using teacher-developed 'free recall' comprehension tests.

As with READ180, this programme might just have been included in the section on what we know does not work. The longest, largest and most recent study based on standardised norm-referenced assessments found no effect. An older study, conducted by the programme producers themselves, found an effect only with a specially created test of free-recall.

Peer-Assisted Learning

Peer-Assisted Learning Strategies (PALS) is a peer-tutoring instructional programme that supplements the primary reading curriculum from first grade onwards. Students work in pairs on reading activities aimed to improve reading accuracy, fluency and comprehension. For the purposes of this book, only studies that evaluate the impact of the PALS programme for students in fifth and sixth grade, and which meet the WWC evidence standards, are considered. WWC (2012) reviewed 97 studies that examined the effects of PALS, and found only one study that met minimum standards for evidence and design. Fuchs et al. (1997) report a randomised controlled trial involving 12 elementary and middle schools with mixed reading scores and free or reduced-price lunch figures. In each arm, 20 teachers, teaching second to sixth grade and dealing with at least one learning disabled student, were assigned. Each teacher then identified three students to take part in the study – a low achiever with a learning disability, a low achiever without learning disability and an average achiever. Altogether there were 60 students in the PALS group and 60 students in the comparison group. The program was implemented during scheduled reading lessons conducted three times a week for 35 minutes each. The study reported significant gains for the PALS group on reading comprehension. However, WWC (2012) reanalyzed the data, taking account of clustering, and found no significant difference, despite a reasonable effect size. The baseline scores were not equivalent, the authors of the paper were also the developers of PALS and there was a high dropout rate of 45 per cent that was not evenly divided between the groups. The results remain unclear.

Van Keer (2004) reported on a different intervention aimed at linking reading strategy instruction with different models of peer tutoring, including teacher-led whole class activities, same-age peer tutoring activities and cross-age peer tutoring activities. Students ranged from 9 to 12 years old, and 454 were involved in 19 schools with 22 fifth-grade teachers in Flanders. The experimental interventions took place with a matched control group across a school year. Both the whole-class and the cross-age peer tutoring groups made significantly larger pre-test to post-test gains than the control group. No significant differences were detected in the same-age peer tutoring group compared with the control group. Although the students were reportedly aged between 9 and 12 years old, the results were only reported for one age group without specifying which age group that was. Also with three age groups, three conditions and a control, it is not clear that 22 teacher clusters is sufficient. Therefore, while there are suggestions that peer mentoring could assist, the evidence is not strong here.

Response to Intervention

Response to Intervention (RTI) is a school-wide multitier programme, which identifies the reasons for underachievement via a case-by-case analysis and tailoring instruction based on these reasons, combined with a standard treatment protocol administered to struggling students to prevent failure. RTI is delivered in three tiers of increasingly intense instruction. There have been some very weak studies of this (in See et al. 2012). In addition, Graves et al. (2011) reports on a quasi-experimental study that compares Tier 2 intensive reading instruction with a control group ('business as usual') for sixth graders with and without learning disabilities. The study reported that the treatment was more efficacious for students with learning disabilities and for oral reading fluency, but less so for reading comprehension. Leroux et al. (2011) undertook a randomised controlled study to examine the effects of an intensive, small group tutoring treatment on the reading outcomes of 30 students in sixth to eighth grade with severe reading difficulties, in three US middle schools. All had shown little response to two previous years of intensive intervention (RTI Tier 2). The control group included those who were randomly assigned to 'business as usual' in Year 1 of the study (RTI Tier 1). Results show that there were significant differences between treatment and comparison groups on some assessments but not others. The sample of only 30 students is small, and given that the Tier 1 students (control group) were randomised two years prior to the study, there may be questions concerning internal validity.

Again, there is mixed and incomplete evidence here, with small samples and sometimes involving only those with learning disabilities (the term used in the studies themselves). It is not certain that RTI does not work, but neither is it clear that this is the way to go in dealing with young people struggling with literacy. As with a number of other possible approaches discussed in this book, we are currently conducting a larger randomised controlled trial of this intervention in a UK context.

One-off studies

There are a number of other studies evaluating bespoke or one-off literacy interventions. Mostly these are small, find no impact, or are otherwise unconvincing (Brown 2004, Coe et al. 2011). For example, Cantrell et al. (2010) looked at LSC (Learning Strategies Curriculum), a reading intervention to improve reading comprehension for sixth to ninth-grade students, as a supplement to the regular curriculum. The study involved 862 sixth and ninth-grade students in 12 middle and 11 high schools. A random selection of students was exposed to an extra 50 to 60 minutes of LSC per day over the course of the school year. In the final analysis, pre-test and post-test results were available for only 655 students, around half in each group and grade. The sixth grade intervention students outperformed students in the control group, on reading comprehension although effect size is small (0.22). However, no significant differences between treatment and control groups were found on other outcomes or in ninth grade.

Conclusion

Unfortunately, many of the studies here make initially depressing reading, since so little has been found that works. But there are several reasons to be optimistic. The more rigorous trials there are of genuinely new programmes to overcome disadvantage in education, the better developers should get at picking possible winners. In the meantime, knowing that something does not work should be almost as useful as knowing something that does work. At least money and effort can be saved on unlikely solutions, making it slightly more likely that the money and effort will be used fruitfully. We need to get better at accepting the results of a definitive programme of research, discarding ideas and moving on. The barrier here is the reluctance of academic researchers to test their ideas, and the ensuing reluctance of users to accept the results of research. We only get the benefit from showing that something does not work if that result is acted on in practice.

One clear implication from the work in this chapter is a warning against reliance on impressions about treatment efficacy, as reported by people involved in any intervention. The overwhelming view of staff and students involved in the treatment group in Khan and Gorard (2012) was that learning was proceeding well, students were better motivated and enjoying lessons and teachers had been freed to deal with specific literacy difficulties within their classes. When asked, all teachers indicated that they would use the same or similar software in the future, and almost all of them said that they would recommend it to other teachers. Most of these impressions of staff and students about the efficacy of the product were simply incorrect, just as the publisher claims were found to be incorrect. In fact, the summer school, IT studies and many others show that people might believe things are going well, while the more solid evidence of attainment shows the opposite. For the purpose of deciding what works to overcome disadvantage, research based only on asking people what they think – the bulk of publicly-funded studies – is actually worse than useless.

Another consistent finding here is that studies conducted by advocates and those with clear conflicts of interest often stand out as the only ones finding a positive result for any intervention. Evaluation must be independent and conducted by people more concerned about getting the right answer than what that answer is.

In summary, we have found no relevant intervention that has been evaluated more than once as successful without also finding an equivalent or greater body of evidence that it does not work. The interventions that have been tried repeatedly either clearly do not work, or the picture remains unclear. There are some promising individual evaluations of specific bespoke programmes, but in isolation each is not sufficient to decide what works. There is no approach to overcoming low levels of literacy that is known to work for children in mainstream settings. Specific classroom programmes and interventions generally find it hard to shift patterns of low literacy by age ten or 11. Where programmes are more effective, they have been used with younger children. It is not the timing or medium of instruction that matters, it seems. The individual interventions that reported success tended to be single-issue, clearer and simpler in approach and further removed from normal practice than the less successful ones. Examples included emphasis on grammar or how to ask and respond to questions. Any proposed new interventions should be assessed using the same pre-specified instruments, preferably one standardised test, to avoid the temptation of 'fishing' for good news related to one site, grade or outcome measure.

Further examples of interventions, with a focus on individuals rather than programmes, appear in Chapter 10. These include the crucial issue of student motivation.

Chapter 10

The role of individuals

Introduction

So far, this book has suggested that psychological constructs such as learner identity, individual well-being or aspirations are likely outcomes of education. They are less stratified by SES than attainment outcomes, and so are easier to improve even for the most disadvantaged in education. But what is the relationship between such psychological constructs and attainment outcomes themselves? Does increasing aspiration really lead to higher participation, and does improved motivation actually cause better examination results? This chapter discusses what role individuals have to play in their own educational outcomes and what can be done for and by potentially disadvantaged individuals to improve them.

Sources of evidence

The main sources of evidence for this chapter are the reviews of evidence conducted by the authors. These are described more fully in Chapter 2 and in a series of publications including Gorard (2012c) and Gorard et al. (2012a). These reviews concerned the attitudes, aspirations and behaviour of young people and their possible link to educational outcomes.

Behaviour

This chapter starts by summarising the evidence on the possible effect of young people's behaviour on educational outcomes. Individual behaviour that might influence school outcomes encompasses a wide range of possibilities. It includes participation in extra-curricular activities, attendance and engagement, anti-social behaviour, risky behaviour such as smoking, experience of bullying, interaction with peers and experience of suspension or exclusion. These are dealt with in five groups: dangerous behaviour such as substance abuse, attendance, discipline, participation in extra-curricular activities and paid work while at school. The evidence in each group is assessed in terms of the four elements of a good causal model (Chapter 2).

An individual's behaviour is of concern where it is risky or disruptive (including poor attendance and punctuality). Such behaviour is slightly stratified by SES and by the school mix (Goza & Ryabov 2009). A focus on improving behaviour is unlikely to result in improved school outcomes but it may be a necessary pre-condition (Horner et al. 2009). It could also benefit the rest of the students in the teaching group whose learning may otherwise become disrupted. Poor attendance, poor social relationships and disruptive behaviour are all associated with attainment to some extent (Vitaro et al. 2005, Shin 2007, Crede et al. 2010). There is very little evidence relevant to the sequence from behaviour to attainment. For example, the study by Beckett et al. (2012) of a parenting intervention on 171 students in England identified as at-risk showed that it had a large effect on improved behaviour (effect size of 1.25) and a medium effect on improved attainment (0.68). The result is impressive, but it cannot show that the change in attainment is caused by improved behaviour. A similar study by Synder et al. (2010) evaluated the effects of the Positive Action programme targeting student behaviour and character, with 544 students in public elementary schools, and around 25 per cent receiving free or reduced-price lunches. They showed moderate 'effect' sizes for improved behaviour and attainment, but did not test the causal link between the two.

Individual extra-curricular activities

There are several possible ways in which additional activities outside regular school hours could help improve attainment or encourage participation in subsequent education. Children who participate in extra-curricular activities (ECA) may benefit directly from additional instruction, or ECA might provide children with an enriched cultural experience, helping them to understand and interpret teachers' expectations and communication better. Both of these ideas are dealt with in other chapters. ECA may lead students to develop a stronger identification with the school, affecting their academic self-concept or locus of control. The key question is: what is the evidence that ECAs are linked to school outcomes?

Our review found several studies reporting a weak association between individual participation in extra-curricular activities including sports and school attainment (Lipscomb 2007, Stevens et al. 2008). Shulruf et al. (2008) found only two per cent common variance between playing team sports and subject attainment at school; this was in a model that was missing a considerable amount of data, and was a population study yet erroneously used significance testing. Using a sample of 7,002 from the Northern Finland Birth Cohort 1986 and data collected by post in 2001/02, Kantomaa et al. (2010) found higher levels of physical activity to be slightly associated with self-reported academic attainment and future educational plans. There is, therefore, hardly any case to investigate a causal link further.

Similarly, the review found few longitudinal studies on this topic, and all were small or of poor quality (Martin et al. 2007). They generally show the same picture as the associative studies. One such study (Vandell et al. 2007) looked at 35 after-school programmes in eight US states, following 3,000 low-income, ethnically diverse elementary and middle school students. The study reported that students who regularly participated in high-quality after-school programmes had higher standardised maths test scores and better behavioural outcomes than students who regularly spent after-school time without adult supervision. However, data was collected for only 2,300 of the students, from teacher and student surveys and school records. Also the authors did not provide evidence that their groups were initially equivalent. The reported differences between the groups might easily reflect pre-programme differences in their behaviour or academic performance.

The review found one intervention study of an after-school programme, but none of ECA as more traditionally conceived. The intervention included paid internships in a range of professions and organisations for young adults in high schools with a high risk of dropout before the age of 18. Attendance at school was a requirement for participation in the scheme. In the end, 24 schools were included, with 1,289 student participants and 19,081 not participating in the study. These participants were not selected randomly, and already had better attendance records and fewer course failures than non-participants, on average. The results showed that those who were on the programme longest and who participated at the highest levels tended to fail fewer core subjects (English, maths, science and social studies) and had the highest average rates of graduation and lowest dropout rates. However, despite some attempts to control for initial and subsequent differences, this cannot be construed as good evidence that the programme caused these differences (Goerge et al. 2007).

In the absence of clear evidence, the conclusion here has to be that there is no evidence for a causal link from extra-curricular participation to improved educational outcomes. This is not to suggest that ECA, sports and after-school activities do not have other benefits, or that evidence of improved attainment will not be found in the future. Rather, anyone concerned about improving educational outcomes for at-risk students would be advised to seek an intervention elsewhere where there is clearer evidence of a causal effect.

Individual paid work

Undertaking paid work during schooling could be a barrier to attainment. It might influence attendance, punctuality for lessons, extra-curricular participation, homework and general well-being. The poorest students are often those under the greatest pressure to work for money while still at school, and 15 hours or more work per week replaces something that the less advantaged children could do.

Our review found a few studies suggesting a weak association between work intensity and educational outcomes (Sy 2006, Staff & Mortimer 2007, Staff et al. 2009). Two full longitudinal studies on this topic disagree with each other in their findings. One suggests that the more hours of paid work a young person does while in compulsory schooling, the weaker their academic results will be (Singh & Ozturk 2000). They used data from the first and second follow-up of the US National Education Longitudinal Study (NELS) to explore the effect of work intensity during high school on the number of courses taken in maths and science, and on twelfth-grade achievement. They found that the more hours students worked, the fewer the number of maths/science courses completed, which is associated with subsequent lower achievement in maths/ science (after controlling for SES and prior achievement). The other study suggests that there is no difference in the level of education achieved for any number of hours of paid work up to and including 15 hours per week (Bachman et al. 2011). Our review found no reports of controlled interventions to improve educational outcomes by adjusting work intensity. With no clear evidence on the effects of paid work on attainment, intervening to alter the amount of paid work students do as an approach to overcoming educational disadvantage cannot be justified.

Individual substance abuse

An individual's use or abuse of substances such as drugs, alcohol and tobacco could also influence school outcomes. They could cause cognitive impairment in early adolescence, or an amotivational syndrome or lethargy. Lynskey and Hall (2000) claimed that there is little evidence for either of these mechanisms, especially since at least some of the highest attainers have been involved in substance abuse. It may be more likely that a link between early cannabis use and educational attainment arises because of the social context within which cannabis, in particular, is used. Early cannabis use is associated with the adoption of an anti-conventional lifestyle, characterised by affiliations with delinquent and substance-using peers, and sometimes the precocious adoption of adult roles including early school leaving, leaving the parental home and early parenthood.

Substance abuse (heavy drinking, taking powerful or illegal drugs and, increasingly, smoking tobacco) is often considered as characteristic of families with serious behavioural difficulties (Goodman & Gregg 2010). Our review found only one study that suggested an association between early substance abuse and educational outcomes. This was based on a cross-sectional survey of 29,393 teenagers aged 17 in France, asking retrospective questions (Legleye et al. 2010). Early school dropout was associated with less elevated family socio-economic status, coming from a single-parent family, early grade repetition and daily tobacco smoking. Early daily cannabis and alcohol use (aged under 14) was not related to attainment or dropout, but its later use was actually positively linked to school attainment, depending on the level of use. If valid, the latter findings may be more to do with pre-existing differences among drug users at that age rather than a direct influence of drug use. There are three full longitudinal studies suggesting that this might be the case.

The first study suggested that heavy drinking (alcohol) at an early age was unrelated to (or evenly positively associated with) participation and attainment for most students, except for working-class boys. Staff et al. (2008) used 9,107 cases from the National Child Development Study, a longitudinal birth cohort study of British children born in 1958, to examine whether heavy alcohol use from age 16 predicted lower educational qualifications by age 42. 12,006 cases remained by the time of their study, but the author only included respondents for whom information on alcohol use at age 16, sex and father's occupation were available. Results showed that for girls, there was no association between heavy drinking and the chances of obtaining a degree. The same was also true for boys from middle-class backgrounds. In fact, Schvaneveldt (2000) found that alcohol use was positively associated with educational attainment for Caucasian youth and those from higher SES backgrounds.

Other studies suggested that early cannabis use is linked to increased likelihood of drop out from education, and decreased likelihood of post-secondary participation (Fergusson et al. 2003). Horwood et al. (2010) used data from three Australasian cohort studies involving over 6,000 participants to compare findings about cannabis use across studies, and obtain pooled estimates of association. There were associations between age of onset of cannabis use and all outcomes such that rates of attainment were highest for those who had not used cannabis by age 18 and lowest for those who first used cannabis before age 15. These findings were evident for each study and for the pooled data, and persisted after controlling for possible confounds.

There is some evidence for a sequence from early cannabis use to poorer outcomes, but less evidence of a sequence from early alcohol use to depressed outcomes. Overall, therefore, there is insufficient evidence here for a complete causal link from an individual's substance abuse to their educational outcomes. This is not to condone substance abuse, or deny that it has other possible dangers, but for the immediate future, attention and energy could be focused on other interventions that have clear evidence of causal influence.

Individual poor behaviour

As with many sections in this chapter, a number of explanatory mechanisms are possible to explain why poor behaviour would result in lower educational outcomes. For example, simply turning up for school and learning in a peaceful environment is envisaged to lead to better attainment at school than non-attendance or disorderly classes (Gottfried 2010). The main outcome of most of these studies was student behaviour, rather than their academic achievement. Any effect on academic achievement appears to be incidental, such as a result of improvement in the school learning environment by increasing the amount of time students are in school, or the proportion of time classrooms are engaged in instruction (Horner et al. 2009). This section looks at evidence of a relationship or effect of children's behaviour on their school outcomes. The evidence suggests that interventions to counter social, emotional and behavioural problems have more chance of success in improving outcomes than those that target ECAs, paid work or substance abuse.

Some studies show that a child's behaviour as early as pre-school is related to later school outcomes. For example, Fantuzzo et al. (2003) found that problems with emotional and behavioural adjustment at the start of the pre-school year were associated with later disengagement, poor emergent literacy and classroom learning outcomes.

A review of research on the impact of social and emotional learning programmes on elementary and middle school students in the US looked at 317 studies involving 324,303 children (Payton et al. 2008). It suggested that such programmes are generally effective and can improve school engagement, classroom behaviour and academic performance. This is powerful evidence but the causal link from behaviour to attainment is not clear.

In a large-scale randomised trial of the US School-wide Positive Behaviour Support (SWPB) intervention, intended to deal with bad and risky behaviour at school, Bradshaw et al. (2010) reported that the intervention resulted in lower incidence of student suspensions and discipline referrals. In these schools the fifth-grade students also made slightly greater gains since third grade in reading and maths than comparison schools. The study involved 37 elementary schools, carried out over five years. Lassen et al. (2006) found similar results with the same behavioural intervention in lower secondary schools in one urban inner-city middle school in the Midwest, over a three-year period.

Jones et al. (2011) conducted a two-year experimental study of the impacts of a school-wide literacy and social-emotional learning programme, involving 1,184 third-grade children in 18 schools in New York City. The only attainment effects noted were for those children identified at baseline by their teachers as being at highest behavioural risk. There were more general improvements in reports of aggression, attention, depression and socially competent behaviour. It is not clear that the attainment changes are the result of the changes in behaviour, as opposed to the direct teaching of literacy that took place. Flay and Allred (2003) reported an evaluation of the Positive Action Program, an intervention to develop positive behaviour to improve achievement from primary to high school in the US. At elementary level, violent behaviour and suspensions, but not absenteeism, were reduced by positive action. Children in positive action schools performed 45 per cent better than children in matched control schools on the Florida Reading test, but no better on the aptitude test. These results largely carried forward to the middle schools attended by these students. The same direction of difference was also seen in the high schools attended by these students, but the size of the differences was small.

However, the evidence for the positive effect of counselling for bad or risky behaviour is rather weak. Reback (2010), for example, used a form of regression discontinuity to estimate the effects of school counsellors and counselling on student behaviour, well-being and achievement, and found no link between the level of school funding for behaviour counsellors and student attainment. However, if such interventions can lead to better behaviour, they are desirable in their own right.

In general, the evidence on interventions to improve poor behaviour at school is quite promising, and worth further attention and development. What is needed is to isolate the part of the intervention that targets behaviour from other aspects of the intervention that target teaching styles and approaches adopted to deal with it.

Attitudes, aspirations, motivations and similar constructs

The influence of aspirations and attitudes can be complex. Aspirations can be linked to living in a deprived area (Carson 2009), family SES (Geckova et al. 2010), parental education and ethnicity (Schlechter & Milevsky 2010). Also, aspirations and expectations have been linked as outcomes *of* achievement at school (Wiley 2006, Ahmavaara & Houston 2007), teacher or parent stereotypes (Tiedemann 2000) and structural features of the educational system (Buchmann & Dalton 2002). Motivation might be affected by instructional strategies (Frampton 2010). Those students with better and more favourable attitudes to education tend to perform better in assessments of learning. The problem for policy is to decide whether such attitudes and aspirations are a key link between socio-economic background and school outcomes. A vital next step is therefore to find the possible causal links involved before rushing in, as some writers have in claiming that attitudes or mental concepts are fundamental in explaining differential attainment (Roth & Salikurluk 2012). There is already considerable policy expenditure committed on the premature assumption that aspirations and attitudes can be influenced to improve educational outcomes. For example, in 2009 the UK government introduced plans to lift the aspirations of 2.4 million children (St Clair & Benjamin 2011). This is just one of many worldwide, national and local initiatives.

Few controlled interventions have so far been conducted that show changing attitudes could lead to better school outcomes. The studies that claim success are often the weakest. For example, Ben-Avie and Steinfeld (2001) reported success for a three-year evaluation of the Institute for Student Achievement (ISA) programme for students at risk of failure or dropping out. Support was given to enhance motivation, personal accountability, parental involvement and student relationship with school. The study involved only four schools, had no comparator for most outcomes and the report does not even include the number of students involved. Using an approach like instrumental variables, claimed to mimic an experimental design, with a large dataset and contextual information, suggests that these correlations then disappear (Vignoles & Meschi 2010).

The following section focuses on eight 'mental' concepts, based on definitions found in the literature reviewed. Identifying the influence of these concepts is problematic because their definitions are vague and can vary over time and between regions of the world. They are also often inter-related.

'Well-being'

Well-being is a relatively new and disputed concept. Here it is assumed to encompass enjoyment and happiness, safety, psychological health and social and emotional competence. It has been linked to improvements in academic outcomes, social skills, motivation, self-esteem, self-control, positive attitudes to school and critical thinking. Like several outcomes other than attainment, well-being is not particularly stratified by SES (Gutman & Vorhaus 2012). A number of studies have shown that students' pro-social behaviour predicts performance on standardised tests (Zins et al. 2004). Studies have also shown positive associations between socio-emotional skills and academic success. Many of these studies of association fail to rule out the possibility of other covariates (social class, parental attitudes), which may be related to socio-emotional skills. As with many affective characteristics, the sequence between them and attainment is unclear (Noble et al. 2008). Hence it is difficult to say if there was a causal effect of such interventions on academic outcomes.

Those factors that make a school successful academically may not be the same as those that support well-being (Gray et al. 2011), and vice versa. For example, Wright et al. (2010) evaluated a Teaching for Personal and Social Responsibility (TPSR) programme for a Wellness course in an inner city high school, with 122 African-Americans aged 14 to 18, of whom 99 per cent were in receipt of free or reduced price lunches. They reported slight improvement in behaviour, punctuality and attendance of the treatment group, but there was no clear impact on academic outcomes. However, there is some promise. Durlak et al. (2008) conducted a meta-analysis of 213 projects involving 270,034 students who were involved in a combination of programmes such as character education, anti-bullying prevention and conflict resolution training. Students were from kindergarten to eighth grade (age 14). On average, participation in social-emotional learning (SEL) programmes was linked to an 11 percentile points higher score on standardised achievement tests compared to those who did not, and the effects persist over time among studies where follow-up data were available. Possible confounds include extra teacher attention and more time to have better relationships with students. Across the projects there was no standardised measurement of social emotional skills. Nevertheless, one of the most interesting findings is that only those SEL programmes conducted solely by teachers were found to be effective. Those conducted by researchers and others including parents were not.

Individual aspirations and expectations

In most studies, 'expectation' was taken to mean what an individual believes will happen in the future, while 'aspiration' refers to what individuals hope, rather than believe, will happen in the future. Our review confirmed the association between children's aspirations and their attainment. Many studies suggest that young people with higher educational aspirations have somewhat higher educational attainment than their peers. Blaver (2010) looked at 1,391 Hispanic youth from the 2003 Trends in International Mathematics and Science Study (TIMSS), and found that self-reported competence in maths was associated with future educational aspirations and also with maths achievement. Using Longitudinal Study of Young People in England (LSYPE) data, Cuthbert and Hatch (2008) found that the aspirations of young people and their parents were associated with their educational attainment.

Yet, there are several studies that suggest that this simple association between aspirations or expectations and school outcomes might be something else. Some reports showed very similar patterns of aspirations for different social groups, such as rich and poor students, despite their different levels of attainment (Calder & Cope 2005, McKendrick et al. 2007, Turok et al. 2008). Marjoribanks (2005) used an Australian dataset (LSAY) and found that adding student expectations to a regression model to 'predict' educational attainment reduced the apparent association with student SES. This means that each variable acts as a proxy for the other, and any analyses not using SES are in danger of over-estimating the association of outcomes with expectations.

The sequence in the relationship between educational outcomes and aspirations is also far from clear (Beal & Crockett 2010). Aspirations can be both a predictor of educational achievement and an outcome of it, and might be influenced by self-esteem or self efficacy, personal traits, experiences and mediating family factors (Gutman & Akerman 2008) or linked to beliefs about ability (Phillipson & Phillipson 2007). Moreover, young peoples' aspirations and expectations are not always a constant and can change rapidly during their school years (Gottfredson 2002). It is therefore not surprising that there is little consensus among these studies about the link between expectations and outcomes.

There are many examples of studies attempting to show a link between students' aspirations and school outcomes, which fail to consider the possibility of other covariates. Liu (2010), for example, used a nationally representative sample from the Education Longitudinal Study of 2002 and reported that students who retained high stable aspirations from tenth grade to the end of high school were the most likely to continue in education. Lin et al. (2009) looked at the progress of 2,000 students from seventh to eleventh grade, and found that the rate of progress was positively related to the expectations of students in Year 7. However, these studies had no measures of SES context. Freeney and O'Connell (2012) claim that their evidence reveals that an intention to leave school early is 'predicted' by attitudes to school. However, their study uses intention to leave rather than leaving itself as the outcome, so it is really associating one mental concept with another.

Bui (2007) used NELS data to examine the relationship between educational expectations and academic achievement among 10,261 students in eighth, tenth and twelfth grade. The author claimed that a cross-lagged analysis shows that there is evidence of reciprocal effects between educational expectations and academic achievement, but that the path from academic achievement to educational expectations is stronger than, and pre-determines, the reverse path. In this case, attainment seems to come first in the sequence.

Interestingly, our review found no rigorous evaluations of interventions explicitly concerned with changing aspirations or expectations to influence educational outcomes. There will, presumably, have been many attempts to intervene with policy or practice to influence aspirations/expectations, but none was found as part of a randomised controlled trial or similar. There is therefore insufficient evidence for a causal link to justify any intervention to raise aspiration in order to raise attainment.

Individual motivation

'Motivation' is generally defined as a reason why an individual makes a decision, and their resolve in carrying it out. A number of studies have suggested weak associations between learner motivation and attainment (Ream & Rumberger 2008, Quirk et al. 2009, Somers et al. 2009). Hayenga and Corpus (2010) found that among 343 middle school students those reporting strong intrinsic motivation received higher school grades than students with reported extrinsic or mixed motivation. There is limited evidence of an association between motivation or type of motivation and attainment.

On the other hand, several studies reported no association in the correct sequence (Dowson et al. 2003). Gagne and St Pere (2001) studied 200 students, and showed that cognitive ability, or IQ, was the strongest single predictor of school achievement. If IQ was included in modelling then any association between individual reported motivation and achievement disappears. This result is similar to that for parental expectation, where the addition of prior variables reduces the apparent association, and it suggests that motivation is a proxy variable rather than a cause of attainment. Similarly, Schwinger et al. (2009) found that motivational strategies were not directly related to GPA. There is little good evidence to support a causal sequence from intrinsic motivation to attainment.

Intriguingly, given the shortage of such basic evidence of a causal sequence, there are a number of intervention studies in which extrinsic motivation was a major independent variable. Fryer (2010) examined the effect of financial incentives on student achievement. The study analysed data on approximately 38,000 students from public schools in Chicago, Dallas, New York City and Washington, DC. Students were given monetary payments for performance in school. The study found no statistically significant effects on standardised maths or reading outcomes in Chicago, New York City or Washington, DC. Focus group interviews with students suggested that although students may be excited about the incentives they do not actually know how to improve their grades. This is an important point to note for all attitude and aspiration work. Confidence may be misplaced without competence. However, paying students for behaviour that they know how to alter produces some results. For example, paying students to read books yielded a noticeable increase in number of books read, but not necessarily improvement in reading performance.

Bettinger (2010) evaluated the effects of a financial incentive programme, providing external motivation for academic achievement. Students in third to sixth grade were paid in gift certificates for every good test result in five core subjects. There appeared to be a positive effect on maths scores, with high-scoring students more responsive to the incentives. There was no difference in reading. This may be because extrinsic motivation is more effective for less conceptual tasks. Students can memorise a series of facts, such as rote-learning tables or formulae, to prepare them for the tests, but it is more difficult for students to prepare in the short term for comprehension after reading a specific text or writing on a particular subject.

In another study the educational outcomes of students whose families were randomly assigned to receive cash rewards were compared with those who did not (Riccio et al. 2010). The programme was found to be effective in improving the maths test scores of KS5 students in year two of the study, but the effect size was minimal. It was slightly more effective for high school students. Jones et al. (2002) examined the effects of the School Attendance Demonstration Project (SADP), which involved giving students financial incentives for attending school on a full-time basis. The study involved 2,744 at-risk students. The study reported success in improving attendance rates, but not in completion rates.

Monetary incentives and sanctions have also been used to improve post-16 participation and retention among high school students. In one intervention, students in the treatment group were paid a monthly stipend if they met the set academic eligibility criteria (Spencer et al. 2005). This was a randomised controlled trial involving 541 students. All participants were high-achieving students from poor families with diverse ethnic backgrounds. At the end of one year, students in receipt of stipends showed a ten per cent higher retention rate than those who did not receive monetary incentives. In one evaluation of an intervention to improve post-secondary participation, students were paid for work-based experiences (Goldberger 2000). This is Boston's Pro-Tech programme, which integrated classroom and worksite learning. Students were paid as in a real world situation. Mixed results were reported. In the first year, participants' grades and GPA were positively associated with the programme, but in the second year programme participation seemed to be negatively associated with grades and GPA.

Because motivation is intertwined with other issues such as attitude and self-esteem, it is hard to synthesize the body of evidence available. However, there may be enough promise from the work already done, and enough evidence here of an association between extrinsic motivation and school outcomes, to investigate further through a large and rigorous trial, if an appropriate intervention can be devised. Payment seems to work for simple changes in behaviour, of the kind that the recipient already knows how to do.

Individual self-concept/self-esteem

Like the other affective measures, there is no agreed definition or measurement for 'self-concept' and 'self-esteem'. It is therefore unsurprising that evidence on the link between self-concept/self-esteem on academic outcomes is mixed. Some studies suggest a link between academic self-concept and achievement, but these are largely based on correlational or observational data (Skaalvik & Skaalvik 2009, Bong et al. 2012). For example, Zand and Thomson (2005) found that African American adolescents with high levels of self-worth were more likely to report having higher grades at school. Gonzalez-Pienda et al. (2002) used data for 503 12 to 18-year-old adolescents, and reported that their self-concept was statistically related to their academic achievement. Singh et al. (2002) reported a slight association between self-reported grades and self-concept, and a slightly stronger link between school outcomes and students' sense of school belonging. However, in a major and widely-cited re-analysis of such previous work, Baumeister et al. (2003, 2005) have suggested that high self-esteem, in terms of the global self-concept, is not associated with better performance once other factors are accounted for. An analysis of TIMSS showed that neither academic self-concept nor motivation are correlated with ability or enjoyment of science in East Asian countries, and are actually negatively correlated in the US (Yu 2012). Therefore, there is only disputed evidence of an association between self-concept and attainment.

There are also large numbers of studies relating to the order of life history events involving self-concepts and attainment (Liew et al. 2008, Whitesell et al. 2009). Eight of these longitudinal studies presented evidence and models suggesting that self-concept (and self-esteem to a lesser extent) do not lead to attainment or participation in the way that a causal model would require. For example, Tang (2004) used 12,144 students from the base year, and second and fourth-year follow up of the US NELS 1988–2000 database. Variables included socio-economic status, prior achievement, self-concept, locus of control, educational aspirations, parental expectations, parental involvement, peer influence, college plans, average grades, test scores, coursework completion and educational attainment. Prior attainment and SES were the strongest predictors. Once other measures were accounted for, locus of control and self-concept were not linked to subsequent attainment.

Scott (2004) analysed interviews with 11 to 15-year-olds in the sample households in the 1994–99 British Household Panel Study (BHPS), looking also at their educational achievements in later years (aged 16–19). In context, self-esteem was unrelated to subsequent public examination results. This study is important because the multivariate analysis includes factors such as family income, mothers' occupation, family structure, housing tenure and parental education (all strongly linked to attainment). In fact, the more explanatory variables any study includes in the analysis the less likely it seems that a mental concept like self-esteem is associated with educational outcomes.

Chowdry et al. (2010) used LSYPE data. They found that around two-thirds of the socio-economic gap in attainment at age 16 can be accounted for by prior attainment at age 11 and long-term family background characteristics. This means that little variations in outcomes can be explained by constructs such as self-concept, motivation or locus of control Therefore, simply increasing self-esteem or locus of control would seem to be unlikely to be effective. It could even be dangerously misleading.

A few studies have proposed that self-concept led to school outcomes in the correct sequence for a causal relationship (Cheng & Ickes 2009, Zanobini & Usai 2010). For example, Guay et al. (2004) used a sample of 465 primary school children whose progress was followed over ten years. They found that children who perceived themselves as academically competent in early schooling had higher subsequent school achievement. Marsh et al. (2005) used a sample of 5,000 early secondary school students, and presented evidence of a link between academic self-concept and future grades, after taking prior achievement into account. However, there were no other context measures such as SES, and it is important therefore to contrast both of these with the even larger studies that had more background variables and found no impact from self-concept.

A number of studies even claimed a causal relationship between such mental concepts and achievement. For example, Marsh and O'Mara (2008) used Youth in Transition data to present what they call a 'definitive test' (p.542) of claims that academic self-concept is reciprocally causally linked. However, even this reciprocal analysis is really only an association, where self-concept 'predicts' attainment at the next stage and so on. No context variables were used so there was a lot of unexplained variation for self-concept measures to soak up. Correlations were as low as 0.14. Less than 73 per cent of the sample was still included in the final analysis. Since school dropout is linked to academic self-concept, the latter could be acting as a proxy for school attendance. Chamorro-Premuzic et al. (2010) assessed 5,957 UK twins aged nine for cognitive ability, academic achievement and self-perceived abilities. Once cognitive ability was accounted for, self-perception and achievement at age nine predicted both self-perception and achievement at age 12. The link between prior achievement and later self-perception was about the same strength as the link between prior self-perception and later achievement. The authors claimed that this was evidence of insight (children's accounts of their previous performance) and self-efficacy. High performing students apparently adjust their self-perception upwards, which might have a subsequent influence on their attainment.

Pinxten et al. (2010) used a sample of 1,753 students who were tracked from seventh grade, through eight, tenth and twelfth grade. The authors concluded that the results of causal ordering studies have to be interpreted very carefully as different measures of academic achievement can give different apparent causal patterns between academic self-concept and achievement. Baumert et al. (2005) analysed longitudinal data from two nationally representative samples of German seventh-grade (13-year-old) students (with 5,649 and 2,264 cases respectively).

The prior self-concept of the student explained some of the variation in subsequent maths interest, school grades and standardised test scores. The authors concluded that self-concept is both an effect and a cause of school attainment.

In summary, the evidence from studies of association and sequence is ambiguous. First, the theoretical and empirical distinctions between self-esteem (or global self-concept) and academic self-concept have been radically altered over time as advocates find that one or more operational versions of their ideas are ineffective. Second, some studies now present the hypothesised relationship between self-concept constructs and attainment as reciprocal. However, it has proved difficult to find ways of separating the two hypothesised relationships empirically, and therefore it is not possible to rule out the causation being entirely from achievement to self-concept. Third, a majority of these studies have investigated relationships between academic self-concept and attainment for children in secondary school. Some studies focused on students close to the completion of compulsory education. Therefore, it might be argued that any effects of academic self-concept or of prior attainment are already embedded in the children's prior attainment, which is used as a baseline in these studies.

We found five interventions involving changing self-concept or self-esteem to influence attainment. None provide very strong evidence of a causal link. Three have very few cases, especially when analysed by sub-group in the ways presented by their authors (Good et al. 2003, Cohen et al. 2009, Gordon et al. 2009). Oyserman et al. (2006, 2007) studied a US School-to-Jobs intervention, based on the idea that individuals have internal 'academic possible selves'. The goals of the intervention were, reportedly, to help students develop possible selves, provide them with the strategies to attain these and insulate them against 'off-track selves' such as involvement in gangs, drugs and pregnancy. It was expected that in the long term the behaviour relevant to academic possible selves (doing homework) would increase, leading to better academic outcomes and grade point averages. The study concluded that the intervention had direct positive effects on possible selves as well as a direct negative effect on school absences (reducing absences). Intervention effect sizes on attainment (GPA) by end of ninth grade were 'small-to-moderate'.

Possible reasons for the inconsistent results in this field could be that studies used different instruments for measuring self-concepts, and the questions asked were not comparable and may even have been measuring different constructs. They also used different indicators of achievement such as standardised tests or teacher ratings. However, the single biggest difference lies in the use of contextual and possible confounding variables. The more and better these additional measures the less association is found between self-concepts and school outcomes. It is also possible that academic self-concept and academic performance are measuring nearly the same thing. This is especially so where one's academic self-concept is based on other people's opinions about one's academic performance (Baumeister et al. 2003). Although the evidence of a causal influence of self-concept or self-esteem is weak, there is sufficient promise here for trial interventions that can separate the impact of self-concept from all else. What are needed are not more longitudinal studies and more sophisticated analyses, since these will be unable to resolve the central issue about causation.

Individual self-efficacy/locus of control

'Self-efficacy' is an individual's belief in their own ability to achieve something. 'Locus of control' refers to an individual's belief that their own actions can make a difference. Our review found a few studies that suggested a correlation between young peoples' reports of an internal locus of control or self-efficacy and their school attainment (Da 2005, Speight 2010). A study of 400 US high school students, selected through cluster random sampling, indicated that an informational identity style was positively related to academic achievement, while a diffuse/avoidance identity style was negatively related. Hejazi et al. (2009) proposed that the personality style is the cause of the attainment, through the mediation of academic self-efficacy. However, there are several difficult and hypothetical concepts in such a complex and therefore possibly tenuous chain of reasoning.

Although the evidence is sparse and neither high quality nor large-scale, there is perhaps sufficient here for a prima facie case of a causal model. There were four studies linking self-efficacy/locus of control in a plausible sequence (Bandura et al. 2001, Yailagh 2003). In the US, Gifford et al. (2006) reported that prior scores and locus of control were both associated with university students' subsequent academic results. Students who entered university with lower scores on the locus of control scale obtained significantly higher GPAs than those who scored higher on this same scale. Two further studies suggested that there is no sequence. Tang (2004) presented strong evidence that once other measures such as prior achievement were accounted for, then locus of control was not linked to subsequent attainment. Also, Grabowski et al. (2001) found evidence that global self-efficacy was not related to subsequent attainment. Overall, the evidence for a sequence is limited and inconclusive. It is as likely that educational outcomes lead to self-efficacy/locus of control as vice versa.

Four interventions were found that related to alterations in self-efficacy or locus of control and subsequent attainment. Together, these studies provide very weak evidence of an impact from self-efficacy. For example, Hughes et al. (2006) conducted an intervention aimed at developing students' self-perceptions, academic self-efficacies and academic performance. It involved Year 6 students in 12 UK primary schools. How cases were selected and allocated is not clear. Psychometric tests (including general self-efficacy, subject specific self-efficacy, self-esteem and academic motivation) were administered. The intervention did not show any effect on self-perception and self-motivation, and a small effect on self-efficacy. Intervention schools had higher KS2 scores, after controlling for KS1 scores. However, this improvement was isolated to SEN (special educational needs) students, who may have felt better about themselves because of the attention given to them as a result of the trial – a kind of Hawthorne factor. Effect sizes, where they were reported, were small.

Blackwell et al. (2007) examined the academic trajectories of learners with different implicit theories of intelligence and other achievement-related beliefs. Using four cohorts of students as they progressed from seventhth to eighth grade, academic achievement was measured using a standardised maths achievement test. The study showed that students who thought their intelligence was malleable were more likely to believe that working hard was necessary and effective in raising achievement, than students who thought that intelligence was fixed. Blackwell et al. (2007) then used an intervention to teach half of the 99 seventh-grade students in a second school the belief that intelligence is malleable. There was a slight gain in achievement for the experimental group, especially those who had not believed in malleable intelligence at the outset. This is a very small sample, and the report is missing key information in places (such as when the initial assessments took place).

Miles (2010) used a controlled pre- and post-test design study to test the effects of a 'mastery goal approach' to mathematics instruction on the performance of eighth-grade students. Only 79 students took part, of which only 57 were tested, and it is not clear if the allocation to control and treatment group was randomised. The report suggests that the mastery goal approach to instruction brought about a positive change in students' motivation and achievement, but did not provide evidence of the causal direction.

These interventions form a strange combination of approaches, generally with older students, on a very small scale and with far from convincing results. Together they provide little solid evidence that either self-efficacy or locus of control can influence attainment or educational participation. Altering self-efficacy or locus of control may not be effective if the real underlying difference is actual competence rather than beliefs about competence. Simply making people believe that they are more competent than they actually are may be ineffective or worse, but making people more competent at gaining positive school outcomes is no different to improving their school outcomes. Self-efficacy by itself could be a red herring.

Other individual attitudes

There are few studies of association between any other individual attitudes, such as respect for education and educational outcomes. As a whole these are not convincing that there is any strong correlation. Hillman (2010) reported an association between positive student attitudes towards engagement with school and their achievement. Abu-Hilal (2000) used a sample of 280 pupils across ninth, eleventh and twelfth grade from one high school in California, and measured their attitudes to school subjects, level of aspiration ('How far do you think you will go in school?') and standardised achievement tests in four core subjects. There was only a very weak association between attitudes and achievement (0.04). Twist et al. (2007) found some links between attitudes to reading and reading attainment for 200,000 nine and ten-year-old children in 41 countries.

Although there were longitudinal studies that establish sequence, the evidence of a sequence was not clear. One suggests a link, one is of poor quality (Harris 2008) and two others both suggest that the sequence moves from attainment to attitude, rather than the other way round. Mattern and Schau's (2002) study of 458 White seventh and eighth-grade students in New Mexico showed the reverse sequence, where students' attitudes at the end of the year were linked to their achievement at the beginning of the year, and that their prior attitudes did not have a strong link with later achievement. In another longitudinal study, Ma and Xu (2004) analysed data from the Longitudinal Study of American Youth (LSAY) in secondary school grades seven to twelve involving 50 middle and high schools. The results also showed the sequence to be reversed, where prior achievement predicted later attitude, but prior attitude did not predict later achievement. For an individual's entire secondary school career, achievement preceded attitudes. This suggests that an institution's ability to affect students' level of achievement via attitudinal change is minimal.

Our review found no school-based study that involved an intervention to improve general attitude and therefore attainment. In summary, the review found little solid evidence that intervening to alter attitudes can lead to improvements in educational outcomes.

The volatility of intentions

If the key to patterns of participation is not so much barriers as the subjective filtering of actual opportunities, then perhaps the key to widening post-compulsory participation lies partly in raising aspirations. This has been tried on a small scale in Aimhigher, for example, with claims of success despite no rigorous evaluation (Chilosi et al. 2010). A review of such studies by Gorard et al. (2007) found no robust evidence that raising aspirations makes any difference to actual patterns of participation. However, a more fundamental issue is whether reported aspirations mean anything at all. If aspirations actually translate into participation then early attitudes of young people would provide a sound basis for planning and intervention, and it is probably right that public money is invested in attempting to raise the aspiration of those currently under-represented in later education. If not, we may be misled into wasting time and resources on what children simply say at an early age rather than on minimising the very real influence of social and economic background, and maximising the chances that students enjoy education and get the best qualifications possible. Young people from poor families are more likely to say at age 11 that they want to continue to HE, even though children from the poorest backgrounds are less likely to continue to HE in practice (Vaughan 2009). It seems as though expressed aspirations from an early age are an inaccurate and unreliable indicator of later participation.

Predictions of school outcomes based on aspirations, intentions and expectations are very volatile. In most social research the term 'predictions' is often used to mean calculations done after the occurrence of the events they are meant to be predicting. Predicting the arrival of a comet or the winner of a race must be done beforehand in order to be a true prediction (Gorard 2013). Parcelling out the variation in a set of already established outcomes cannot be prediction in the sense needed to demonstrate a causal model.

For example, Frisco (2008) used data from the National Education Longitudinal Study (NELS) 1988 to 1994, and demonstrated that the timing of sexual initiation and the non-use of contraceptives predict students' subsequent academic attainment. However, the analysis was conducted afterwards, and it is on this basis that they match a pattern of earlier events to a result. Jacob and Wilder (2010, p.10) meant the same thing when they said, 'Even after we control for a host of individual, family and school characteristics, tenth-grade expectations are strongly predictive of eventual enrollment'. Almost all of the longitudinal cohort analyses encountered in our reviews did something similar. This may be a valuable way of initially identifying the possible determinants of school outcomes, but the field needs to move on and use such results to make testable and falsifiable predictions for the as yet unknown future. Each generation of researchers appears to rediscover or confirm what is already known – that aspiration, for example, can both predate and be associated with a school outcome. The next step, if the model is truly causal, is to predict events in the real future, and so make at least some social science predictions more like predictions of the appearance of comets.

Strangely, even those studies claiming to be able to 'predict' retrospectively were not correct in their claims. Croll (2009), for example, in his analysis of data from prior years of the Youth Survey, says, 'The results show that most children can express intentions with regard to future participation very early in their secondary school careers and that these intentions are good predictors of actual behaviour five years later' (p.400). However, the evidence presented does not match this claim. For example, 52 per cent of 11-year-olds said they wanted to stay on and eventually did so, while seven per cent of 11-year-olds said they did not want to stay on and eventually did not stay on. This means that in total only 59 per cent of 11-year-olds acted out their previously-reported intentions at age 16. Of the remainder, 22 per cent at age 11 did not know whether they wanted to stay on or not when aged 16, and 19 per cent did the opposite at age 16 to what they reported at age 11. Every year, every cohort has a 72 per cent to 74 per cent staying-on rate, and the historical trend is upwards, with variation chiefly in the nature of the post-compulsory routes available (Payne 2003). Put simply, a gambler betting who would stay on using only students' expressed intentions at age 11 would be right 59 per cent of the time. However, because so many students did stay on in fact and do so every year, this gambler would lose to another gambler who simply bet that all and any students would stay on. The latter would be correct over 72 per cent of the time. Knowing the expressed intentions actually makes any prediction of the future less accurate than not knowing it, and this means that Croll (2009, p.400) is quite wrong to say that 'intentions are good predictors of actual behaviour five years later'. In addition, only 41 per cent of students expressed the same intention when asked repeatedly from Year 7 to Year 11, and 93 per cent expressed, at least once, an intention to stay on. Jacob and Wilder (2010) also reported that around 60 per cent of students in their dataset updated their educational expectations at least once, and that expectations have become less predictive of school attainment over past decades. Whatever it is that reported intentions are expressing, it is very volatile. There is no basis for a causal model here.

Conclusion

Most of the mental constructs covered in this chapter have such an unpromising evidence base that it is not worth pursuing them at present, unless the reason for doing so is for purposes other than to improve educational outcomes. Continuing with such interventions may be anti-educational and even dangerous. Consider an intervention that made more young people falsely believe that their future was under their control to a large extent when the world is not actually under their control. Children might become demoralised if they find that they cannot actually achieve what they were told they could. There is some evidence that children's aspirations are realistic (which is perhaps why they show some signs of correlation with outcomes). Children are aware of what they can and cannot achieve. Thus, any suggestion to increase them further might be more than any labour market and higher education system can cope with (St Clair & Benjamin 2011). For many students, aspirations are un-stratified by class, ethnic origin and attainment at school (Gorard & Smith 2010). This is an important point because if aspirations were stratified by SES then raising aspirations for children from lower SES families would be fairer even if the 'system' could not cope. However, if they are not stratified, then falling short of one's early expectations and aspirations might perhaps lead to lower emotional and psychological well-being in adulthood (Hardie 2010). There are, therefore, possible dangers in raising aspirations without raising competence. And if competence is raised, is there still a need to raise aspirations artificially?

There is also the problem that intentions, aspirations and expectations are very changeable. While this might seem desirable for any intervention intended to change them, the actual level of volatility makes them unreliable as indicators. If there is little link between intentions and real outcomes then there is little point in interfering with them in order to improve outcomes.

It is hard to prove the effectiveness of varied psychological constructs such as aspirations and attitudes. The association between such concepts and educational outcomes tends to disappear when high quality contextual data is available. The strongest claims made for the impact of aspirations and attitudes by authors in this review tend to emerge from studies in which measures of prior attainment or SES background or cognitive ability are missing. When these datasets have sometimes been re-analysed with fuller contextual data, and have shown a reduced or missing association, the same authors sometimes changed the construct. Self-esteem becomes global self-concept, then academic self-concept, then academic self-concept for a specific curriculum area, and so on. It makes their ideas almost impossible to test. It is as though they are marketing an inefficient product, and are constantly re-packaging it to make it appealing to the market. This is not how social science should proceed.

Overall, there was no clear evidence that intervening to change the educational attitudes of otherwise disadvantaged students leads to enhanced attainment. Some of the suggested ideas, such as external motivation, show promise and could be developed further. Others, such as locus of control, show little promise and could even be dangerous if used without care. Given that there are other approaches that can help to overcome the poverty gradient in schools, it is clear that raising aspirations and similar is not the way for policy to go. As shown in the book so far, the stratification of educational outcomes is more likely to be structural than mental. The current evidence is that attitudes do not cause variation in attainment, and so policies and practices based on a belief that they do are, and will continue to be, ineffective. Such policies also present opportunity costs, using budgets that could be used for more promising approaches, and leaving the poverty gradient largely untouched for yet another generation.

Chapter 11

The role of 'parents'

Introduction

This chapter considers the role of parents, carers or guardians in the educational outcomes of their children. The term 'parent' is used here to encompass all of these more precise relationships, and others like them. It is clear that the characteristics of parents are strongly related to the education and participation of their children. There is a high level of predictability from one to another, in all countries where such data have been assessed and reported. In fact, parental characteristics, occupations and prior experiences may be the best single predictor of children's lifelong learning trajectory (Gorard & Rees 2002). This is so even for nations such as Denmark, which have reportedly high levels of social mobility (Tverborgvik et al. 2012). Around the world, Wobmann (2003) found that students' performance in maths and science was strongly related to their parents' educational level and the number of books at home. Marks (2007) showed that students' performance in literacy and numeracy in 30 countries was related to parental SES characteristics. All other things being equal, more educated parents tend to have children who are more successful in education. Conversely children from families living in poverty, on average, tend to do less well than their peers.

As explained in Chapter 2, it is useful to distinguish those factors that can be altered from those that cannot. Parents offer examples of both kinds. In the long term, reducing poverty or increasing levels of education might make a difference for subsequent generations. Indeed, there is evidence from some countries and studies that the correlation between family background characteristics and achievement gaps at school weakens with historical changes to family structures, levels of education and so on (Grissmer & Flanagan 1998, Hedges & Nowell 1998). But for a child in formal education now, their parents' characteristics are more fixed than malleable; therefore, this chapter focuses instead on what can be done in the short term to improve parental behaviour and attitudes, and so improve their children's educational outcomes. In the long run these children may become parents in turn, and hopefully the cascading effect of such changes will also be realised in future generations.

Sources of evidence

The evidence in this chapter stems largely from a research synthesis of the causal impact of parental behaviour on children's attainment, conducted for the Joseph Rowntree Foundation, and a follow up research synthesis of the most promising interventions to enhance parental engagement in children's education, conducted for the Nuffield Foundation. The methods are described more fully in Chapter 2, and a series of publications including Gorard et al. (2011) and Gorard (2012c).

Parental involvement

Recent studies in the UK have shown that parental involvement is more evident in families of higher social class (Harris & Goodall 2006). US studies suggest that parents from less advantaged households are less likely to be involved in the help and supervision of children's work at home, and in school activities and support (Zill 1994). Parental involvement in education has been linked to their income and education (Suizzo & Stapleton 2007), social class and ethnic origin (Bodovski 2010). Where parents in unskilled manual jobs or on state benefits have reported being involved in their child's schooling, their involvement mostly concerned school trips and helping with dinner duties (Moon & Ivins 2004). This stratification matters because parental involvement has a likely effect on children's achievement and adjustment even after all other available explanatory factors have been accounted for (Desforges & Abouchaar 2003). There are several ways in which parental involvement in their child's education could influence attainment and participation, for example discipline that encourages 'good' educational behaviour such as attendance and punctuality. Parents can also be a kind of resource or teaching assistant, helping the child with their work directly. A parent who is knowledgeable about the education and assessment system may be in a better position to assist their child with homework, coursework, revision and choice of appropriate subjects. Alternatively, they can behave in ways that align the cultural norms of communication and behaviour at home with those in school, for example, by making the rules of communication and behaviour at home similar to those expected at school, or more powerfully by playing a role in school itself so that it becomes more like an extension of home.

Several studies show a medium association between some measure of parental behaviour, and the school readiness or performance of their child (Yan & Lin 2005). This included encouragement for parents to read at home with their young children, and help for some parents in providing reading activities (Siraj-Blatchford 2010). Positive associations have been reported between early parenting and 'school-readiness'. Using observational data on mothers reading with their children, Korat (2009) reported positive associations between a mother's education and the sophistication of their interaction with their child's reading, which was also associated with the child's reading level. Morrison et al. (2003), using a sample of 142 families, reported a positive association between the observed quality of mother–child interaction in problem solving, and the child's contextualised school performance. Cooper et al. (2010) used the Early Childhood Longitudinal Study-Kindergarten Cohort (20,356 children) and measured parental involvement through resources for learning available in the home and the frequency of the child's participation in learning activities within and beyond the home. The authors reported that these measures of parental involvement mediate the association between family poverty and children's maths and reading achievement in early school.

Similarly, positive associations are reported for parental behaviour that is seen as supporting children's achievement during their schooling. School engagement is apparently linked to parental support for schooling (Benner et al. 2008, Dearing et al. 2008) and child motivation to mother–child interaction (Vincson 2008). Gottfried et al. (2008) suggested that parental motivational practices (such as encouraging children to be mastery-oriented, curious and persistent in school work) are related to children's intrinsic academic motivation from childhood onwards. Plunkett et al. (2009) found a modest relationship between a mother's homework help and monitoring, and her child's academic orientation. Feinstein and Symons (1999) found that early parental interest in their child's education, as reported by teachers, was strongly associated with school progress. Martin and Martin (2007) described the 'Williamson Project', which involved parents, community leaders and school personnel in a comprehensive effort to improve achievement for African American students at one urban elementary school. The results indicated improvement in academic achievement in state-mandated achievement testing, and a decrease in behavioural problems. One suggestion that emerged from this study was that school environments should be restructured to resemble more closely the family environments and cultures of all children. Topor et al. (2010) used a sample of 158 seven-year-olds to investigate the mechanism that explains the relationship between parental involvement and children's academic achievement, such as the child's perception of cognitive competence, and the quality of the student–teacher relationship. There was a correlation between parental involvement and the child's academic performance over and above the impact of cognitive ability. After controlling for socioeconomic status, there was some evidence that even minimally increased parental involvement had a positive impact on pre-schoolers' early development and mastery of basic skills (Marcon 1999). The review uncovered many more such studies of correlation (Aikens & Barbarin 2008, Bodovski 2010, Zhai et al. 2011).

There are many studies, particularly in the US that show that, irrespective of a child's background, parental involvement has a positive impact on academic achievement (Epstein et al. 1997, Dryfoos 2000). For example, a US Department of Education report (1997) found that students whose parents are involved in their school work are more likely to take challenging mathematics courses early in their academic careers. Patel (2006) suggests that parental involvement has beneficial effects during the middle school years, particularly with respect to maths achievement.

On the other hand, Wang et al. (1996) found that in the US parents' involvement with children's homework had a negative relationship with achievement. It is difficult to interpret this result if parents' educational background is not known. If parents are not highly educated, they may not be able to help their children with their homework. It is also possible that parents are more likely to help their children with their homework if the children are struggling. How parents are involved can also make a difference. In some studies it is not clear what kind of parental involvement is being studied. Ho and Willms (1996), for example, found that parents talking with their children about school and planning their education programmes had more effect on student achievement than merely volunteering for and attending school activities. Ma (1999) reported that the effect of parental involvement varies depending on the grade level and the kind of parental involvement. For example, volunteer work for school is the most important school-level variable in the early grades (age eight to ten), but home discussion is especially important in the middle grades (age ten and 11). The effect of home-school communication, on the other hand, has a short-term but strong effect in ninth grade.

A study by Jeynes (2005) on the effects of parental involvement on the academic achievement of African American youth found that the apparent importance of parental involvement on educational outcomes disappeared when variables for SES were included in the analysis. It is possible that social class rather than parental involvement as such explains differences in academic performance. Supporting this finding is a study by Okpala et al. (2001), which indicated that expenditure on instructional supplies per student and parental volunteer hours were not significant in explaining test scores. Low family income was related negatively to students' academic performance in mathematics. Better-educated, middle-class parents are apparently more able to provide the guidance and home environment conducive to study than less educated parents. Some commentators would say that these variables represent cultural capital. In the US, Hogrebe et al. (2006) used participation in free or reduced school lunch programmes as an indicator of parental poverty. It was clearly, but not invariably, linked to low attainment.

Lara-Cinisomo et al. (2004) found that the most important factors associated with the educational achievement of children are socio-economic ones, in particular mothers' educational level on students' performance in maths. Over 90 per cent of students whose mothers completed a college education scored in the high and middle ranges on the maths test, while 40 per cent of students whose mothers had no more than a high school education had low scores on the maths test. Even in poor neighbourhoods, students are likely to perform well in reading and maths if they have well-educated mothers, and even when mothers' reading scores are held constant. This is quite a powerful finding. Raising mothers' educational level is thus something worth considering.

Shaver and Walls (1998) looked at eighth graders' mathematics and reading achievement and concluded that parental involvement, regardless of the child's gender or SES, was a positive influence on academic success. Wang et al. (1996) show that parental education and encouragement are strongly related to seventh-grade students' performance in mathematics. They obtained significant predictors of mathematics achievement using backwards elimination. Similar results appear in Cotton and Wikelund (1989). Again, we have no way of knowing the causal model here. This study uses teachers' and parents' perceptions of students' ability, rather than their actual performance, and it uses no measure of SES.

To establish a causal influence, we also looked at the sequence of influence. A considerable number of longitudinal studies suggested that parental involvement and interest in their child's learning from an early age through schooling were related to successful outcomes, and in the correct sequence for a causal model (Son & Strasser 2002, Sylva et al. 2008). Most importantly, no studies reported the absence of such a link. Dearing et al. (2009), with a longitudinal sample of 1,398, found that higher levels of participation by parents in early childcare were followed by a weakened link between social class and subsequent educational achievement. Kiernan and Mensah (2011) analysed data from the UK Millennium Cohort Study, and reported that the parenting index score for positive parenting was linked to the child's foundation stage achievement, regardless of poverty or other disadvantage.

Based on the US Study of Early Child Care Youth Development, children from high SES backgrounds had more exposure to stimulating environments of the kind that might enhance learning (Crosnoe et al. 2010). Children identified as having been exposed to cognitive stimulation at home, in preschool child care and first-grade classrooms, net of socio-economic selection into different settings, had higher subsequent maths and reading achievement. The observed benefits of consistent environmental stimulation across settings tended to be more pronounced for low-income children. The authors argued that policies targeting only one setting might not be as effective as those interventions that target across multiple settings in improving outcomes for children at risk. Some potential confounding variables, such as parenting skills and types of schools or child-care centres, were not included in the analysis. The link between SES and quality of child care was also omitted, as was the potential influence of pre-existing genetic differences.

Using 1,364 randomly selected 15-month-old toddlers followed through to age 15, Burt and Roisman (2010) found that the mothers' response to and interaction with their very young children predicted greater social competence, school engagement and then achievement. However, it was unclear from the report how much background and context variation was accounted for in the analysis. Hango (2007) suggested that greater parental involvement can mediate the negative effects of low SES. They used data from the UK National Child Development Study (NCDS), which is a longitudinal study of 98 per cent of all births in one week in 1958. Whether the child had any qualifications or not by age 33 varied substantially by parental involvement. Two factors, fathers' interest and going on outings with the mother at any age, were associated with the largest decrease in the odds of a child having no qualifications. It would appear that the best predictors of educational attainment are father's social class, living in owner-occupied homes and the child's sex, behaviour and reading ability. The authors claim that fathers' interest in school had the biggest impact on reducing the effect of economic hardship. The outcome measure here is an odd one, since the authors could have used qualifications achieved, and actual educational trajectory at age 16 as well. Several key indicators are based on self and subjective reports, despite the existence of other more objective measures in the dataset. Furthermore, only 2,658 of the initial 17,000 families were involved.

Bates (2009) used data from four waves of the Early Childhood Longitudinal Study, Kindergarten Class of 1998–99, looking at the educational trajectories of children from kindergarten through to US fifth grade. Parental educational expectations, frequency of reading outside of school and number of children's books in the home were positively associated with children's reading and maths scores in kindergarten, and with the change in those scores over time. Gfellner et al. (2008) evaluated the Parent–Child Home Program in Manitoba for the 20 years since the program was introduced. The aim of the intervention was to reduce negative school outcomes for disadvantaged children. The programme used the parent–child bond to facilitate verbal interactions between parents and pre-school children with an emphasis on toys and books introduced into the home. Home visitors and volunteers or paid service providers demonstrated to parents the styles of play and reading that facilitate verbalisations. A total of 185 families were enrolled but data were available for only 86 cases because of missing forms or drop-outs. The authors reported an improvement in the quality of home environment, parent–child interaction and child behaviour conducive to learning. However, there was no report of any control, or randomisation, and there was over 50 per cent dropout. Many of the outcomes were judged by the visitors, who may have had an interest in the success of the intervention.

Schvaneveldt (2000) examined parental involvement in their children's academic activities and parental regulation of adolescents' behaviours in eighth grade, and the possible effects of these on academic achievement in tenth grade. Data were drawn from the US National Education Longitudinal Study (NELS), which included 13,116 participants. The study claimed strong evidence that for all sex, ethnicity and SES groups, post-secondary educational attainment can be enhanced through greater parental discussion of academic activities with their child during early adolescence. UK NCDS 1958 data showed an association between reports of father's involvement in their child's education at age seven and school outcomes at age 16. Involvement included reading with the child, going on outings with the child, being interested in the child's education and 'father manages the child'. The UK British Cohort Study (BCS) 1970 data also portrayed a strong association between parental interest in their child's education aged ten, and educational outcomes at age 26 when controlling for other factors used (Flouri 2006). However, the 'parental interest' item was completed by teachers, which is not ideal.

It is clear that despite doubts about the quality and rigour of some of these studies, and some reasonable evidence that parental involvement is not necessarily linked to SES (Hartas 2011), there is an even more considerable body of evidence that parental interest and involvement in their child's education is associated with, and appears in the correct sequence to cause, educational and occupational outcomes. This is true from pre-school to post-16 participation. This is by some way the most promising area relevant to parents in overcoming educational disadvantage. Therefore, the next section focuses on identifying the most likely interventions to assist.

Parental involvement interventions

One aspect of this theme is that there is evidence that interventions can lead to greater involvement by parents, and apparently to changes in the behaviour and attitudes of children. The key question is whether this makes any difference to subsequent outcomes at school. There are already many such programmes on the market. It makes sense for policy and practice to invest money and effort to identify those interventions that hold the greatest promise of success for the most marginalised and disadvantaged young people.

The nature of the evidence

Research on the impact of parental involvement on children's school outcomes has so far produced some mixed results. Some programmes are found to be effective for younger children, but not for older ones, while others have found quite the reverse. Some interventions appear to have an effect on some components of certain ability tests but not on others. There are also studies that suggest that parenting skills and behaviour alone have little or no impact on children's school outcomes (Hartas 2012). One of the main reasons for the mixed results may be the varied definitions of 'parental involvement' or types of parental involvement (Jeynes 2012). Parental involvement can mean a wide range of things, from parental behaviours, parenting styles and aspirations to helping with homework and attending school activities. Another possible reason is the lack of any agreed measure of parental involvement. Many studies used parent self-report, student or even teacher reports. Other reasons for these mixed results included the difference in the duration and focus of the intervention, and the age group or school phase of the children involved. For example, Terzian and Mbwana (2009), in a synthesis of 47 parent involvement interventions for adolescents aged 12 to 17, found that generally successful interventions were those that:

- develop skills
- involved therapeutic interventions with a focus on the family and teens
- specifically focus on both parents and teens
- provided at least five sessions.

On the other hand, programmes that only offered information with no practical training for parents were most likely to fail; those aimed at changing behaviour, such as substance abuse and reproductive health outcomes, were equally less likely to succeed. Home-based interventions, clinic-based therapeutic interventions and community-based interventions were also shown not to work.

In much research there was also little or no attempt to control the influence of other variables, thus making it difficult to conclude definitively that any programme works. The main issue with research on parental involvement programs is the lack of rigour in research design. In one review of 200 parental involvement studies, Baker and Soden (1997) found only three studies that were experimental in design. Although students may be matched on demographics and academic ability, other confounding variables such as differences in teachers, types of schools or school-mix, which provided plausible alternative explanations for the differences in test scores, were not controlled for. These problems are not unique to studies of parenting.

Currie (2001), in her review of early childhood intervention programmes, found only seven that were randomised controlled trials or near equivalent. Among these were four very high profile ones: the Perry Preschool Project, the Carolina Abecedarian Project, the Early Training Project and the Milwaukee Project. These cases all involved random allocation of children to intervention and control groups and had low attrition. Another review of 20 studies on school readiness initiatives (Brown & Scott-Little 2003) found only one experimental design. In a review of research reports on the impact of school, family and community, only five were experimental. As usual, the majority were correlational studies (Henderson & Mapp 2002). A review of best practice in parental engagement for young people across a wide age range (aged five to 19) also noted the lack of 'robust' studies, 'too little to provide evidenced based judgements about many of the key variables, or the relative effectiveness of work in different key stages of children's development' (Goodall and Vorhaus 2011, p.12). A bibliography of research on the impact of parent/family involvement on student outcomes (Carter 2002) identified 66 distinct studies, of which only four were experimental studies with comparison groups. One had a sample size of only eight children, and the outcomes were based on informal assessments by teachers (Faires et al. 2000). Another reported non-attainment outcomes such as participation in learning activities, developing responsibility and level of parent–child interaction. Moreover, these outcomes were based on participants' self-report (Van Voorhis 2001). The rest were ex-post facto or correlational studies or reviews of research. Very often the use of the word 'impact' in the title of the review is quite misleading, in that the reader assumes that the studies included would establish causal impact, but this was clearly not the case.

Our own review (Chapter 3) found 70 relevant studies that satisfy the research design requirements. The quest was for studies where there is evidence of robust evaluations of interventions, including randomised controlled trials, quasi-experiments or alternates such as regression discontinuity that have pre- and post-test comparisons of outcomes and comparison groups. Of these, 28 were interventions targeting pre-school/kindergarten children (age zero to five), 23 were aimed at primary school-age children (age six to ten) and 11 were interventions to improve outcomes of secondary school-age children (age 11/12 to 18). Eight studies were across age groups. Only a selection is discussed below.

Pre-school

Most of the interventions for pre-school age children involved parental training (11/28) or a combination of parental training and home support (8/28). Most of these interventions reported positive effects on young children's school readiness and academic outcomes. Four involved parental support. Of these, three reported positive effects while one showed a negative impact on young children's school outcomes. Two interventions on shared reading appeared to have mixed effects. The results of one study were not considered valid (Stevens 1996). This is because although the researcher concluded that because test scores for the experimental group had improved significantly between pre- and post-test, the treatment had a positive effective, there was no similar analysis carried out for the control group. It is therefore not possible to attribute the improvement to the treatment. The study had many other problems, with a 25 per cent response rate, the inclusion of only English speaking parents and no pre- and post-test comparisons between groups.

A second study showed no effects (Baker 2010). Parent implementation (controlling for teacher implementation) was not associated with changes in children's language and pre-literacy skills on all measures and sub-scales. There were also no significant differences between children whose parents achieved the recommended number of reading and those who did not, but children whose parents achieved the optimal number of reading days had significantly higher pre-test and post-test scores for four of the six measures. This suggests that the active ingredient could be something related to the parents, such as parental attitude towards reading or education, rather than background in general. This factor, however, was not explored in the study. Zevenbergen et al. (2003) evaluated the impact of a shared reading intervention programme on the reading skills of four-year-old children from low SES families enrolled in Head Start. However, because the intervention was conducted in the classroom as well as at home, it is hard to untangle the outcomes.

Ford et al. (2003) evaluated an initiative in Wales called the Tandem Project, to encourage parents from low-SES backgrounds to play a greater role in preparing their children for school, as part of the Sure Start initiative. The intervention lasted six weeks, and parents were given a series of games to play with their children, designed to develop basic pre-reading and numerical skills. A total of 128 children took part (only ten per cent of those invited), aged 33 months to 46 months, from socially and economically deprived backgrounds. Of these, 63 lived in the designated Sure Start area, were less likely to have families with earned income, and more likely to have single mothers and mothers who had left school before the age of 16 than the other 65 children. The children were divided into four roughly equal groups, including Sure Start delivered by parents, other parents as a control, children with Sure Start delivered at nursery and other nursery children as a control. Children were assessed on each of the skills (such as recognising letters or numerals) before and after the intervention and again six weeks after the intervention. The results were mixed. In general, the treatment groups made greater gains than the controls in some tasks or skills. The nature of these gains differed in the different treatment groups, and also differed in the same group in the post-test and after six weeks. The amount of parental effort in support of the intervention was largely unrelated to the eventual reading results. The cell sizes are small, and the gains measured are short term.

Reynolds et al. (2004) used 1,404 children from low-income families taking part in the Chicago Longitudinal Study of the Chicago Child–Parent Centers, aimed at improving educational attainment and reducing delinquency. The original sample included those who entered the CPC pre-school and completed kindergarten, and those who participated in government-funded kindergarten programmes without CPC pre-school experience. Pre-school participation was associated strongly with higher rates of high school completion by age 20, and significantly lower rates of juvenile arrest by age 18. It is hard to rule out threats to the validity of the findings in such quasi-experimental designs.

School-age and beyond

While parental interventions for pre-school children are most likely to involve parental training of some kind, those for older children (primary to secondary school age) are more likely to involve home–school collaborations (n=16) or a combination of parental training and home support (n=5). Our current review of the most promising interventions identified 42 such interventions for children from primary (n=23), secondary (n=11) and across age group (n=8). However, the effects of many of these were inconclusive. Of the eight studies that evaluated home–school partnerships among primary school age children, only two reported positive effects, four showed no effects and two had mixed results.

Kyriakides (2005) conducted a comparison study of a parent–school partnership programme in Cyprus, getting parents to work with their children in the classroom while teaching was going on. The intention was to encourage close communication with parents and help them understand and value the purposes of school activities. Parents acted as advisors, learners and teacher aides, in collaboration with the teachers. The intervention took place in one primary school with 92 Year 5 students, and comparisons were made with a similar school in another village with 95 Year 5 students. Written and teacher assessments were made of mathematics, Greek language and social science before the intervention, as a post-test and then again six months later in both schools. After the intervention, students in the intervention group achieved higher grades than the control school in teacher and external assessments in the three core subjects. The intervention was effective for all socio-economic groups, but especially so where the mother was a housewife (and perhaps had more time to commit to the programme). The study was small, contained no randomisation and so the authors were incorrect to quote probabilities instead of effect sizes.

Portillo Pena (2009) examined the potential effects of a reading intervention called the Power Lunch Program (a paired inter-generational reading aloud activity) on reading attitudes, reading motivation and reading achievement for children from first grade to third grade (age six to nine). The programme emphasised reading as an interactive and collaborative process between a child and a caring adult. Participants were taken from 12 public schools in the US, involving four cohorts, and all were African American. Of the initial 1,866 students only 866 were included in the analysis (if they were matched with control or treatment condition within school/grade level, within the grade criteria and had longitudinal data available). This study used a quasi-experimental design and examined results up to four years after the intervention. It suggested that the intervention had a positive effect on academically at-risk elementary students' reading attitudes, motivation and achievement up to four years later, with small to medium effects. Because of the multiple components targeted by the programme (reading attitude, motivation and reading achievement) it is not clear what the direction of the effect is.

Moon and Callahan (2001) discussed the project Support to Affirm Rising Talent (START), which was a collaborative research effort between a university and a large urban school district. The authors suggested that parental involvement had no impact on the academic achievement of the primary grade students from low socio-economic environments who participated.

Magnuson (2003) used an instrumental variables approach with data from the random-assignment National Evaluation of Welfare to Work Strategies Child Outcomes Study to estimate the effect of maternal education on young children's school readiness. Further analyses were conducted with two sets of nationally representative data from the National Longitudinal Survey of Youth Child Supplement (NLSY-CS). These suggest that when mothers themselves returned to school on their own initiation, their children's reading achievement improved, but not their maths. This was true regardless of the mothers' prior educational level. Return to school also predicted improvements in the quality of the home learning environments for the children.

Kratochwill et al. (2004) conducted a randomised controlled trial of a multi-family group program called FAST (Families and Schools Together), involving parents more in their children's education, to improve classroom behaviour and academic performance. The study matched 50 pairs of Native American children aged between five and nine, and each was randomly assigned to the treatment or the control. Pre-test, immediate post-test and nine to 12-month follow-up data were collected. Teacher ratings indicated that FAST students showed greater improvement in academic competence after one year, while immediate post-test results showed improvement in behaviour measured on the teacher-rated Aggressive Behaviour Scale and Child Behaviour Checklist. Improved classroom behaviour by the child due to parental involvement may be an intermediary step or simply a correlate of the outcome. The study was small, ethnically specific, and relied on teacher reports. FAST has been tried in the UK and the early signs are encouraging, but in both the US and UK, the evaluations have only found very weak differences in actual attainment results (Crozier et al. 2010).

Topping et al. (2004) considered a maths tutoring method used by peers, parents and other volunteers. Thirty children aged nine and ten years of below-average mathematical ability were randomly allocated to experimental or control conditions. Experimental tutees (17) were tutored in mathematical problem-solving at home by their parent using the method, while control children (13) received traditional maths problem homework. Pre- and post-test assessment of both groups involved a criterion-referenced mathematics test in parallel forms and a scale of attitudes to mathematics. Experimental tutees showed gains on the attainment test while the control group did not. The study was small, and not only about parental involvement, making the results hard to interpret.

For secondary school age children, the most common interventions trialled were home school collaborations (7/11) where schools worked together with parents to engage children in homework or in providing home support. Of these interventions, only two reported positive effects on children's academic outcomes. Three, in fact, showed negative effects and two were not able to demonstrate positive results. Two studies were about parents working with children at home using computers. Effects of the use of computers at home with parental engagement showed mixed effects. While one reported positive effects (Sirvani 2007), the other (Tsikalas et al. 2008) showed no effects at all. Another study involved training of parents in interacting with their children, communication skills and modelling behaviour (Spoth et al. 2008). The study reported that the intervention increased parenting competencies and reduced students' substance-related risks in the sixth grade, which in turn improved academic performance in the twelfth grade and school engagement in the eighth grade. However, if we compare the effect size of gain scores on student-reported grade of experimental (ES = 0.05) and control group (ES = 0.02) six years after intervention, there is little difference between the groups.

One study that used a combination of strategies also reported positive effects on children's academic outcomes (Gonzales et al. 2012). This is a family-focused preventive intervention to reduce problems associated with transition to secondary school. The intervention involved parenting intervention, adolescent coping and joint family sessions with parent and child instructions plus family support. The study concluded that the intervention was particularly effective in improving academic outcomes (measured using GPAs) of students with low baseline GPAs. However, because only 62 per cent of eligible parents agreed to participate there is a danger of bias due to self-selection. Also the relatively high attrition rate

(27 per cent) in the third wave (one year after intervention) may have jeopardised the validity of the experiment. Again, because of the multiple strategies involved, it is hard to pinpoint the active ingredient.

Eight of the intervention studies were for children across age groups. Of these, seven reported positive effects on some outcomes (three of which had mixed results showing positive for some, negative or no effects for other measures) and one reported negative effects. These interventions tended to be about parental training and home-support or a combination of the two.

Other parental behaviour

Considerable space has been devoted to parental involvement, because this is one of the most promising interventions discussed in the book so far, with the most complete evidence base. The next section looks at a number of other ways that parents might influence their children's educational outcomes.

Parental substance abuse

One possible cause of the impact of disadvantage in education could be substance abuse by parents. Substance abuse might reduce the capacity of parents to engage in positive behaviours, they may foster substance abuse by children or they may cause neo-natal damage, producing long-term differences in learning ability.

Some older research has shown that children's subsequent cognitive ability is associated with pre-natal exposure to alcohol (Coles et al. 1991, Olson et al. 1997), but the sizes of the correlations are small. Otherwise, the review found no studies of cross-sectional association between parental substance abuse and the child's educational outcomes. Part of the reason for this could be that by its nature an association between pre-natal events and attainment must be from a longitudinal study.

The review found three full longitudinal studies on this topic. The Mater-University of Queensland Study of Pregnancy (Australia) followed 7,223 children born to mothers enrolled at pre-natal classes. After 14 years, around 71 per cent were still involved, although only 52 per cent of the young people provided assessment data. This suggested no link from pre-natal alcohol use to educational outcomes (O'Callaghan et al. 2007). Another much smaller study suggested a lowering of ability and subsequent achievement for 265 15-year-olds mostly born to mothers in one pre-natal clinic in Atlanta, Georgia. Young people exposed to alcohol pre-natally had lower IQs than others, and performed slightly worse on mathematics tests (Howell et al. 2006). An even smaller study suggested no influence from pre-natal cocaine use (Hurt et al. 2005). The study found that 62 children exposed to cocaine during pregnancy and 73 control children did not differ substantially in school performance, in terms of successful grade progression, grade point average, reading below grade level and standardised test scores in reading, maths and science.

No reports were found of controlled interventions to improve children's educational outcomes by adjusting parental substance abuse. Ethically, it is difficult to envisage what these could have been. Perhaps some kind of regression discontinuity design could be used, involving those just above and just below a threshold for enforced drug treatment. There is, in summary, very little solid evidence here for a sequence leading from pre-natal parental substance abuse to the child's educational outcomes. This is not to condone substance abuse during pregnancy, or deny that it has other possible dangers; but at present, anyone with a sole concern to improve educational outcomes for those most at risk would be advised to seek an intervention elsewhere.

Parenting style

Parenting styles have been categorised in terms of the extent to which they are authoritarian or dialogic, and authoritative or neglectful. Different parents have different styles of bringing up children, which could be differentially effective for education, and correlated with SES backgrounds. However, because parenting style is intertwined with other issues, such as parental involvement (as discussed previously), it is hard to synthesise the evidence available.

Goodman and Gregg (2010) showed that simple differences in parenting styles and rules (such as having regular bedtimes or family mealtimes) are linked to poverty, with poorer children often facing less regularity in their lives. By the age of three, infants' test scores are already slightly linked to whether they have a regular bedtime or not. Some studies have shown a link between parenting style and school outcomes, with the 'authoritative' style associated with most success (Terry 2008, Sektnan et al. 2010). Brown and Iyengar (2008) conducted a literature review on parenting styles and achievement, suggesting that what they termed 'behavioural' and 'psychological' control were the two parenting styles most closely related to higher academic achievement. Hill (2001) found that low parent SES and parenting strategies, such as 'hostile and non-supportive', were associated with each other and with lower literacy scores for the children. Nuijens et al. (2000) employed self-reports from seventh and tenth graders to examine parents' level of education and features of parent–adolescent relationships as predictors of adolescents' academic performance. There was little pattern in the seventh grade, but by the tenth grade academic performance was highly correlated with the closeness of parent–adolescent relationships. There is, therefore, a prima facie case for a causal model linking parenting style and school outcomes.

Our review found three further relevant longitudinal studies. All three suggest a link between parenting style and outcomes, when considered in the necessary sequence for a causal model (i.e. where the parenting style precedes the educational outcome). Flouri (2007) used UK BCS 1970 data, and found mothers' authoritarian parenting negatively associated with educational outcomes when the child was aged 26. Gregory and Rimm-Kaufman (2008), with a small sample of 142 children and observation of parenting practices, found no link between mothers' behaviour when the child was at an early age and subsequent Year 9 SATs, but a later link to the likelihood of graduating from high school. Blondal and Adalbjarnardottir (2009) conducted a longitudinal study of 427 Icelandic youths. The study examined the relationship between the young peoples' perceptions of parenting style and parental involvement in their education and their chance of dropping out of school. Results indicated that adolescents at age 14 who characterised their parents as authoritative (showing acceptance and supervision) were more likely to have completed upper secondary school by age 22 than adolescents from non-authoritative families, after controlling for adolescents' sex, SES, temperament and parental involvement. Therefore, although the evidence is sparse, there is enough evidence here for the field to move on to controlled intervention studies.

The search yielded no studies that attempted to alter parenting style and so influence children's later attainment or participation. The conclusion here has to be that parenting style is not the solution to overcoming disadvantage. The style might as easily be an outcome of SES as attainment is. At present, anyone with a sole concern to improve educational outcomes for those most at risk would be advised to seek an intervention elsewhere.

Parental expectations

There are several mechanisms through which parents' expectations might conceivably affect children's attainment. Expectations might affect the resources (time and money) parents devote to supporting their children's education, frame their children's expectations or direct the way in which parents respond to any opportunities and problems their children encounter in school.

Our review found a number of studies all showing a positive link between parental expectations and child's school outcomes (Qi 2006, Senler & Sungur 2009). Children seem to perform better at school when their mothers, in particular, expect them to (Mistry et al. 2009). Hong and Ho (2005) used US NELS data, and found a strong association between parental aspiration/expectation and student achievement. Cook (2010) involved 77 care-givers enrolled in Head Start, and found that high parental expectations were strongly linked to school readiness scores. Grinstein-Weiss et al. (2009) used a sample of over 12,000 children aged between five and 17, from three different datasets. Their study found that self-reported parental expectations for their children were associated with student outcomes at school. Jeynes (2007), in a review of studies, also found a strong link between school grades and parental expectations (0.9 'effect' size). Fan and Chen (2001) reviewed a number of studies and reported a stronger association between parental expectation and achievement than between parental involvement and achievement. Therefore, there is considerable evidence that parental expectations are linked to their children's school outcomes of different kinds and at different stages.

Our review also found a number of reports relating to parental expectations for their child's education, and the subsequent attainment or participation of the child (Kiernan & Huerta 2008, Rogers et al. 2009, Johnson et al. 2010). Taningco and Pachon (2008) used data from the Early Childhood Longitudinal Study (ECLS). They found mothers' education and parental expectations to be consistently and positively associated with later test scores. In each of these studies, the association appeared in the correct sequence for a causal relationship.

However, it is remarkable that none of these studies included parental SES or student prior attainment in their analyses. Where such contextual factors are included then the apparent link with expectations weakens or disappears. Englund et al. (2004) found no association between parents' expectations and child school performance in first and third grade. Skokut (2010) found that only SES was linked to school completion for Latino English language learners in California. Parent expectations, parent–child communication, school connectedness and extra-curricular activities made no difference to either outcome. Even though there are several studies looking at simple associations between parental expectations and outcomes, the link between parental expectations and child success is less stable when viewed in the proper sequence for a causal model with appropriate prior contextual factors.

Our review found no controlled interventions explicitly intended to alter parental expectations in order to assess their influence on a child's school outcomes. Apparently, no one has reported testing this out. There is no good evidence that changing parental expectations will lead to improved attainment by their children later.

Conclusion

There is very little evidence that educational outcomes for disadvantaged families will be fundamentally affected by combating parental substance abuse, changing parenting styles or raising parental expectations. These might all be good things in themselves, and may even lead to other benefits, but they are not important causes of low attainment or under-representation in post-compulsory education. Any areas of promise could be subsumed within the more fruitful line of work on parental involvement.

The one area for which there is enough evidence to test for a causal influence is parental involvement in their child's learning, but this is only for attainment, not participation. There is a reasonable amount of evidence to suggest that parental involvement is partly a causal influence on children's school readiness and slightly less so for subsequent attainment. The questions that follow from this are whether parental involvement is malleable, whether intervening can improve educational outcomes for disadvantaged children and what the vital elements of any programme would have to be. This will be picked up again in the next and final chapter.

Chapter 12

The way forward in overcoming educational disadvantage

Introduction

Discovering what does not work in overcoming disadvantage in education can be just as important as identifying what does work, in order to be able to make well-founded judgements about the difference between the two. That is what this book has done. Along the way, some approaches and techniques lauded by others have been shown not to work, meaning that the opportunity costs and likely damage caused by such approaches should cease. Some ideas have shown promise, and need to be developed further by ethical rigorous programmes of design and evaluation. Some approaches might work, are desirable in their own right and would be so cheap and easy to implement that they are a reproach to any society that does not do them. Finally, a small number of very promising interventions have survived critical scrutiny. This chapter sorts out which is which, and thus points to the way forward for research, education systems and wider society. It deals first with some suggestions for research.

Suggestions for research and evidence collection

One of the firm conclusions from this book must be that there is a need for better research and evaluation than currently occurs in education (especially outside the US). Whether it is the misuse of large datasets or the weak studies encountered in reviews, a lot of the worst research reported could be eliminated easily. It could be eliminated by the funders, following the lead of those such as the IES in the US or EEF in the UK, who target their budget on finding out what works. It could be eliminated by pressure applied through consideration of ethics (Gorard 2013). The most unethical research is weak research that tells us nothing of value. Poor studies, with conflicts of interest or lack of concern about clarity and logic, do considerable damage. They waste the time of everyone involved in them, and everyone who has to try to read them. They also waste the money of the taxpayers and charity-givers that fund them; most crucially, they damage the life chances of those disadvantaged students that their authors often claim to care about – by forcing out or obscuring good research, and by offering incorrect answers to real-life questions. The opportunity cost is that students who might have done better have lost their one shot at success. The quality controls for education research do not work well, mostly because poor work is so prevalent that its creators inevitably play important roles in 'safeguarding' it, through various review processes. This situation is a scandal.

Mixed in with this games-playing approach to research are a minority of genuine, if flawed, attempts to explain and overcome problems. In a time of economic downturn it is perhaps even more important that policy-makers commission and abide by rigorous independent evaluations of their ideas. The cost of proper research, of a kind that is rare in education, is minimal in comparison to the cost of policy interventions of the kind that happen almost continuously. So it is possible to save money on ineffective solutions before they go national and to improve provision by backing those schemes with the most chance of success. Governments need to pay more attention to rigorous research evidence than they are doing now.

There has been very little rigorous work on the causes of post-compulsory participation in education, which is quite surprising since widening participation has been a favoured policy for more than a decade in the UK and elsewhere. Prior reviews of specific areas of participation such as post-16 (See et al. 2011) and HE (Gorard et al. 2007) largely confirm this gap. Work could be commissioned in the most promising areas. However, given that these same reviews also note that participation is closely related to prior attainment at school, measures to improve experiences of school could have a longer-term impact on participation as well.

In general, there was no consistent reporting of effect sizes in the studies of compulsory schooling reviewed here. This is partly because the evidence in most areas is generally too immature at present, and partly because most authors still rely inappropriately on significance testing. Without more consistent use of effect sizes, it is not possible to conduct either a good meta-analysis of impacts or a cost-benefit analysis of interventions in each area. It is important that future work moves towards estimates of both, and that funders and researchers realise the importance of this step. For the same reason, even where there is evidence for the impact of an intervention, without effect sizes there can be no differential effectiveness estimates for specific sub-groups of potentially disadvantaged learners such as low SES, low attaining or SEN students. Some studies focused on specific sub-groups by design and these are noted throughout. This is very different from statistical dredging for differences by sub-groups after the research has been conducted.

Another really simple improvement that could be made in studies that involve statistical modelling would be to end the schisms between fields and disciplines. One of the biggest threats to the validity of such analyses lies in omitted variable bias (Gorard 2013). Yet psychologists continue to work with almost no consideration of SES or prior attainment, sociologists with no measures of motivation, and so on. Using a fuller range of possible explanatory variables inevitably leads to a smaller possible causal claim for any one of them – which is perhaps why the schisms suit so many of the authors cited in this book. Psychologists can claim predominance of mental processes over structural factors, and sociologists can claim the opposite, but neither group actually tests this in any way. Of course, the problem is more widespread than this simple example, encompassing all of the social sciences and beyond.

A particular concern is that any area of research may become dominated by only one style of work, contributing to only one part of a causal model (the longitudinal work on self-concept is a clear example). On the other hand, an intervention study in any area would generally be premature and unethical unless there is a prima facie case that the intervention would be effective. Therefore, each iteration of the research cycle legitimately starts with exploratory development work, which is often small-scale and tentative, or based on existing data. However, in the same way that it would be unethical to move to intervention studies with only this preliminary basis to justify it, it is also unethical not to pursue promising developments into efficacy and cost-effectiveness trials and, depending on results, to national rollout and monitoring (Gorard & Cook 2007). Inevitably, even many promising ideas will not work; but this is no reason not to test them, as appears to happen too often at present.

The principles of overcoming disadvantage

Before summarising the practical and user implications of this book, it is worth being a little clearer about what we are all trying to achieve, perhaps by taking a lesson from the students in Chapter 7. Overcoming disadvantage does not mean that all educational outcomes should be equal or equivalent for everyone. That would not be fair, because it would not allow for recognition of choice, merit, effort or talent. Equally, overcoming disadvantage means that differences in outcomes should not be systematically stratified in terms of indicators of disadvantage. That would not be fair because initial disadvantage does not allow true equality of opportunity. Therefore, we need to distinguish between outcomes that should be equal, and those that are entitlements or requirements based on a universal principle of justice, from outcomes that can legitimately be distributed unevenly because they are deemed the responsibility of the individual involved.

This leads quickly to three important questions for readers of this book. Collectively, these questions should become topics of widespread debate. It appears that many commentators and policy-makers hold latent views on these key questions that are in tension if not blatantly contradictory when spelt out. These questions are not for us as authors, or any individuals or groups, to answer alone. Yet, until they are settled, much of the apparent debate about how to overcome disadvantage will be distorted by commentators with different but undeclared views on these questions. There are other such questions about what a just and fair education system would look like, but these three will do for now.

Question 1: At what age or stage does initial education cease to be a threshold entitlement and become a resource differentiated by merit?

Increasingly, all countries have planned an initial education system that is compulsory for all, and that only becomes partial after a certain age (or stage). In the UK, for example, schooling has traditionally been compulsory until the age of 16. The crucial cut-off has risen since 1945 from age 14 to 15, then to 16, and now to 17 soon to be 18. After this, access to education or training becomes voluntary, and the various routes through post-compulsory education become selective, especially the opportunities for higher education. It is not clear which, if any, of these ages is the correct one, or whether the cut-off should be based on age at all rather than achievement or satisfaction. It is anyway not at all clear why education should be universal in one year for an individual and then so suddenly become selective in the next year. In fact, policies such as widening participation in higher education suggest dissatisfaction with the existing selection process, even for young adults. Practices such as grade retention at school, which are widespread in many countries, suggest dissatisfaction with age-related criteria even for young children. Is there an age up to which it is fair for the state to intervene to equalise outcomes or to ensure that all citizens reach a threshold of literacy or numeracy, for example? Or is such intervention fair over the entire life course?

There are three contradictory principles underlying the provision of most education systems. To some extent, opportunities must be equal and open to all as discussed in Chapter 4, meaning that some outcomes will tend to be unequal (dependent upon luck, talent and effort perhaps). To some extent, outcomes such as a threshold competence in literacy and numeracy are entitlements, which mean deploying unequal resources as discussed in Chapter 9. Both of these ideas are clearly fair, and the task is to decide the domains in which they apply. To some extent, opportunities are based on past performance in education. It is not so clear that this is fair.

Question 2: Are qualifications obtained through merit?

As illustrated in Chapter 8, the qualifications obtained by young people are stratified in terms of their earlier attainment, and family and background characteristics. It is well known that males in developed countries are less likely to obtain any high level generic form of qualification, for example. This means that any selection of students on the basis of qualifications would lead to the under-representation of males. The same argument could be made for variables about social class, some ethnic groups, the age of the applicant and many others. Using the socially-stratified variable of prior qualification to select people for future education or employment must lead to these same patterns of inequality appearing in education and employment. Yet in many countries, it is illegal to select on the basis of sex, age etc. but legal to use qualification as a proxy that amounts to practically the same thing.

This is an issue that societies need to debate urgently. Currently, many commentators and policy-makers adopt the contradictory stance of allowing or encouraging the use of qualifications as a determinant, while at the same time admitting that qualifications could be unfairly awarded and asking that this unfairness is somehow taken into account. Two principles of justice are clashing here and it is important to be much clearer about which applies to which domain. One possibility is to reject qualifications as not being an outcome of merit (talent or effort) and so not to allow selection on that basis, or even not allow selection at all. This means that males and females can be accepted equally, for example, even though the average qualifications of the former may be lower. This is fair if previous qualifications have been awarded unfairly. If not, then the only real alternatives are to continue to use a flawed and unfair mechanism, or to make a stand that qualifications are fair and that we must accept the stratified consequences. Does this mean that stratification is inevitable in a free society?

Question 3: Should an individual be permitted to assist others, by using an advantage they may have gained through their own talent?

If one individual can genuinely help another, then the second individual gains an advantage relative to anyone without that help. If the first individual is in a position of advantage then their advantage becomes 'inherited' by the second, and this could lead to stratification of outcomes, on average. On the other hand, if we deny that an individual is permitted to help another of their own choosing then we are creating an unpleasant-sounding society, and perhaps reducing the motivation to do well in life or to do good things such as helping others. We might demotivate those who want to do well in order to help others, but not demotivate those who want to do well in order to be selfish. This seems perverse.

An example might clarify the problem. Money has been invented as a cypher that can be exchanged conveniently for goods and services. It is generally permissible for an individual to use money earned through their own effort or success to pay for food, shelter, travel etc. They could also use it for luxuries, holidays and they can even waste it. Currently, they could also use it to assist their child's education, or leave this money to their child after death. If they do this, the child will gain a likely advantage in life that is not merited by their own talent or effort. Yet if society bans either of these last two actions as unfair, then the value of money is markedly less, and it will become less attractive to those who are meant to be earning it. We will also have created a situation where waste and luxury are condoned, but helping some others such as children is frowned upon. The same kind of argument as that used with money could be advanced about the transfer of skills, knowledge or taste from one person to another. An individual can pass such useful things on to others. Indeed, Chapter 10 advocates this and it is after all what formal education is about. But this also means that the recipient might then be advantaged, because it will be hard to overcome the influence of parental occupation or education on a child's opportunities. If this kind of parental assistance were banned (as if that were enforceable) then part of the beautiful parent–child relationship of co-operative learning has been destroyed. Perhaps it should be permitted, but the state should intervene to give the same advantages to all? Perhaps this is what universal, compulsory, free education is intended to do. If it is not doing this, or not even attempting to do this, perhaps schools should lose their special status as the only compulsory state treatment for all citizens, and one of the most expensive investments to boot. This brief outline begins to reveal some of the complexity involved in answering this and the previous questions, and also the importance of the answers for overcoming disadvantage in a coherent manner.

A further issue concerns the indicators of disadvantage themselves. To be officially poor in the UK, as denoted by eligibility for FSM, is very different from being poor in sub-Saharan Africa (Chapter 2). Given welfare payments and many free public services such as the National Health Service, a poor family in the UK might objectively still be among the wealthiest in other societies. In principle, the kind of relative definition of poverty used in the UK would still present inequality even if no one were objectively poor. So, perhaps all of the indicators should be looked at in another way. Some, such as ethnic origin, are not really indicators of disadvantage at all. Objectively and intrinsically, to be of one origin or another is no advantage or disadvantage. Where ethnic 'gaps' show up, such as in achievement, is presumably a result of something else including prior family education, historical patterns of immigration, political control or even discrimination. Other indicators, such as poverty of income perhaps, are only indicators of disadvantage up to a certain threshold. Put another way, if the children of the super-rich have different outcomes to the children of the merely rich this would be a different and more tolerable kind of inequality than between average and the super-poor.

A way forward

For the present, and until there is consensus on such pressing but difficult questions, we will assume that there are at least three kinds of outcomes that we want to make fair – equitable treatments, thresholds of entitlement and equalising interventions. The chapter considers what can and cannot be done to improve the situation in these overlapping categories. Much of the focus is on attainment and participation, but it must be remembered that these are linked to other outcomes, and that these other outcomes may actually be of more value in their own right. Learning has an intrinsic value, and it can be enjoyable and fulfilling. It does not always have to be *for* something else, such as advancement.

Equitable treatments

A lot of state-funded education should be about equitable treatment, as so clearly identified by the students traversing it. Students should always be treated with respect by teachers, even under difficult circumstances (and vice versa of course). This universal principle should be part of initial and continuing teacher development, while persistent misapplication of this ideal strongly suggests unsuitability to be a teacher and should be acted on appropriately. Similarly, teachers should not have 'favourites' in the sense of students who are treated better outside of any domain in which they have merited it. A higher grade because of better work is fair. More interaction with the teacher over a prolonged period, or differential application of uniform regulations because of better work is not fair.

Equitable treatment goes beyond 'rules' for individual interactions however. State-funded education is intended to reduce the influence of background and to provide all children with a good preparation for the future. Everything that can be done to ensure appropriately equitable treatment should be done. In fact, it is so much easier to treat people the same that it is hard to imagine why so much policy attention is devoted to treating them differentially. The expenditure on and allocation of resources to students in schools and other educational institutions should be equivalent (but see exceptions below), as should the per capita funding to educational institutions. The procedure for allocating places at educational institutions should be the same for all institutions and all individuals. The existing school system in England, with regulations about allocation of school places, teacher development, inspections, national curriculum and standard attainment in key stages, is aimed at standardising schools. So it should make little difference which school a child attends. This would be the ideal.

This means no state-funded diversity of schooling. If, for example, Academies in England are really a superior form of school to the 'bog-standard' local comprehensives then why are only some schools made into Academies? Surely, all students are entitled to this better form of education, rather than the state wilfully continuing to provide what they claim is an inferior experience for some. Similar issues arise in other countries with Free Schools, Charter schools, tracking and so on. In fact, as this book shows, it is not clear that Academies are better than other schools and so the money invested in them could have been used more fruitfully elsewhere. Again, the same could be said about most initiatives that tinker with the types of school available. For the same reason there should be no schools for 11- to 16-year-olds alongside those for 11- to 18-year-olds, or indeed any variation in age range. One of these ranges will be the better for any nation or region as a whole, and should be adopted universally. If it is argued that we do not know which is best then that means we have no reason to vary them (unless for the purposes of a genuine attempt to find out). Similarly, there should be no single-sex and co-educational schools in the same system. Again, one of these forms of schooling will be better for the region as a whole and should be adopted.

It means there should be no selection by aptitude or prior attainment within a system that is also compulsory. There should be no differences between schools in terms of their faith-basis, or more simply no faith-basis at all. There should be no private investment (as opposed to welcome charitable giving to the system as a whole), and no curricular specialisms in the compulsory phase (there should be a truly National Curriculum). All young people should be included in mainstream institutions as far as possible (but see possible exceptions discussed in the following pages).

Controlling the school mix like this is one of the most important educational tasks for central and local governments. The changes and simplifications explored previously would make a huge difference to the underlying levels of segregation (Chapter 4). However, in any region there will still be segregation in schools caused by the nature and cost of local housing, transport and the historical number of schools. In the long term, the impact of such structural factors might be reduced by removing all unnecessarily divisive elements, such as those noted previously. For example, the changes could reduce the 'premium' price purportedly added to housing near popular schools. In the medium term, further equitable measures might be needed to reduce segregation of any indicator of disadvantage to its minimum level. School places could be subject to family preference, which could be deemed a right, and is likely to improve the situation to a limited extent. For example, parents in disadvantaged areas will be more likely to express a preference for a school in another area than parents in advantaged areas to express a preference for one in a disadvantaged setting. More importantly, school places must not be allocated in terms of where people live, or any proxy for that such as distance travelled. This means that free public transport (bussing) must be available for all, which could have many other advantages such as less road congestion in rush hours. Disputed places at over-subscribed schools could be determined by lottery or using overall school mix balance (in terms of disadvantage) as the priority criterion – the disadvantaged student gets priority access to the relatively advantaged school and vice versa. This is fair. The purpose is to make a truly national or regional system of equivalent schools, so that the quality of education received depends in no way on where one lives or who one is. Once this is realised, there would be no need to travel further than the nearest school, and almost no need for place allocation criteria at all anyway.

Practical solutions include:

- making schools more comprehensive. There should be no curricular specialist schools, no faith-based schools, no selection by attainment or aptitude, no private investment or control of state-funded schools. The same admissions criteria should be applied to every school. This may be cheaper and more effective than many other measures currently used or suggested;
- offering schools incentives for taking in students from disadvantaged backgrounds;

- using a banding or quota system to ensure that school intakes reflect the social and ethnic mix of the local population;
- using a lottery system rather than distance or residence in allocating places in over-subscribed or popular schools. Free transportation should be made available to those entitled to any feasible school, not simply to the nearest available.

It is not possible to list all possible simplifications here, but because of the importance of teachers (Chapters 6 and 7), it is worth making a few suggestions for the profession. Again, the emphasis should be on equitable treatment and processes. Currently, some applicants to teacher training in England are being rejected on the basis of prior qualifications at some institutions while other applicants with much worse qualifications are being accepted at others. The pass rates into subsequent qualified teacher status are then comparable between the two. This suggests either that qualifications are meaningless (discussed previously) or that there is unfairness and inefficiency in the selection process, including likely loss of some highly qualified applicants to the teaching profession. The profession should be national and so the preparation for it should reflect that characteristic. Schools themselves should not employ teachers, and to some extent and within reason teachers employed by the state should be able to be deployed to meet demand just as many other state employees are. This would help avoid the stratification of teachers between areas, and the shortage of teachers in some. Their salaries must be national not local. This would mean an end, among other things, to incentives or compensatory payments for those living and working in the most popular areas. The local cost of living and housing tends to reflect perceived desirability, so popular locations do not need an incentive or any recompense. They are attractive already. A genuinely national pay scheme provides a kind of incentive for good teachers to work in the less desirable areas. Policies such as the London Allowance in England undercut that fairness and should cease. The problems are far worse outside London. Again, it should be easier to keep things the same than to make artificial and probably harmful distinctions.

Practical solutions include:

- nationalise the selection and development of professional teachers
- introduce a central employment scheme for teachers.

As this book shows, if these changes combined then made any difference to attainment outcomes at all (and this is not their main purpose), they are likely to improve results and reduce the poverty gradient. This is because of the diminishing returns on any 'investment' in the already advantaged learners, and the inefficiency produced by enhancing rather than counteracting 'privileged student bias' (Chiu & Khoo 2005, p.576). Most of the proposals that have been noted also have no obvious cost. In fact, because the system will be simpler, as well as fairer, it will probably be cheaper within a very short time. Quality, equality and cost-effectiveness are firm friends in the educational context.

Thresholds of entitlement

Equitable treatment is a key principle for the organisation of a state education system. However, it will lead to unfairness in some situations, such as those where students are entitled to achieve a certain level of proficiency but do not do so as a direct result of a disadvantage beyond their control, or where a minimum level of input is expected from students.

It is reasonable to ask a state education system that is imposed on all to yield citizens with certain basic skills. Such skills will change over historical time, but currently they might include a level of proficiency in numeracy, literacy, use of technology, knowledge of societal rights and duties and in making important life choices for oneself. Perhaps most obviously from the accounts in this book, students have a right to expect a certain minimum level of competence from their teachers. Teachers should be required to allow learners a certain level of control over their own learning. Students should be required to behave with some level of consideration to teachers and other students, if only to make the whole process work at all. If some form of post-compulsory participation in education or training is open to all, then it makes sense to ensure that this is not overly influenced by early decisions or learner-identities. Something like a voucher system could be implemented. If a young person continues from school to a traditional post-compulsory experience, with or without a gap year perhaps, then their voucher is 'cashed'. If they do not continue at that age, then the voucher can remain valid for use later when a more mature experience is desired.

Overcoming disadvantage in school is not only about improving results, and quality of teaching need not be measured in terms of student attainment. Education should also be about enhancing students' overall well-being and experiences of learning. All children should be entitled to a pleasant and enjoyable education experience. Enjoyment can be wide-ranging and have long-term impact on students' lives, such as attitude towards learning and employment. Enhancing students' learning experience is easier than improving teacher effectiveness, which cannot be easily measured or calibrated anyway. Improving the way teachers interact with their pupils in such a way that it enhances students' general well-being and experiences of learning is one way of overcoming disadvantage if it leads to better citizens. Better behaved, respectful citizens are less likely to get into trouble in society and more likely to find employment. This has implications for teacher training and teacher development in reinforcing good practice such as fairness and respect.

All of these are threshold outcomes or rights. In these domains and others like them, equal outcomes would be fair, yet equitable treatment will sometimes be insufficient to achieve this. Rather, unequal treatment is generally required for universal achievement of the threshold. This could be in the form of equalising interventions.

Equalising interventions

Intervening to improve outcomes for a subset of disadvantaged or struggling students is therefore fair, up to a point and within the framework set out so far. It could also be cost neutral or better, largely because so many interventions are currently taking place that just do not work. The money and effort saved in abolishing these can be diverted to developing and sharing the few initiatives that have more promise. This book has shown that we have no evidence that the following well-meaning and plausible-sounding ideas work to improve attainment or participation.

Approaches showing no promise of overcoming disadvantage:

- differential school effectiveness factors, and the associated generic school improvement approach
- diversity of schooling, including selection and tracking
- raising student aspirations or parental expectations
- improving individual attitudes including self-concept, locus of control and similar
- changing individuals' behaviour in terms of paid work or participation in enrichment activities
- other changes to parental styles, attitudes or behaviour
- use of technology in itself
- use of extra time such as summer programmes, in itself.

There may be cases where a young person could not thrive in a mainstream school setting, and a hospital or similar is preferred. This is not unjust as long as they feel looked after and respected (Gorard & Smith 2010). There are a number of other possible interventions described in detail in the book, including the following, that could be targeted fairly at helping potentially disadvantaged students.

Approaches showing some promise of overcoming disadvantage:

- making schools as uniform as possible
- offering schools 'incentives' for taking in students from disadvantaged backgrounds, with funding following the student, as with the pupil premium policy in England
- using incentives not for extrinsic motivation to achieve, but for rewarding the components of improvement such as attendance and behaviour
- parental training and home support for those with pre-school children
- encouraging parental involvement in education when their child is young, working in collaboration with staff
- prepare and develop interventions to improve students' social and emotional learning
- prepare and develop interventions to improve students' civic participation, happiness and empathy for others

- improving home–school collaboration and minimising the differences between home and school culture for older students
- some targeted literacy catch-up programmes developed in the US
- adult mentoring for struggling students.

Education is more than attainment

Serious inequalities and some difficult social problems may be apparent in the population at large in many countries for the foreseeable future, and despite efforts to deal with them via education and other policies. This would never result in there being no differences in outcomes; that would be both unfair and unrealistic. But the differences should not be at threshold levels, and there should not be such large systematic differences between social groups in terms of other outcomes. Meanwhile, there is no need for any government to transport these wider problems into their state-funded schools. As mini-societies in themselves, schools and colleges could be shaped as the kind of wider society we would like, rather than left to represent only the society we have. They can be designed to minimise the experience and impact of inequalities outside schools, affording children and young people a decade or more with a mixed peer group and mutually respectful relationships with adults. To some extent this is what schools and colleges already try to do, but they are hampered by the red herring of differential attainment as it appears to policy-makers and many other commentators. If schools were engineered for their wider purpose more explicitly than at present, then their benign influence could be much greater.

References

Abbot, A. (1998) The causal devolution, *Sociological Methods and Research*, 27, 2, 148–181

Abu-Hilal, M. (2000) A structural model of attitudes towards school subjects, academic aspiration and achievement, *Educational Psychology*, 20, 1, 75–84

Agirdag, O., Van Houtte, M. and Van Amermaet, P. (2012) Ethnic school segregation and self-esteem, *Urban Education*, 47, 6, 1135–1159

Ahmad, F. (2001) Modern traditions? British Muslim women and academic achievement, *Gender and Education*, 13, 2, 137–152

Ahmavaara, A. and Houston, D. (2007) The effects of selective schooling and self-concept on adolescents' academic aspiration: An examination of Dweck's Self-Theory, *British Journal of Educational Psychology*, 77, 3, 613–632

Aikens, N. and Barbarin, O. (2008) Socioeconomic differences in reading trajectories: The contribution of family, neighbourhood, and school contexts, *Journal of Educational Psychology*, 100, 2, 235–251

Alegre, M. and Ferrer, G. (2010) School regimes and education equity: Some insights based on PISA 2006, *British Educational Research Journal*, 36, 3, 433–461

Alexander, K. and Cook, M. (1979) The motivational relevance of educational plans: Questioning the conventional wisdom, *Social Psychology Quarterly*, 42, 202–213

Allen, R. and West, A. (2011) Why do faith-based schools have advantaged intakes? The relative importance of neighbourhood characteristics, social background and religious identification amongst parents, *British Educational Research Journal*, 37, 4, 631–655

Allen, R., Coldron, J. and West, A. (2012) The effect of changes in published secondary school admissions on pupil composition, *Journal of Education Policy*, 27, 3, 349–366

Amrein-Beardsley, A. (2008) Methodological concerns about the education value-added assessment system, *Educational Researcher*, 37, 2, 65–75

Anders, J. (2012) The link between household income, university applications and university attendance, *Fiscal Studies*, 33, 2, 185–210

Antikainen, A. and Huusko, A. (2008) The impact of information technology on participation in adult education: The case of Finland from a comparative perspective, *International Journal of Contemporary Sociology*, 45, 2, 119–129

Antoniou, P. (2012) The short- and long-term effects of secondary schools upon students' academic success and development, *Educational Research and Evaluation*, 18, 7, 621–639

Bachman, J., Staff, J., O'Malley, P. Schulenberg, J. and Freedman-Doan, P. (2011) Twelfth-grade student work intensity linked to later educational attainment and substance use: New longitudinal evidence, *Developmental Psychology*, 47, 2, 344–363

Baker, A. and Soden, L (1997) *Parent involvement in children's education: A critical assessment of the knowledge base*, Paper presented at the Annual Meeting of the American Education Research Association, 24 March (Chicago)

Baker, C. (2010) *Relationships between contextual characteristics, parent implementation, and child outcome within an academic preventive intervention for preschoolers*, Dissertation Abstracts International, Section B, The Sciences and Engineering

Bandura, A., Barbaranelli, C., Caprara, G. V. and Pastorelli, C. (2001) Self-efficacy beliefs as shapers of children's aspirations and career trajectories, *Child Development*, 72, 1, 187–206

Barber, M. and Mcoursched, M. (2007) *How the world's best-performing school systems come out on top*, UK: McKinsey & Co.

Barker, I. (2010) School closures soar, *Times Educational Supplement*, 26 February, pp.1–4

Barnett, R. (2011) Learning about learning: A conundrum and a possible resolution, *London Review of Education*, 9, 1, 5–13

Bates, L. (2009) *Racial and ethnic differences in educational trajectories: The role of parental involvement, families and schools*, Dissertation Abstracts International, Section A, The Humanities and Social Sciences

Battistich, V. and Hom, A. (1997) The relationship between students' sense of their school as a community and their involvement in problem behaviours, *American Journal of Public Health*, 87, 12, 1997–2001

Battle, J. and Coates, D. (2004) Father-only and Mother-only, single-parent family status of Black girls and achievement in grade twelve and at two-years post High School, *Journal of Negro Education*, 73, 4, 392–407

Baumeister, R., Campbell, J., Krueger. J. and Vohs, K. (2003) Does high self-esteem cause better performance, interpersonal success, happiness, or healthier lifestyles? *Psychological Science in the Public Interest*, 4, 1, 1–44

Baumeister, R., Campbell, J., Krueger. J. and Vohs, K. (2005) Exploding the self-esteem myth, *Scientific American*, 292, 1, 84–92

Baumert, J., Koller, O., Ludtke, O., Marsh, H. and Trautwein, U. (2005) Academic self-concept, interest, grades, and standardised test scores: Reciprocal effects models of causal ordering, *Child Development*, 76, 2, 397–416

Baysu, G. and de Valk, H. (2012) Navigating the school system in Sweden, Belgium, Austria and Germany: School segregation and second generation school trajectories, *Ethnicities*, 12, 6, 776–799

BBC (2004) *Academies getting results at GCSE*. Available at http://news.bbc.co.uk/go/pr/fr/-/1/hi/education/3602818.stm (accessed 17 November 2004)

Beal, S. and Crockett, L. (2010) Adolescents' occupational and educational aspirations and expectations: Links to high school activities and adult educational attainment, *Development Psychology*, 46, 1, 258–265

Beckett, C., Kallitsoglou, A., Doolan, M., Ford, T. and Scott, S. (2012) *Helping children achieve: Summary of the study, 2007–2010*, interim report DFE-RR185b, London: Department for Education

Behnke, A., Gonzalez, L. and Cox, R. (2010) Latino students in new arrival states: Factors and services to prevent youth from dropping out, *Hispanic Journal of Behavioral Sciences*, 32, 3, 385

Ben-Avie, M. and Steinfeld, T. (2001) *The impact of a school-based academic and counselling intervention on the lifepaths of youth: An independent evaluation of the Institute for Student Achievement*, paper presented at the Annual Meeting of the American Educational Research Association, 10–14 April (Seattle, WA)

Benner, A., Graham, S. and Mistry, R. (2008) Discerning direct and mediated effects of ecological structures and processes on adolescents' educational outcomes, *Developmental Psychology*, 44, 3, 840-854

Bettinger, E. (2010) *Paying to learn: The effect of financial incentives on elementary school test scores*, NBER working paper 16333, National Bureau of Economic Research

Billett, S. (2010) The perils of confusing lifelong learning with lifelong education, *International Journal of Lifelong Education*, 29, 4, 401–413

Black, A., Little, C., McCoach, D., Purcell, J. and Siegle, D. (2008) Advancement via individual determination: Method selection in conclusions about program effectiveness, *The Journal of Educational Research*, 102, 2, 111–123

Blackwell, L., Trzesniewski, K. and Dweck, C. (2007) Implicit theories of intelligence predict achievement across an adolescent transition: A longitudinal study and an intervention, *Child Development*, 78, 1, 246–263

Blanden, J., Gregg, P. and Machin, S. (2005) *Intergenerational mobility in Europe and North America: Report for the Sutton Trust*, London: Centre for Economic Performance

Blaver, A. (2010) *An examination of gender, home language, self-appraisals, and mathematics achievement among Hispanic youth*, Dissertation Abstracts International, Section A, The Humanities and Social Sciences

Blondal, K. S. and Adalbjarnardottir (2009) Parenting practices and school dropout: A longitudinal study, *Adolescence*, 44, 176, 729–750

Bodovski, K. (2010) Parental practices and educational achievement: Social class, race, and habitus, *British Journal of Sociology of Education*, 31, 2, 139–156

Boliver, V. and Swift, A. (2011) Do comprehensive schools reduce social mobility? *British Journal of Sociology of Education*, 62, 1, 89–110

Bonal, X. (2012) Education policy and school segregation of migrant students in Catalonia, *Journal of Education Policy*, 27, 3, 401–421

Bong, M., Cho, C., Ahn, H. S. and Kim, H. J. (2012) Comparison of self-beliefs for predicting student motivation and achievement, *The Journal of Educational Research*, 105, 5, 336–352

Borman, G. and Dowling, N. (2006) Longitudinal achievement effects of multiyear summer school: Evidence from the Teach Baltimore Randomized Field Trial, *Educational Evaluation and Policy Analysis*, 28, 1, 25–48

Borman, G., Benson, J. and Overman, L. (2009) A randomised field trial of the Fast ForWord Language computer-based training program, *Educational Evaluation and Policy Analysis*, 31, 82–106

Boulton, M., Duke. E., Holma, G., Laxton, E., Nicholas, B., Spells, R., Williams, E. and Woodmansey, H. (2009) Associations between being bullied, perceptions of safety in classroom and playground, and relationship with teacher among primary school pupils, *Educational Studies*, 35, 3, 255–267

Bowl, M. (2001) Experiencing the barriers: Non-traditional students entering higher education, *Research Papers in Education: Policy & Practice*, 16, 2, 141–160

Bradbury, A. (2011) Equity, ethnicity and the hidden dangers of 'contextual' measures of school performance, *Race, Ethnicity and Education*, 14, 3, 277–291

Bradford-Hill, A. (1966) The environment and disease: Association or causation? *Proceedings of the Royal Society of Medicine*, 58, 285

Bradshaw, G., Mitchell, M. and Leaf, P. (2010) Examining the effects of school-wide positive behavioural interventions and supports on student outcomes: Results from a randomised controlled effectiveness trial in elementary school, *Journal of Positive Behavior Interventions*, 12, 3, 133–148

Breen, R. (2004) *Social mobility in Europe*, Oxford: Oxford University Press

Brooks, G., Miles, J. N. V. and Torgerson, C. J. (2006) Is an intervention using computer software effective in literacy learning? A randomised controlled trial, *Educational Studies*, 32, 2, 33–143

Brown, E. and Scott-Little, C. (2003) *Evaluations of school readiness initiatives: What are we learning?* Tallahassee, FL: SERVE

Brown, G. (2004) *The efficacy of question-answering instruction for improving year 5 reading comprehension*, PhD dissertation, University of Western Sydney (Sydney, Australia)

Brown, L. and Iyengar, S. (2008) Parenting styles: The impact on student achievement, *Marriage & Family Review*, 43, 1–2, 14–38

Bruel, A. and Bartholo, T. (2012) Inequality of educational opportunities in Rio de Janeiro public school system: Transition between segments of elementary school, *Revista Brasileira de Educação*, 17, 50, 303–328

Buchmann, C. and Dalton, B. (2002) Interpersonal influences and educational aspirations in 12 countries: The importance of institutional context, *Sociology of Education*, 75, 2, 99–122

Bui (2007) Educational expectations and academic achievement among Middle and High school students, *Education*, 127, 3, 328–331

Burgess, S., Wilson, D. and Lupton, R. (2005) Parallel lives? Ethnic segregation in schools and neighbourhoods, *Urban Studies*, 42, 7, 1027–1056

Burris, C., Wiley, E., Welner, K. and Murphy, J. (2008) Accountability, rigor, and detracking: Achievement effects of embracing a challenging curriculum as a universal good for all students, *Teachers College Record*, 110, 3, 571–607

Burstein, L., Fischer, K. B., Miller, M. D. (1980) The multilevel effects of background on science achievement: A cross-national comparison, *Sociology of Education*, 53, 4, 215–225

Burt, K. and Roisman, G. (2010) Competence and psychopathology: Cascade effects in the NICHD Study of Early Child Care and Youth Development, *Development and Psychopathology*, 22, 3, 557–567

Caggiano, J. (2007) *Addressing the learning needs of struggling adolescent readers: The impact of a reading intervention program on students in a middle school setting*, EdD dissertation, The College of William and Mary (Williamsburg, VA)

Calder, A. and Cope, R. (2005) *Breaking barriers: Reaching the hardest to reach*, London: Prince's Trust

Campbell, T. and Campbell, D. (1997) Faculty/student mentor program: Effects on academic performance and retention, *Research in Higher Education*, 38, 6, 727–742

Cantrell, S., Almasi, J., Carter, J., Rintamaa, M. and Madden, A. (2010) The impact of a strategy-based intervention on the comprehension and strategy use of struggling adolescent readers, *Journal of Educational Psychology*, 102, 2, 257–280

Carroll, M. (2000) *Exploring the commitments parents make to their children's education*. Dissertation Abstracts International, Section A, The Humanities and Social Sciences

Carson, A. (2009) *A spatial-temporal analysis of factors influencing the postsecondary plans of Indiana public high school graduates; 1996–2006*, Dissertation Abstracts International, Section A, The Humanities and Social Sciences

Carter, S. (2002) *The impact of parent/family involvement on student outcomes: An annotated bibliography of research from the past decade*. Eugene, OR: CADRE

Casey, L., Davies, P., Kalambouka, A., Nelson, N. and Boyle, B. (2006) The influence of schooling on the aspirations of young people with special educational needs, *British Educational Research Journal*, 32, 2, 273–290

Chamorro-Premuzic, T., Harlaar, N., Greven, C. and Plomin, R. (2010) More than just IQ: A longitudinal examination of self-perceived abilities as predictors of academic performance in a large sample of UK twins, *Intelligence*, 38, 4, 385–392

Chaplin, D. and Capizzano, J. (2006) *Impacts of a summer learning program: A random assignment study of Building Educated Leaders for Life (BELL)*, Washington, DC: The Urban Institute. Available at http://www.urban.org/UploadedPDF/411350_bell_impacts.pdf (accessed 22 February 2013)

Chapman, B. and Ryan, C. (2002) Income contingent financing of student higher education charges: Assessing the Australian innovation, *Welsh Journal of Education*, 11, 1, 64–81

Cheng, SC. and Gorard, S. (2010) Segregation by poverty in secondary schools in England 2006–2009: A research note, *Journal of Education Policy*, 25, 3, 415–418

Cheng, W. and Ickes, W. (2009) Conscientiousness and self-motivation as mutually compensatory predictors of university-level GPA, *Personality and Individual Differences*, 47, 8, 817–822

Chilosi, D., Noble, M., Broadhead, P. and Wilkinson, M. (2010) Measuring the effect of Aimhigher on schooling attainment and higher education applications and entries, *Journal of Further and Higher Education*, 34, 1, 1–10

Chiu, M. and Khoo, L. (2005) Effects of resources, inequality, and privilege bias on achievement: Country, school and student level analyses, *American Educational Research Journal*, 42, 4, 575–603

Chowdry, H., Crawford, C. and Goodman, A. (2010) *The role of attitudes and behaviours in explaining socio-economic differences in attainment at age 16*, Institute of Fiscal Studies working paper 10/15

Clarke, L. (2009) *Effects of a school-based adult mentoring intervention on low income, urban high school freshmen judged to be at risk for drop-out: A replication and extension*, PhD dissertation, The Graduate School of Applied and Professional Psychology (Piscataway, NJ)

Clayden, J. and Stein, M. (2002) *The way it is: Young people on race, school exclusion and leaving care*, London: The Prince's Trust.

Clotfelter, C. (2001) Are Whites still fleeing? Racial patterns and enrolment shifts in urban public schools, *Journal of Policy Analysis and Management*, 20, 2, 199–221

Coe, M., Hanita, M., Nishioka, V. and Smiley, R. (2011) *An investigation of the impact of the 6+1 trait writing model on grade 5 student writing achievement: Final Report*, Washington DC: National Center for Education Evaluation and Regional Assistance, Institute of Education Sciences, US Department of Education

Coe, R. (2010) School improvement: Reality and illusion, *British Journal of Educational Studies*, 57, 4, 363–379

Coffield, F. (2012) Why the McKinsey reports will not improve school systems, *Journal of Education Policy*, 27, 1, 131–149

Cohen, G., Garcia, J., Purdie-Vaughns, V., Apfel, N. and Brzustoski, P. (2009) Recursive processes in self-affirmation: Intervening to close the minority achievement gap, *Science*, 324, 5925, 400–440

Coldron, J., Cripps. C. and Shipton, L. (2010) Why are English secondary schools socially segregated, *Journal of Education Policy*, 25, 1, 19–35

Coleman, J., Hoffer, T. and Kilgore, S. (1982) Cognitive outcomes in public and private schools, *Sociology of Education*, 55, 2/3, 65–76

Coles, C., Brown, R., Smith, I., Platzman, K., Erickson, S. and Falek, F. (1991) Effects of prenatal alcohol exposure at school age. I. Physical and cognitive development, *Neurotoxicology and Teratology*, 13, 4, 357–367

Condron, D. (2011) Egalitarianism and educational excellence: Compatible goals for affluent societies? *Educational Researcher*, 40, 2, 47–55

Cook, K. (2010) *Effects of parent expectations and involvement on the school readiness of children in Head Start*, Dissertation Abstracts International, Section A, The Humanities and Social Sciences

Cooper, C., Crosnoe, R., Suizzo, M. A. and Pituch, K. (2010) Poverty, race, and parental involvement during the transition to Elementary School, *Journal of Family Issues*, 31, 7, 859–883

Cosgrove, J. and Gilleece, L. (2012) An international perspective on civic participation in Irish post-primary schools: Results from ICCS, *Irish Educational Studies*, 31, 4, 377–395

Cotton, K. and Wikelund, K. (1989) *Parent involvement in education*, School Improvement Research Series (SIRS), US: Office of Educational Research and Improvement (OERI)

Council of the European Union (2010) *Council conclusions on the social dimensions of education and training*, report of the 3013th Education, Youth and Culture Council Meeting, 11 May (Brussels)

Cox, M., Abbott, C., Webb, M., Blakeley, B., Beauchamp, T. and Rhodes, V. (2003) *ICT and pedagogy: A review of the research literature*, ICT in Schools Research and Evaluation Series No. 18, Coventry/London: Becta/DfES. Available at http://www.becta.org.uk/page_documents/research/ict_pedagogy_summary.pdf (accessed 10 February 2005)

Crede, M., Roch, S. and Kieszczynka, U. (2010) Class attendance in college: A meta-analytic review of the relationship of class attendance with grades and student characteristics, *Review of Educational Research*, 80, 2, 272–295

Crisp, V. (2010) Towards a model of the judgement processes involved in examination marking, *Oxford Review of Education*, 36, 1, 1–22

Croll, P. (2009) Educational participation post-16: A longitudinal analysis of intentions and outcomes, *British Journal of Educational Studies*, 57, 4, 400–416

Crosnoe, R., Leventhal, T., Wirth, R., Pierce, K. and Pianta, R. (2010) Family socioeconomic status and consistent environmental stimulation in early childhood, *Child Development*, 81, 3, 972–987

Croxford, L. and Paterson, L. (2006) Trends in social class segregation between schools in England, Wales and Scotland since 1984, *Research Papers in Education*, 21, 4, 381–406

Crozier, M., Rokutani, L., Russett, J., Godwin, E. and Banks, G. (2010) A multisite program evaluation of Families and Schools Together (FAST): Continued evidence of a successful multifamily community-based prevention program, *The School Community Journal*, 20, 1, 187–207

Currie, J. (2001) Early childhood education programs, *Journal of Economic Perspectives*, 15, 2, 213–238

Cuthbert, C. and Hatch, R. (2008) *Aspiration and attainment amongst young people in deprived communities: Analysis and discussion paper*, DCSF, Cabinet Office Social Exclusion Task Force, Short studies

Da, H. (2005) A research into the causality model affecting junior high school students' English academic achievement, *Psychological Science*, 28, 4, 984–988

Dale, A., Shaheen, N., Kalra, V. and Fieldhouse, E. (2000) Routes into education and employment for young Pakistani and Bangladeshi women in the UK, *Ethnic and Racial Studies*, 25, 6, 942–968

Davis, T. (2012) School choice and segregation: 'Tracking' racial equality in magnet schools, *Education and Urban Society*, doi 10.1177/0013124512448672

De Corte, E., Verschaffel, L. and Van De Ven, A. (2001) Improving text comprehension strategies in upper primary school children: A design experiment, *British Journal of Educational Psychology*, 71, 4, 531–559

Dearden, L., McGranahan, L. and Sianesi, B. (2004) *The role of credit constraints in educational choices: Evidence from NCDS and BCS70*, London: London School of Economics and Political Science, Centre for the Economics of Education

Dearing, E., Kreider, H. and Weiss, H. (2008) Increased family involvement in school predicts improved child–teacher relationships and feelings about school for low-income children, *Marriage and Family Review*, 43, 3/4, 226–254

Dearing, E., McCartney, K. and Taylor, B. (2009) Does higher quality early child care promote low-income children's math and reading achievement in middle childhood? *Child Development*, 80, 5, 1329–1349

Desforges, C. with Abouchaar, A. (2003) *The impact of parental involvement, parental support and family education on student achievements and adjustment: A literature review*, Department for Education and Skills report RR433, London: Department for Education and Skills

DfE (2010) *Youth cohort study and longitudinal study of young people in England: The activities and experiences of 17 year olds: England 2009.* Available at http://www.education.gov.uk/rsgateway/DB/SBU/b000937/index.shtml (accessed 21 January 2012)

DfE (2011) Statistical First Release SFR 15/2011: *Participation in education, training and employment by 16–18 year olds in England.* Available at http://www.education.gov.uk/rsgateway/DB/SFR/s001011/index.shtml (accessed 21 January 2012)

DfES (2002) *Citizenship: The National Curriculum for England.* Available at http://www.dfes.gov.uk/citizenship_(accessed August 2003)

DfES (2003a) *The future of higher education*. Norwich: The Stationery Office

DfES (2003b) *Towards a unified learning e-learning strategy*, London: HMSO. Available at http://www.dfes.gov.uk/consultations/downloadableDocs/ towards%20a%20unified%20e-learning%20strategy.pdf (accessed 22 March 2005)

Dobbie, W. and Fryer, R. (2009) *Are high-quality schools enough to close the achievement gap? Evidence from a social experiment in Harlem*, NBER working paper 15473, National Bureau of Economic Research

Domovic, V. and Godler, Z. (2005) Educational systems' efficiency evaluation on the basis of student performance: Comparison Finland-Germany, *Drustvena Istrazivanja*, 14, 3, 439–458

Dowson, M., Barker, K., McInerney, D. (2003) *The chicken and the egg: Causal ordering of goals and self-concept and its effect on academic achievement*, paper presented at the joint AARE/NZARE conference, December 2003 (Auckland, New Zealand)

Dryfoos, J. (2000) *Evaluations of community schools: Findings to date*, Hastings-on-Hudson, NY: Coalition for Community Schools

Dugdale, G. (2009) *Enjoyment, confidence and reading: The keys for the success of writing in the 21st century*, London: National Literacy Trust. Available at http://www.literacytrust.org.uk/policy/writingthefuture.pdf (accessed 14 November 2009)

Duncan, G. and Magnuson, K. (2005) Can family socioeconomic resources account for racial and ethnic test score gaps? *The Future of Children*, 15, 1, 35–54

Duncan, O., Cuzzort, R. and Duncan, B. (1961) *Statistical geography: Problems in analyzing area data*, Glencoe IL: Free Press

Dupriez, V. and Dumray, X. (2006) Inequalities in school systems: Effect of school structure or of society structure? *Comparative Education*, 42, 2, 243–260

Durlak, J., Weissberg, R., Dymnicki, A., Taylor, R. and Schellinger, K. (2008) The impact of enhancing students' social and emotional learning: A meta-analysis of school-based universal interventions, *Child Development*, 82, 1, 405–432

Dynarski, M., Agodini, R., Heaviside, S., Novak, T., Carey, N., Campuzano, L., et al. (2007) *Effectiveness of reading and mathematics software products: Findings from the first pupil cohort* (Publication No. 2007–4005), Washington, DC: US Department of Education, Institute of Education Sciences. Available at http://ies.ed.gov/ ncee/pdf/20074005.pdf (accessed 23 February 2013)

Education Commission (2004) *The educational experiences and achievements of Black boys in London schools 2000–2003*, London: London Development Agency

Edwards, R. and Weller, S. (2010) Trajectories from youth to adulthood: Choice and structure for young people before and during recession, *21st Century Society*, 5, 2, 125–136

Englund, M., Luckner, A., Whaley, G. and Egeland, B. (2004) Children's achievement in early elementary school: Longitudinal effects of parental involvement, expectations, and quality of assistance, *Journal of Educational Psychology*, 96, 4, 723–730

Epstein, J., Clark, L. Salinas, K. and Sanders, M. (1997) Involving parents in homework in the middle grades, Baltimore, MD: Johns Hopkins University.

European Commission (2001) *Making a European area of lifelong learning a reality*, DG Education and Culture, European Commission Communication

European Group for Research on Equity in Educational Systems (2008) *Developing a sense of justice among disadvantaged students: The role of schools*, Birmingham: European Group for Research on Equity in Education Systems

European Group for Research on Equity in Educational Systems (2005) Equity in European Educational Systems: A set of indicators, *European Educational Research Journal*, 4, 2, 1–151

Eurydice (2007) *The information network on education in Europe*. Available at http://www.eurydice.org/portal/page/portal/Eurydice (accessed 23 February 2013)

Exley, S. (2011) Seven out of 10 academies fail to meet admission procedures, *Times Educational Supplement*, 3 June, p.6

Faires, J. Nichols, W. and Rickelman, R. (2000) Effects of parental involvement in developing competent readers in first grade, *Reading Psychology*, 21, 195–215

Fan, X. and Chen, M. (2001) Parental involvement and students' academic achievement: A meta-analysis, *Educational Psychology Review*, 13, 1, 1–22

Fantuzzo, J., Bulotsky, R., McDermott, P., Mosca, S. and Lutz, M. (2003) A multivariate analysis of emotional and behavioral adjustment and preschool educational outcomes, *School Psychology Review*, 32, 2, 185–203

Feinstein, L. and Symons, J. (1999) Attainment in secondary school, *Oxford Economic Papers*, 51, 2, 300–321

Feinstein, L., Duckworth, K. and Sabates, R. (2004) *A model of inter-generational effects of parental education*, Research Brief RCB01-04, Nottingham: DfES

Felouzis, G. and Charmillot, S. (2012) School tracking and educational inequality: A comparison of 12 education systems in Switzerland, *Comparative Education*, 10.1080/03050068.2012.706032

Fergusson, D., Horwood, L. and Beautrais, A. (2003) Cannabis and educational achievement, *Addiction*, 98, 12, 1681–1692

Fisher, P. (2011) Performativity, well-being, social class and citizenship in English schools, *Educational Studies*, 37, 1, 49–58

Flay, B. and Allred, C. (2003) Long-term effects of the Positive Action program, *American Journal of Health Behavior*, 27, 1, S6–S21

Flouri, E. (2006) Parental interest in children's education, children's self-esteem and locus of control, and later educational attainment: Twenty-six year follow-up of the 1970 British birth cohort, *British Journal of Educational Psychology*, 76, 1, 41–55

Flouri, E. (2007) Early family environments may moderate prediction of low educational attainment in adulthood: The cases of childhood hyperactivity and authoritarian parenting, *Educational Psychology*, 27, 6, 737–751

Ford, R., Evans, D. and McDougall, S. (2003) Progressing in tandem: A Sure Start initiative for enhancing the role of parents in children's early education, *Educational and Child Psychology*, 20, 4, 80–95

Frampton, S. (2010) *The effectiveness of an integrated conceptual approach to teaching middle school science: A mixed methods investigation*, Dissertation Abstracts International, Section A, The Humanities and Social Sciences

Freeney, Y. and O'Connell, M. (2012) The predictors of the intention to leave school early among a representative sample of Irish second-level students, *British Educational Research Journal*, 38, 4, 557–574

Frisco, M. (2008) Adolescents' sexual behavior and academic attainment, *Sociology of Education*, 81, 3, 284–311

Fritz, C. and Morris, P. (2012) Effect size estimates: Current use, calculations, and interpretations, *Journal of Experimental Psychology*, 141, 1, 2–18. Available at http://www.wisecampaign.org.uk/ (accessed 23 February 2013)

Fryer, R. (2010) *Financial incentives and student achievement: Evidence from randomised trials*, NBER working paper 15898, National Bureau of Economic Research

Fuchs, T. and Wobmann, L. (2004) What accounts for international differences in student performance? A re-examination using PISA, *Empirical Economics*, 32, 2–3, 433–464

Fuchs, D., Fuchs, L., Mathes, P. and Simmons, D. (1997) Peer-assisted learning strategies: Making classrooms more responsive to diversity, *American Educational Research Journal*, 34, 1, 174–206

Gagne, F. and St Pere, F. (2001) When IQ is controlled, does motivation still predict achievement? *Intelligence*, 30, 1, 71–100

Gayle, V., Berridge, D. and Davies, R. (2002) Young people's entry into higher education: Quantifying influential factors, *Oxford Review of Education*, 28, 1, 5–20

Geckova, A., Tavel, P., van Dijk, J., Abel, T. and Reijneveld, S. (2010) Factors associated with educational aspirations among adolescents: Cues to counteract socioeconomic differences? *BMC Public Health*, 10, 154. Available at http://www.biomedcentral.com/1471-2458/10/154 (accessed 21 February 2013)

Gfellner, B., McLaren, L. and Metcalfe, A. (2008) The parent–child home program in Western Manitoba: A 20-year evaluation, *Child Welfare: Journal of Policy, Practice and Program*, 87, 5, 49–67

Gifford, D., Briceno-Perriott, J. and Mianzo, F. (2006) Locus of control: Academic achievement and retention in a sample of University first-year students, *Journal of College Admission*, 191, 18–25

Gillborn, D. and Youdell, D. (2000) *Rationing education: Policy, practice, reform and equality*, Buckingham: Open University Press

Ginsburg, H. and Pappas, S. (2004) SES, ethnic, and gender differences in young children's informal addition and subtraction: A clinical interview investigation, *Journal of Applied Developmental Psychology*, 25, 2, 171–192

Glass, D. (1954) *Social mobility in Britain*, London: Routledge

Glass, G. (2004) *Teacher evaluation: Policy brief*, Tempe, AZ: Education Policy Research Unit

Gleason, P., Clark, M., Tuttle, C. and Dwoyer, E. (2010) *The evaluation of charter school impacts*, final report ED510574, National Center for Education Evaluation and Regional Assistance

Glenn, W. (2011) A quantitative analysis of the increase in public school segregation in Delaware: 1989–2006, *Urban Education*, 46, 4, 719–740

Goerge, R., Cusick, G., Wasserman, M. and Gladden, R. (2007) After-school programs and academic impact: A study of Chicago's after school matters, *Chaplin Hall Center for Children: Issue Brief*, 112, January

Goldberger, S. (2000) *School-to-career as a strategy to improve education and employment outcomes for urban youth: An impact evaluation of the ProTech Program*, Dissertation Abstracts International, Section A, The Humanities and Social Sciences

Goldsmith, P. (2011) Coleman revisited: School segregation, peers, and frog ponds, *American Educational Research Journal*, 48, 3, 508–535

Goldstein, H. (2001) Using pupil performance data for judging schools and teachers: Scope and limitations, *British Educational Research Journal*, 27, 4, 433–442

Goldthorpe, J. and Jackson, M. (2007) Intergenerational class mobility in contemporary Britain, *British Journal of Sociology*, 58, 4, 525–546

Gonzalez-Pienda, J., Carlos, N., Gonzalez-Pumariega, S., Alvarez, L., Roces, C. and Garcia, M. (2002) A structural equation model of parental involvement, motivational and aptitudinal characteristics, and academic achievement, *Journal of Experimental Education*, 70, 3, 257–287

Gonzalez, N., Dumka, L., Millsap, R., Gottshall, A., McClain, D., Wong, J., German, M., Mauricio, A., Wheeler, L., Carpentier, F. and Kim, S. (2012) Randomised trial of a broad preventive intervention for Mexican American adolescents, *Journal of Consulting and Clinical Psychology*, 80, 1, 1–16

Good, C., Aronson, J. and Inzlicht, M. (2003) Improving adolescents' standardised test performance: An intervention to reduce the effects of stereotype threat, *Journal of Applied Developmental Psychology*, 24, 6, 645–662

Goodall, J. and Vorhaus, J. (2011) *Review of best practice in parental engagement*, London: Department for Education

Goodman, A. and Gregg, P. (2010) *Poorer children's educational attainment: How important are attitudes and behaviour?* York: Joseph Rowntree Foundation

Gorard, S. (2000) *Education and social justice*, Cardiff: University of Wales Press

Gorard, S. (2001) *Quantitative methods in educational research: The role of numbers made easy*, London: Continuum

Gorard, S. (2004) The international dimension: What can we learn from the PISA study? In H. Claire (Ed.) *Gender in education 3–19: A fresh approach* (pp.26–32), London: Association of Teachers and Lecturers

Gorard, S. (2005) Academies as the 'future of schooling': Is this an evidence-based policy? *Journal of Education Policy*, 20, 3, 369–377

Gorard, S. (2006a) Does policy matter in education? *International Journal of Research and Method in Education*, 29, 1, 5–21

Gorard, S. (2006b) Is there a school mix effect? *Educational Review*, 58, 1, 87–94

Gorard, S. (2006c) Value-added is of little value, *Journal of Educational Policy*, 21, 2, 233–241

Gorard, S. (2008a) Who is missing from higher education? *Cambridge Journal of Education*, 38, 3, 421–37

Gorard, S. (2008b) *Quantitative research in education: Volumes 1 to 3*, London: Sage

Gorard, S. (2008c) Research impact is not always a good thing: A re-consideration of rates of 'social mobility' in Britain, *British Journal of Sociology of Education*, 29, 3, 317–324

Gorard, S. (2008d) The value-added of primary schools: What is it really measuring? *Educational Review*, 60, 2, 179–185

Gorard, S. (2009a) Does the index of segregation matter? The composition of secondary schools in England since 1996, *British Educational Research Journal*, 35, 4, 639–652

Gorard, S. (2009b) What are Academies the answer to? *Journal of Education Policy*, 24, 1, 1–13

Gorard, S. (2010a) Measuring is more than assigning numbers. In G. Walford, E. Tucker, and M. Viswanathan (Eds) *Sage handbook of measurement* (pp.389–408), Los Angeles: Sage

Gorard, S. (2010b) Serious doubts about school effectiveness, *British Educational Research Journal*, 36, 5, 735–766

Gorard, S. (2010c) All evidence is equal: The flaw in statistical reasoning, *Oxford Review of Education*, 36, 1, 63–77

Gorard, S. (2010d) Education *can* compensate for society – a bit, *British Journal of Educational Studies*, 58, 1, 47–65

Gorard, S. (2011) The potential determinants of young peoples' sense of justice: An international study, *British Journal of Sociology of Education*, 32, 1, 35–52

Gorard, S. (2012a) Who is eligible for free school meals? Characterising FSM as a measure of disadvantage in England, *British Educational Research Journal*, 38, 6, 1003–1017

Gorard, S. (2012b) Experiencing fairness at school: An international study in five countries, *International Journal of Educational Research*, 3, 3, 127–137

Gorard, S. (2012c) Querying the causal role of attitudes in educational attainment, *ISRN Education*, 2012, Article ID 501589

Gorard, S. (2013) *Research design: Robust approaches for the social sciences*, London: Sage

Gorard, S. and Cheng, S. C. (2011) Pupil clustering in English secondary schools: One pattern or several? *International Journal of Research and Method in Education*, 34, 3, 327–339

Gorard, S. and Cook, T. (2007) Where does good evidence come from? *International Journal of Research and Method in Education*, 30, 3, 307–323

Gorard, S. and Fitz, J. (1998a) The more things change: The missing impact of marketisation, *British Journal of Sociology of Education*, 19, 3, 365–376

Gorard, S. and Fitz, J. (1998b) Under starter's orders: The established market, the Cardiff study and the Smithfield project, *International Studies in Sociology of Education*, 8, 3, 299–314

Gorard, S. and Rees, G. (2002) *Creating a learning society*, Bristol: Policy Press

Gorard, S. and See, B. H. (2009) The impact of SES on participation and attainment in science, *Studies in Science Education*, 45, 1, 93–129

Gorard, S. and See, B. H. (2011) How can we enhance enjoyment of secondary school? The student view, *British Educational Research Journal*, 37, 4, 671–690

Gorard, S. and See, B. H. (2012) *The affective influence of teachers*, Birmingham: Teach First.

Gorard, S. and Smith, E. (2010) *Equity in education: An international comparison of pupil perspectives*, London: Palgrave

Gorard, S. and Taylor, C. (2001) *Student funding and hardship in Wales: A statistical summary*, Report to the National Assembly Investigation Group on Student Hardship, Cardiff: National Assembly for Wales

Gorard, S. and Taylor, C. (2002) What is segregation? A comparison of measures in terms of strong and weak compositional invariance, *Sociology*, 36, 4, 875–895

Gorard, S., Fevre, R. and Rees, G. (1999a) Patterns of participation in lifelong learning: do families make a difference? *British Educational Research Journal*, 25, 4, 517–532

Gorard, S., Fevre, R. and Rees, G. (1999b) The apparent decline of informal learning, *Oxford Review of Education*, 25, 4, 437–454

Gorard, S., Hordosy, R. and Siddiqui, N. (2013) How stable are 'school effects' assessed by a value-added technique? *International Education Studies*, 6, 1, 1–9

Gorard, S., Rees, G. and Salisbury, J. (2001) The differential attainment of boys and girls at school: Investigating the patterns and their determinants, *British Educational Research Journal*, 27, 2, 125–139

Gorard, S., See, B. H. and Davies, P. (2011) *Do attitudes and aspirations matter in education? A review of the research evidence*, Saarbrucken: Lambert Academic Publishing

Gorard, S., See, B. H. and Davies, P. (2012a) *The impact of attitudes and aspirations on educational attainment and participation*, York: Joseph Rowntree Foundation

Gorard, S., Siddiqui, N. and See, B. H. (2012b) *Process and summative evaluation of the Edmonton 'BELL' Summer School Programme 2012*, London: Educational Endowment Foundation

Gorard, S., Taylor, C. and Fitz, J. (2003) *Schools, markets and choice policies*, London: RoutledgeFalmer

Gorard, S., See, B. H., Smith, E. and White, P. (2006) *Teacher supply: The key issues*, London: Continuum

Gorard, S. with Adnett, N., May, H., Slack, K., Smith, E. and Thomas, L. (2007) *Overcoming barriers to HE*, Stoke-on-Trent: Trentham Books

Gorard. S., Lumby, J., Briggs, A., Morrison, M., Hall, I., Maringe, F., See, B. H., Shaheen, R. and Wright, S. (2009) *14–19 reforms: QCA Centre Research Study, commentary on the baseline of evidence 2007–2008*, London: QCA

Gordon, D., Iwamoto, D., Ward, N., Potts, R. and Boyd, E. (2009) Mentoring urban Black middle school male students: Implications for academic achievement, *Journal of Negro Education*, 78, 3, 277–289

Gordon, I. and Monastiriotis, V. (2006) Urban size, spatial segregation and inequality in educational outcomes, *Urban Studies*, 43, 1, 213–236

Gottfredson, L. (2002) Gottfredson's theory of Circumspection, Compromise and Self Creation. In D. Brown (Ed.) *Career choice and development* (4th ed, pp. 85–148), San Francisco, CA: Jossey-Bass

Gottfredson. L. (2004) Intelligence: Is it the epidemiologists' elusive 'fundamental cause' of social class differences in health? *Journal of Personality and Social Psychology*, 86, 174–199

Gottfried, A. E., Gottfried, A. W., Morris, P. and Cook, C. (2008) Low academic intrinsic motivation as a risk factor for adverse educational outcomes: A longitudinal study from early childhood through early adulthood. In C. Hudley and A. E. Gottfried (Eds) *Academic motivation and the culture of school in childhood and adolescence* (pp. 36–69), New York: Oxford University Press

Gottfried, M. (2010) Evaluating the relationship between student attendance and achievement in urban and middle school: An instrumental variables approach, *American Educational Research Journal*, 47, 2, 434–465

Goza, F. and Ryabov, I. (2009) Adolescents' educational outcomes: Racial and ethnic variations in peer network importance, *Journal of Youth and Adolescence*, 38, 9, 1264–1279

Grabowski, L., Call, K. and Mortimer, J. (2001) Global and economic self-efficacy in the educational attainment process, *Social Psychology Quarterly*, 64, 2, 164–179

Graves, A., Brandon, R., Duesbery, L., McIntosh, A. and Pyle, N. (2011) The effects of tier 2 literacy instruction in sixth grade: Toward the development of a response-to-intervention model in middle school, *Learning Disability Quarterly*, 34, 1, 86

Gray, J., Galton, M., McLaughlin, C., Clarke, B. and Symonds, J. (2011) *The supportive school: Well-being and the young adolescent*, Newcastle: Cambridge Scholars Publishing

Gray, J., Goldstein, H. and Thomas, S. (2001) Predicting the future: The role of past performance in determining trends in institutional effectiveness at A level, *British Educational Research Journal*, 27, 4, 39–406

Gregory, A. and Rimm-Kaufman, S. (2008) Positive mother–child interactions in kindergarten: Predictors of school success in high school, *School Psychology Review*, 37, 4, 499–515

Griffiths, M. (2012) Why joy in education is an issue for socially just policies, *Journal of Education Policy*, 27, 5, 655–670

Grinstein-Weiss, M., Yeo, YH, Irish, K. and Zhan, M. (2009) Parental assets: A pathway to positive child educational outcomes, *Journal of Sociology and Social Welfare*, 36, 1, 61–85

Grissmer, D. and Flanagan, A. (1998) *Exploring rapid score gains in Texas and North Carolina*, commissioned paper, Washington, DC: National Education Goals Panel

Guay, F., Larose, S. and Boivin, M. (2004) Academic self-concept and educational attainment level: A ten-year longitudinal study, *Self and Identity*, 3, 1, 53–68

Guthrie, J., McRae, A., Coddington, C., Lutz Klauda, S., Wigfield, A. and Barbosa, P. (2009) Impacts of comprehensive reading instruction on diverse outcomes of low- and high-achieving readers, *Journal of Learning Disabilities*, 42, 3, 195–214

Gutman, L. and Akerman, R. (2008) *Determinants of aspirations*, Centre for Research on the Wider Benefits of Learning Research Project 27, London: Institute of Education

Gutman, M. and Vorhaus, J. (2012) *The impact of pupil behaviour and wellbeing on educational outcomes*, Department for Education research report DFE-RR253, London: Department for Education

Haahr, J., with Nielsen, T., Hansen, E. and Jakobsen, S. (2005) *Explaining pupil performance: Evidence from the international PISA, TIMSS and PIRLS surveys*, Danish Technological Institute. Available at http://www.danishtechnology.dk (accessed 22 February 2013)

Hagenauer, G. and Hascher, T. (2010) Learning enjoyment in early adolescence, *Educational Research and Evaluation*, 16, 6, 495–516

Hango, D. (2007) Parental investment in childhood and educational qualifications: Can greater parental involvement mediate the effects of socio economic disadvantage? *Social Science Research*, 36, 34, 1371–1391

Hardie, J. (2010) *How aspirations are formed and challenged in the transition to adulthood and implications for adult well-being*. PhD dissertation. Available at ProQuest, http:// gateway.proquest.com/openurl%3furl_ver=Z39.88-2004%26res_dat=xri:pqdiss%26rft _val_fmt=info:ofi/fmt:kev:mtx:dissertation%26rft_dat=xri:pqdiss:3366345 (accessed 12 June 2011)

Harris, A. (2008) Optimism in the face of despair: Black–White differences in beliefs about school as a means for upward social mobility, *Social Science Quarterly*, 89, 3, 608–630

Harris, A. and Goodall, J. (2006) *Parental involvement in education: An overview of the literature*, Coventry: University of Warwick

Harris, D. and Williams, J. (2012) The association of classroom interactions, year group and social class, *British Educational Research Journal*, 38, 3, 373–397

Harris, N. and Gorard, S. (2010) The education system of the United Kingdom. In H. Döbert, H. Wolfgang, B. von Kopp, and L. Reuter (Eds) *Die bildungssysteme Europas*, Baltmannsweiler: Schneider Verlag Hohengehren

Harris, R. (2010) *Segregation by choice? The debate so far*, CMPO working paper 10/251, Bristol: Centre for Market and Public Organisation

Harris, R. (2012) Geographies of transition and the separation of lower and higher attaining pupils in the move from primary to secondary school in London, *Transactions of the Institute of British Geographers*, doi 10.1111/j.1475-5661. 2012.519.x

Harris, R. and Haydn, T. (2006) Pupils' enjoyment of history: What lessons can teachers learn from their pupils? *Curriculum Journal*, 17, 4, 315–333

Hartas, D. (2011) Families' social backgrounds matter: Socio-economic factors, home learning and young children's language, literacy and social outcomes, *British Educational Research Journal*, 37, 6, 893–914

Hartas, D. (2012) Inequality and the home learning environment: Predictions about seven-year olds' language and literacy, *British Educational Research Journal*, 38, 5, 859–879

Harvard Family Research Project (2006) *Evaluation of the BELL (Building Educated Leaders for Life) accelerated learning summer program*. Available at http://www.hfrp.org/out-of-school-time/ost-database-bibliography/database/bell-accelerated-learning-summer-program/evaluation-1-2002-national-evaluation-report (accessed 21 February 2013)

Harwell, M. and LeBeau, B. (2010) Student eligibility for a free lunch as an SES measure in Education Research, *Educational Researcher*, 39, 2, 120–131

Hattie, J. (2009) *Visible learning: A synthesis of over 800 meta-analyses relating to achievement*, New York: Routledge

Haworth, C., Asbury, K., Dale, P. and Plomin, R. (2011) Added value measures in education show genetic as well as environmental influence, *PLoS ONE*, 6, 2

Hayenga, A. and Corpus, J. (2010) Profiles of intrinsic and extrinsic motivations: A person-centered approach to motivation and achievement in middle school, *Motivation and Emotion*, 34, 34, 371–383

Hedges, L. and Nowell, A. (1998) Black–White test score convergence since 1965. In C. Jencks and M. Phillips (Eds) *The Black–White test score gap*, (pp. 149–182) Washington DC: The Brookings Institution Press

Hejazi, E. Shahraray, M., Farsinejad, M. and Asgary, A. (2009) Identity styles and academic achievement: Mediating role of academic self-efficacy, *Social Psychology of Education*, 12, 1, 123–135

Henderson, A. and Mapp, K. (2002) *A new wave of evidence: The impact of school, family, and community connections on student achievement*, Austin, TX: Southwest Educational Development Laboratory

Higher Education Funding Council for England (2005) *Young participation in higher education*, Bristol: Higher Education Funding Council for England

Hill, N. (2001) Parenting and academic socialization as they relate to school readiness: The roles of ethnicity and family income, *Journal of Educational Psychology*, 93, 4, 686–697

Hillman, K. (2010) *Attitudes, intentions and participation in education: Year 12 and beyond. LSAY Briefing Number 20*, Australian Council for Educational Research, ED512541

Ho, S. and Willms, J. (1996) Effects of parental involvement on eighth-grade achievement, *Sociology of Education*, 69, 2, 126–141.

Hobbs, G. and Vignoles, A. (2010) Is children's free school meal 'eligibility' a good proxy for family income, *British Educational Research Journal*, 36, 4, 673–690

Hogrebe, M. C., Kyei-Blankson, L. and Zou, L. (2006) *Using GIS to examine science and mathematics attainment. Report for the Centre for Inquiry in Science Teaching and Learning (CISTL)*, St Louis, MO: Washington University Department of Education

Holt, L., Bry, B. and Johnson. V. (2008) Enhancing school engagement in at-risk, urban minority adolescents through a school-based, adult mentoring intervention, *Child & Family Behaviour Therapy*, 30,4, 297–318

Hong, S. and Ho, HZ (2005) Direct and indirect longitudinal effects of parental involvement on student achievement: Second-order latent growth modeling across ethnic groups, *Journal of Educational Psychology*, 97, 1, 32–42

Hoover, E. (1941) Interstate redistribution of population 1850–1940, *Journal of Economic History*, 1, 199–205

Hope, M. (2012) Small and perfectly formed? Is democracy an alternative approach to school leadership? *School Leadership and Management*, 32, 3, 291–305

Hornby, G. and Lafaele, R. (2011) Barriers to parental involvement in education: An explanatory model, *Educational Review*, 63, 1, 37–52

Horner, R., Sugai, G., Smolkowski, K., Eber, L., Nakasato, J., Todd, A. and Esperanza, J. (2009) A randomised, wait-list controlled effectiveness trial assessing school-wide positive behaviour support in elementary schools, *Journal of Positive Behavior Interventions*, 11, 3, 133–144

Horsfall, S. and Santa, C. (1994) *Project CRISS: Validation report for the program effectiveness panel*, Unpublished manuscript. In WWC (2010) *Project CRISS® (CReating Independence through Student-owned Strategies), What Works Clearing House intervention report*, Washington: US Department of Education, Institute of Education Sciences

Horwood, L., Fergusson, D., Hayatbakhsh, M., Najman, J., Coffey, C., Patton, G., Silins, E. and Hutchinson, D. (2010) Cannabis use and educational achievement: Findings from three Australasian cohort studies, *Drug and Alcohol Dependence*, 110, 3, 247–253

Howell, K., Lynch, M., Platzman, K., Smith, G. and Coles, C. (2006) Prenatal alcohol exposure and ability, academic achievement, and school functioning in adolescence: A longitudinal follow-up, *Journal of Pediatric Psychology*, 31, 1, 116–126

Hoyle, R. and Robinson, J. (2003) League tables and school effectiveness: A mathematical model, *Proceedings of the Royal Society of London B*, 270, 113–199

Hughes, A., Torrance, M. and Galbraith, D. (2006) *Evaluation of the Pacific Institute's 'It's up to me!' intervention for motivational development in students at Key Stage 2, final report*, Staffordshire: Institute for Educational Policy Research and Centre for Educational Psychology Research, Staffordshire University

Hume, D. (1962) *On human nature and the understanding*, New York: Collier

Hurt, H., Brodsky, N., Roth, H., Malmud, E. and Giannetta, J. (2005) School performance of children with gestational cocaine exposure, *Neurotoxicology and Teratology*, 27, 2, 203–211

Ichou, M. and Vallet, L. (2011) Do all roads lead to inequality? Trends in French upper secondary school analysed with four longitudinal surveys, *Oxford Review of Education*, 37, 2, 167–194

Interactive Inc. (2002) *An efficacy study of READ 180, a print and electronic adaptive intervention program. Grades 4 and above*, New York: Scholastic Inc. Evaluated in WWC (2009) *READ 180. What Works Clearing House intervention report*, Washington, DC: US Department of Education, Institute of Education Sciences

Interim Report (2012) *Seven key truths about social mobility*, Westminster: All-party parliamentary group on social mobility

Jacob, B. and Wilder, T. (2010) *Wilder educational expectations and attainment*, NBER working paper 15683, National Bureau of Economic Research

Jacobs, N. (2011) Racial, economic and linguistic segregation: Analyzing market supports in the District of Columbia's public charter schools, *Education and Urban Society*, 45, 1, 120–141

Jacobs, N. (2013) Racial, economic and linguistic segregation, *Education and Urban Society*, 45, 1, 10–141

James-Burdumy, S., Mansfield, W., Deke, J., Carey, N., Lugo-Gil, J., Hershey, A., Douglas, A., Gersten, R., Newman-Gouchar, R., Dimino, J. and Faddis, B. (2009) *Effectiveness of selected supplemental reading comprehension interventions: Impacts on a first cohort of fifth-grade students* (NCEE 2009–4032), Washington, DC: National Center for Educational Evaluation and Regional Assistance, Institute of Education Sciences, U.S. Department of Education

Jerrim, J. (2012) The socio-economic gradient in teenagers' reading skills: How does England compare with other countries? *Fiscal Studies*, 33, 2, 159–184

Jeynes, W. (2005) The effects of parental involvement on the academic achievement of African American youth, *Journal of Negro Education*, 74, 3, 260–274

Jeynes, W. (2007) The relationship between parental involvement and urban secondary school student academic achievement: A meta-analysis, *Urban Education*, 42, 1, 82–110

Jeynes, W. (2012) A meta-analysis of the efficacy of different types of parental involvement programs for urban students, *Urban Education*, 47, 4, 706–742

Johnson, R. and Howard, C. (2003) The effects of the accelerated reader program on the reading comprehension of pupils in grades 3, 4, and 5, *The Reading Matrix*, 3, 3, 87–96

Johnson, W., McGue, M. and Iacono, W. (2010) How parents influence school grades: Hints from a sample of adoptive and biological families, *Learning and Individual Differences*, 17, 3, 201–219

Jones, L., Harris, R. and Finnegan, D. (2002) School attendance demonstration project: An evaluation of a programme to motivate public assistance teens to attend and complete school in an urban school district, *Research on Social Work Practice*, 12, 2, 222–237

Jones, S., Aber, J. and Brown, J. (2011) Two-year impacts of a universal school-based social-emotional and literacy intervention: An experiment in translational developmental research, *Child Development*, 82, 2, 533–544

Joseph Rowntree Foundation (2006) A comparison of how young people from different ethnic groups experience leaving school, *Findings*, 426, July, 1–4

Kantomaa, M., Tammelin, T., Demakakos, P., Ebeling, H. and Taanila, A. (2010) Physical activity, emotional and behavioural problems, maternal education and self-reported educational performance of adolescents, *Health Education Research*, 25, 2, 368–379

Kay, H. and Sundaraj, A. (2004) Are undergraduate mature students widening participation students? *Learning transformations: changing learners, organisations and communities*. Saunders et al. London: Forum for the Advancement of Continuing Education: 255–260

Kelly, S. and Monczunski, L. (2007) Overcoming the volatility in school-level gain scores: A new approach to identifying value-added with cross-sectional data, *Educational Researcher*, 36, 5, 279–287

Kemple, J. and Snipes, J. (2000) *Career academies: Impacts on students' engagement and performance in high school*, New York: Manpower Demonstration Research Corporation

Khan, M. and Gorard, S. (2012) A randomised controlled trial of the use of a piece of commercial software for the acquisition of reading skills, *Educational Review*, 64, 1, 21–35

Kiernan, K. and Huerta, M. (2008) Economic deprivation, maternal depression, parenting and children's cognitive and emotional development in early childhood, *British Journal of Sociology*, 59, 4, 783–806

Kiernan, K. and Mensah, F. (2011) Poverty, family resources and children's early educational attainment: The mediating role of parenting, *British Educational Research Journal*, 37, 2, 317–336

Kim, J. (2006) Effects of a voluntary summer reading intervention on reading achievement: Results from a randomized field trial, *Educational Evaluation and Policy Analysis*, 28, 4, 335–355

Kim, J., Samson, J., Fitzgerald, R. and Hartry, A. (2010) A randomized experiment of a mixed-methods literacy intervention for struggling readers in grades 4–6: Effects on word reading efficiency, reading comprehension and vocabulary, and oral reading fluency, *Reading and Writing: An Interdisciplinary Journal*, 23, 9, 1109–1129

Kishiyama, M., Boyce, W., Jimenez, A., Perry, L. and Knight, R. (2009) Socioeconomic disparities affect prefrontal function in children, *Journal of Cognitive Neuroscience*, 21, 6, 1106–1115

Kloosterman, R. and de Graaf, P. (2010) Non-promotion or enrolment in lower track? The influence of social background on choices in secondary education for three cohorts of Dutch pupils, *Oxford Review of Education*, 36, 3, 363–384

Knowles, E. and Evans, H. (2012) *PISA 2009: How does the social attainment gap in England compare with countries internationally?* Research report DFE-RR206, London: Department for Education

Korat, O. (2009) The effect of maternal teaching talk on children's emergent literacy as a function of type of activity and maternal education level, *Journal of Applied Developmental Psychology*, 30, 1, 34–42

Koucky, J., Bartusek, A. and Kovarovic, J. (2010) *Who gets a degree? Access to teriary education in Europe 1950–2009*, Prague: Charles University

Kratochwill, T., McDonald, L., Levin, J., Youngbear-Tibbetts, H. and Demaray, M. (2004) Families and schools together: an experimental analysis of a parent mediated multi-family group program for American Indian children, *Journal of School Psychology*, 42, 5, 359–383

Kyriakides, L. (2005) Evaluating school policy on parents working with their children in class, *Journal of Educational Research*, 98, 5, 281–298

Kyriakides, L. (2008) Testing the validity of the comprehensive model of educational effectiveness: A step towards the development of a dynamic model of effectiveness, *School Effectiveness and School Improvement*, 19, 4, 429–446

Lambert, P. (2002) Handling occupational information, *Building Research Capacity*, 4, 9–12

Lamprianou, I. (2009) Comparability of examination standards between subjects: An international perspective, *Oxford Review of Education*, 35, 2, 205–226

Lang, L., Torgersen, J., Petscher, Y., Vogel, W., Chanter, C. and Lefsky, E. (2008) *Exploring the relative effectiveness of reading interventions for high school students*, paper presented at the annual research conference of the Society for Research on Education Effectiveness (Crystal City, VA)

Lara-Cinisomo, S., Pebley, A. R., Vaiana, M. E., Maggio, E., Berends, M. and Lucas, S. R. (2004) A matter of class: Educational achievement reflects family background more than ethnicity or immigration, *A RAND review*, 28, 3

Lassen, S., Steele, M. and Sailor, W. (2006) The relationship of school-wide positive behaviour support to academic achievement in an urban middle school, *Psychology in the Schools*, 43, 6, 701–712

Leckie, G., Pillinger, R., Jones, K. and Goldstein, H. (2012) Multilevel modelling of social segregation, *Journal of Educational and Behavioural Statistics*, 37, 1, 3–30

Leckie, G. and Goldstein, H. (2009) *The limitations of using school league tables to inform school choice*, working paper 09/208, Bristol: Centre for Market and Public Organisation

Lee, C. (2003) Why we need to re-think race and ethnicity in educational research, *Educational Researcher*, 32, 5, 3–5

Lee, M. and Madyun, N. (2008) School racial composition and academic achievement: The case of Hmong LEP pupils in the USA, *Educational Studies*, 34, 4, 319–331

Legleye, S., Obradovic, I., Janssen, E., Spilka, S., LeNezet, O. and Beck, F. (2010) Influence of cannabis use trajectories, grade repetition and family background on the school-dropout rate at the age of 17 years in France, *European Journal of Public Health*, 20, 2, 157–163

Lei, J. and Zhao, Y. (2005) Technology uses and pupil achievement: A longitudinal study, *Computers and Education*, 49, 2, 284–296

Leroux, A., Vaughn, S., Roberts, G. and Fletcher, J. (2011) *Findings from a three year treatment within a response to intervention framework for students in grades 6 with reading difficulties*, paper presented at the Society for Research on Educational Effectiveness Conference (no details about place and date of conference). Available at http://www.eric.ed.gov/PDFS/ED518866.pdf (accessed 1 March 2013)

Li, Y. and Lerner, R. (2011) Trajectories of school engagement during adolescence: Implications for grades, depression, delinquency, and substance use, *Developmental Psychology*, 47, 1, 233–247

Liew, J., McTigue, E., Barrois, L. and Hughes, J. (2008) Adaptive and effortful control and academic self-efficacy beliefs on achievement: A longitudinal study of 1st through 3rd graders, *Early Childhood Research Quarterly*, 23, 4, 515–526

Lin, KS., Cheng, YY., Chen, YL. and Wu, YY. (2009) Longitudinal effects of educational expectations and achievement attributions on adolescents' academic achievement, *Adolescence*, 44, 176, 911–924

Lindborn, A. (2010) School choice in Sweden: Effects on student performance, school costs and segregation, *Scandinavian Journal of Education*, 54, 6, 615–630

Lingard, T. (2005) Literacy acceleration and the Key Stage 3 English strategy: Comparing two approaches for secondary-age pupils with literacy difficulties, *British Journal of Special Education*, 32, 2, 67–77

Lipscomb, S. (2007) Secondary school extracurricular involvement and academic achievement: A fixed effects approach, *Economics of Education Review*, 26, 4 463–472

Liu, L. (2010) *From educational aspirations to college enrollment: A road with many paths*, Dissertation Abstracts International, Section A, The Humanities and Social Sciences

Livingstone, D. (2000) Researching expanded notions of learning and work and underemployment: Findings of the first Canadian survey of informal learning practices, *International Review of Education*, 46, 6, 491–514

Lizzio, A., Wilson, K. and Hadaway, V. (2007) University pupils' perceptions of a fair learning environment: A social justice perspective, *Assessment and Evaluation in Higher Education*, 32, 2, 195–213

Logan, J., Minca, E. and Adar, S. (2012) The geography of inequality: Why separate means unequal in American public schools, *Sociology of Education*, 85, 3, 287–301

Long, L. and Nucci, A. (1997) The Hoover Index of Population Concentration: A correction and update, *Professional Geographer*, 49, 4, 431–440

LTS Scotland (2009) *Reading for interest and enjoyment.* Available at http://www.ltscotland.org.uk/curriculumforexcellence/languages/modernlanguages/outcomes/reading/readingforinterestandenjoyment/index.asp (accessed 14 November 2009)

Lubienski, S. and Lubienski, C. (2006) School sector and academic achievement: A multi-level analysis of NAEP Mathematics data, *American Educational Research Journal*, 43, 4, 651–698

Lykins, C. (2012) Why 'What works?' still doesn't work: How to improve research syntheses at the What Works Clearing House, *Peabody Journal of Education*, 87, 4, 500–599

Lynskey, M. and Hall, W. (2000) The effects of adolescent cannabis use on educational attainment: A review, *Addiction*, 95, 11, 1621–1630

Ma, X. (1999) Dropping out of advanced mathematics: The effects of parental involvement, *Teachers College Record*, 101, 1, 60–81

Ma, X. and Xu, J. (2004) Determining the causal ordering between attitude toward mathematics and achievement in mathematics, *American Journal of Education*, 110, 3, 256–280

MacNab, D. (2000) Raising standards in mathematics education: Values, vision, and TIMSS, *Educational Studies in Mathematics*, 42, 1, 61–80

Maddern, K. (2010) 'Perverse incentive' spurs heads to up SEN figures, *Times Educational Supplement*, 7 May 2010, p.14

Magnuson, K. (2003) *The intergenerational benefits of maternal education: The effect of increases in mothers' educational attainment on children's academic outcomes*, Dissertation Abstracts International, Section B, The Sciences and Engineering

Magnuson, K. (2007) Maternal education and children's academic achievement during middle childhood, *Developmental Psychology*, 43, 6, 1497–1512.

Maitlies, H. (2011) Citizenship initiatives and pupil values: a case study of one Scottish school's experience, *Educational Review*, 62, 4, 391–406

Marcon, R. (1999) *Impact of parent involvement on children's development and academic performance: A three-cohort study*, paper presented at the Meeting of the Southeastern Psychological Association, March 1999 (Savannah, GA)

Marjoribanks, K. (2005) Family background, academic achievement, and educational aspirations as predictors of Australian young adults' educational attainment, *Psychological Reports*, 96, 3, 751–754

Marks, G. (2007) Are father's or mother's socioeconomic characteristics more important influences on student performance? Recent international evidence, *Social Indicators Research*, 85, 2, 293–309

Marley, D. (2009) A third of schools bore their classes, *Times Educational Supplement*, 9 January 2009, p.12

Marsh, H. and O'Mara, A. (2008) Reciprocal effects between academic self-concept, self esteem, achievement, and attainment over seven adolescent years: Unidimensional and multidimensional perspectives of self-concept, *Personality and Social Psychology Bulletin*, 34, 4, 542–552

Marsh, H., Trautwein, U., Ludtke, O., Baumert, J. and Koller, O. (2007) The big-fish-little-pond effects of selective high schools on self-concept after graduation, *American Educational Research Journal*, 44, 3, 631–669

Marsh, H., Trautwein, U., Ludtke, O., Koller, O. and Baumert, J. (2005) Academic self-concept, interest, grades and standardised test scores: Reciprocal effects models of causal ordering, *Child Development*, 76, 2, 397–416

Marsick, V. and Watkins, K. (1990) *Informal and incidental learning in the workplace*, London: Routledge

Martin, D. and Martin, M. (2007) Implementing a family/school partnership in an urban elementary school to reduce negative behavior and increase academic achievement, *Family Therapy*, 34, 3, 141–152

Martin, D., Martin, M., Gibson, S.S. and Wilkins, J. (2007) Increasing prosocial behavior and academic achievement among adolescent African American males, *Adolescence*, 42, 168, 689–698

Marzano, R., Marzano, J. and Pickering, D. (2003) *Classroom management that works*, Alexandria: ASCD

Massey, D. and Denton, N. (1998) *American apartheid: Segregation and the making of the underclass*, Harvard: Harvard University Press

Massey, D. and Fischer, M. (2006) The effect of childhood segregation on minority academic performance at selective colleges, *Ethnic and Racial Studies*, 29, 1, 1–26

Mattei, P. (2012) Policy studies, raising educational standards: National testing of pupils in the United Kingdom 1988–2009, *Policy Studies*, 33, 3, 231–247

Mattern, N. and Schau, C. (2002) Gender differences in science attitude–achievement relationships over time among White middle school students, *Journal of Research in Science Teaching*, 39, 4, 324–340

Maunder, R., Harrop, A. and Tattersall, A. (2010) Pupil and staff perceptions of bullying in secondary schools, *Educational Research*, 52, 3, 263–282

Maxi-pedia (2012) *Robin Hood Index*. Available at http://www.maxi-pedia.com/ Robin+Hood+index (accessed 25 May 2012)

Mayhew, K., Deer, C. and Dua, M. (2004) The move to mass higher education in the UK, *Oxford Review of Education*, 30, 1, 65–82: 94

McCoy, S., Banks, J. and Shevlin, M. (2012) School matters: How context influences the identification of different types of special educational needs, *Irish Educational Studies*, 31, 2, 119–138

McKendrick, J., Scott, G. and Sinclair, S. (2007) Dismissing disaffection: Young people's attitudes towards education, employment, and articulation on a deprived community, *Journal of Youth Studies*, 10, 2, 139–160

Meehl, P. (1967) Theory testing in psychology and physics: A methodological paradox, *Philosophy of Science*, 34, 103–115

Mensah, F. and Kiernan, K. (2010) Gender differences in educational attainment: Influences of the family enviromment, *British Educational Research Journal*, 36, 2, 239–260

Metcalf, H. (2005) Paying for university: The impact of increasing costs on student employment, debt and satisfaction, *National Institute Economic Review*, 191, January, 106–117

Meyer, B., Wijekumar, K., Middlemiss, W., Higley, K., Lei, P., Meier, C. and Spielvogel, J. (2010) Web-based tutoring of the structure strategy with or without elaborated feedback or choice for fifth- and seventh-grade readers, *Reading Research Quarterly*, 45, 1, 62–92

Middleton, S., Rennison, J., Cebulla, A., Perren, K. and DE-Beaman, S. (2005) *Young people from ethnic minority backgrounds: Evidence from the education maintenance allowance database*, DfES research report RR627, Nottingham: Department for Education and Skills

Miles, K. (2010) *Mastery learning and academic achievement*, Dissertation Abstracts International, Section A, The Humanities and Social Sciences

Mill, J. (1882) *A system of logic, ratiocinative and inductive, being a connected view of the principles of evidence, and the methods of scientific investigation* (8th ed), New York: Harper & Brothers

Mistry, R., White, E., Benner, A. and Huynh, V. (2009) A longitudinal study of the simultaneous influence of mothers' and teachers' educational expectations on low-income youth's academic achievement, *Journal of Youth and Adolescence*, 38, 6, 826–838

Molinair, L., Speltini, G. and Passini, S. (2013) Do perceptions of being treated fairly increase students' outcomes? *Educational Research and Evaluation*, 19, 1, 58–76

Moon, N. and Ivins, C. (2004) *Parental involvement in children's education*, research report DfES RR589, Nottingham: Department for Education and Skills

Moon, T. and Callahan, C. (2001) Curricular modifications, family outreach, and a mentoring program: Impacts on achievement and gifted identification in high-risk primary students, *Journal for the Education of the Gifted*, 24, 4, 305–321

Moreau, M. (2010) The societal construction of 'boys' underachievement' in educational policies: A cross-national comparison, Journal of Education *Policy*, 26, 2, 161–180

Morgan, S. (2004) Methodologist as arbitrator: Five models for Black–White differences in the causal effect of expectations on attainment, *Sociological Methods & Research*, 33, 1, 43–53

Morrison, E., Rimm-Kauffman, S. and Pianta, R. (2003) A longitudinal study of mother–child interactions at school entry and social and academic outcomes in middle school, *Journal of School Psychology*, 41, 3, 185–200

Mwetundila, P. (2001) *Gender and other student level factors influencing the science achievement of 13–14 year old Australian.* MA (Ed) thesis, Flinders University of South Australia

Nagda, B., Gregerman, S., Jonides, J., von Hippel, W. and Lerner, J. (1998) Undergraduate student-faculty research partnerships affect student retention, *Review of Higher Education*, 22, 1, 55–72

National Audit Office (2002) *Widening participation in higher education in England*, London: The Stationery Office

National Literacy Trust (2010) Are children's literacy skills improving or getting worse? Available at http://www.literacytrust.org.uk/about/faqs/filter/about%20 literacy%20in%20the%20uk#q713 (accessed July 2010)

Newton, X. (2010) End-of-high-school mathematics attainment: How did students get there? *Teachers College Record*, 112, 4, 1064–1095

Ni, Y. (2011) The sorting effect of charter schools on student composition in traditional public schools, *Educational Policy*, 26, 2, 215–242

Nielsen, F. (2006) Achievement and ascription in educational attainment: Genetic and environmental influences on adolescent schooling, *Social Forces*, 85, 1, 193–216

Noble, J., Roberts, W. and Sawyer, R. (2006) Student achievement, behaviour, perceptions and other factors affecting ACT scores, *ACT Research Report Series*, 2006–1

Noble, T., McGrath, H., Wyatt, T., Carbines, R. and Robb, L. (2008) *Scoping study into approaches to student wellbeing: Literature review*, report to the Department of Education, Employment and Workplace Relations PRN 19219, Australia: ACU National Australian Catholic University and Erebus International

Nuijens, K., Mrozak, K., Zhe, E., Chadha, J., Repinski, D. and Zook, J. (2000) *Parents' education and features of parent–adolescent relationships as predictors of adolescents' academic performance: Report ED442556*, paper presented at the Annual Meeting of the Eastern Psychological Association (Baltimore, MD)

O'Callaghan, F., O'Callaghan, M., Najman, J., Williams, G. and Bor, W. (2007) Prenatal alcohol exposure and attention, learning and intellectual ability at 14 years: A prospective longitudinal study, *Early Human Development*, 83, 2, 115–123

OFSTED (2004) *ICT in schools: The impact of government initiatives*, School Portraits Eggbuckland Community College, London: Ofsted. Available at http://www. ofsted.gov.uk/publications/index.cfm?fuseaction=pubs. displayfile&id=3704&type=pdf (accessed 26 March 2006)

OFSTED (2007) *Ofsted TellUs2 Survey Summary and Technical Manual.* Available at http://www.ttrb.ac.uk/viewArticle2.aspx?contentId=14193 (accessed 7 January 2009)

Okpala, C., Okpala, A. and Smith, F. (2001) Parental involvement, instructional expenditures, family socioeconomic attributes, and student achievement, *Journal of Educational Research*, 95, 2, 110–115

Olson, H., Streissguth, A., Sampson, P., Barr, H., Bookstein, F. and Theide, K. (1997) Association of prenatal alcohol exposure with behavioural and learning problems in early adolescence, *Journal of the American Academy of Child and Adolescent Psychiatry*, 36, 9, 1187–1194

Orr, D., Gwosc, C. and Netz, N. (2011) *Social and economic conditions of student life in Europe*, Bielefeld: Bertelsmann Verlag

Ortloff, D. (2011) Moving the borders: Multiculturalism and global citizenship in the German Social Studies classroom, *Educational Research*, 53, 2, 137–149

Oyserman, D., Brickman, D. and Rhodes, M. (2007) School success, possible selves and parent school involvement, *Family Relations*, 56, 5, 479–489

Oyserman, D., Bybee, D. and Terry, K. (2006) Possible selves and academic outcomes: How and when possible selves impel action, *Journal of Personality and Social Psychology*, 91, 1, 188–204

Padgett, V. and Reid, J. (2002) Five year evaluation of the Student Diversity Program: A retrospective quasi-experiment. *Journal of College Student Retention*, 4, 2, 135–145

Park (2000) *Voodoo science*, Oxford, OUP

Patel, N. (2006) *Perceptions of student ability: Effects on parent involvement in middle school. Doctoral thesis*, Dissertation Abstracts International, Section A, The Humanities and Social Sciences

Paterson, L. (2009) Civic values and the subject matter of educational courses, *Oxford Review of Education*, 35, 1, 81–98

Payne, G. (2012) A new social mobility? The political redefinition of a sociological problem, *Contemporary Social Science*, 7, 1, 55–71

Payne, J. (2003) *Choice at the end of compulsory schooling: A research review*, research report DfES 414, Nottingham: Department for Education and Skills

Payton, J., Weissberg, R., Durlak, J., Dymnicke, A., Taylor, R., Schellinger, K. and Pachan, M. (2008) *The positive impact of social and emotional learning for kindergarten to eighth-grade students: Findings from three scientific reviews*, technical report ED505370, Chicago: Collaborative for Academic, Social, and Emotional Learning

Phillipson, S. and Phillipson, S. (2007) Academic expectations, belief of ability, and involvement by parents as predictors of child achievement: A cross-cultural comparison, *Educational Psychology*, 27, 3, 329–348

Pinxten, M., De Fraine, B., Van Damme, J. and D'Haenens E. (2010) Causal ordering of academic self-concept and achievement: Effects of type of achievement measure, *British Journal of Educational Psychology*, 80, 4, 689–709

Pittard, V., Bannister, P. and Dunn, J. (2003) *The big pICTure: The impact of ICT on attainment, motivation and learning*, London: DfES. Available at http://www.dfes.gov.uk/research/data/uploadfiles/ThebigpICTure.pdf (accessed 22 November 2005)

Plunkett, S., Behnke, A., Sands, T. and Choi, B. (2009) Adolescents' reports of parental engagement and academic achievement in immigrant families, *Journal of Youth and Adolescence*, 38, 2, 257–268

Pong, S. (1997) The school compositional effect of single parenthood on 10th-grade achievement, *Sociology of Education*, 71, 1, 23–42

Portillo Pena, N. A. (2009) *The power of reading: A multilevel study of the longitudinal effect of a paired intergenerational reading aloud program on academically at-risk elementary students' reading attitudes, reading motivation and academic achievement*, Dissertation Abstracts International, Section B, The Sciences and Engineering

Print, M. and Coleman, D. (2003) Towards understanding of social capital and citizenship education, *Cambridge Journal of Education*, 33, 1, 123–149

Proud, S. (2010) *Peer effects in English primary schools: An IV estimation of the effect of a more able peer group on age 11 examination results*, CMPO working paper 10/248, Bristol: Centre for Market and Public Organisation

Pugh, K. and Bergin, D. (2005) The effect of schooling on pupils' out-of-school experience, *Educational Researcher*, 34, 9, 15–23

Puma, M., Tarkow, A. and Puma, A. (2007) *The challenge of improving children's writing ability: A randomised evaluation of writing wings*, Washington DC: Institute of Education Sciences, US Department of Education

Qi, S. (2006) Longitudinal effects of parenting on children's academic achievement in African American families, *Journal of Negro Education*, 75, 3, 415–429

Quillian, L. (2012) Segregation and poverty concentration: The role of three segregations, *American Sociological Review*, 77, 3, 364–379

Quintelier, E. (2010) The effect of schools on political participation: A multilevel logistic analysis, *Research Papers in Education*, 25, 2, 137–154

Quirk, M., Schwanenflugel, P. and Webb, M. (2009) A short-term longitudinal study of the relationship between motivation to read and reading fluency skill in second grade, *Journal of Literacy Research*, 41, 2, 196–227

Raffe, D., Croxford, L., Ianelli, I. Shapira, M. and Howieson, C. (2006) *Social class inequalities in education in England and Scotland*, Edinburgh: Education Youth and Transitions Project

Raty, H., Karkkainen, R. and Kasanen, K. (2010) To be or not to be? Pupils' explanation of the malleability of their academic competencies, *Educational Research*, 52, 3, 247–261

Ready, D. (2012) Associations between student achievement and student learning: Implications for value-added accountability models, *Educational Policy*, 27, 1, 92–120

Ream, R. and Rumberger, R. (2008) Student engagement, peer social capital, and school dropout among Mexican American and non-latino white students, *Sociology of Education*, 81, 2, 109–139

Reback, R. (2010) Noninstructional spending improves noncognitive outcomes: Discontinuity evidence from a unique Elementary School Counselor Financing System, *Education Finance and Policy*, 5, 2, 105–137

Reidel, J., Tomaszewski, T. and Weaver, D. (2003) *improving student academic reading achievement through the use of multiple intelligence teaching strategies*, Master of Arts Research Project, Saint Xavier University and Skylight Professional Development Field-Based Master's Program

Reynolds, A., Ou, S. and Topitzes, J. (2004) Paths of effects of early childhood intervention on educational attainment and delinquency: A confirmatory analysis of the Chicago Child–Parent Centers, *Child Development*, 75, 5, 1299–1328

Riccio, J., Dechausay, N., Greenberg, D., Miller, C., Rucks, Z. and Verma, N. (2010) *Toward reduced poverty across generations: Early findings from New York City's conditional cash transfer program*, New York: MDRC

Richardson, H. (2012) *Segregated UK school 'toxic for poor'*, BBC News, 4 April 2012

Rider, L. (2010) *The impact of direct reading instructional strategies on reading achievement in 8th grade students*, EdD dissertation, Walden University (Baltimore, MD)

Ridgway, R. and Ridgway, J. (2011) Crimes against statistical inference, *On-line Educational Research Journal*. Available at http://www.oerj.org (accessed 23 February 2013)

Riley, K. (2004) Voices of disaffected pupils: Implications for policy and practice, *British Journal of Educational Studies*, 52, 2, 166–179

Robinson, D., Levin, J., Thomas, G., Pituch, K. and Vaughn, S. (2007) The incidence of 'causal' statements in teaching-and-learning research journals, *American Educational Research Journal*, 44, 2, 400–413

Robinson, J. (2010) The effects of test translation on young English learners' mathematics performance, *Educational Researcher*, 39, 8, 582–590

Roemer, J. (1996) *Theories of distributive justice*, Cambridge, MA: Harvard University Press

Rogers, M., Theule, J., Ryan, B., Adams, G. and Keating, L. (2009) Parental involvement and children's school achievement: Evidence for mediating processes, *Canadian Journal of School Psychology*, 24, 1, 34–57

Roth, T. and Salikurluk, Z. (2012) Attitudes and expectations: Do attitudes towards education mediate the relationship between social networks and parental expectations? *British Journal of Sociology of Education*, 33, 5, 701–722

Rudd, P., Gardiner, C. and Marson-Smith, H. (2010) *Local authority approaches to the school admission process*, Slough: NFER

Rutter, M., Maughan, B., Mortimore, P. and Ouston, J. (1979) *Fifteen thousand hours: Secondary schools and their effects on children*, London: Open Books

Sacerdote, B. (2004) *What happens when we randomly assign children to families?* NBER working paper 10894, National Bureau of Economic Research

Sainsbury, M., Whetton, C., Keith, M. and Schagen, I. (1998) Fallback in attainment on transfer at age 11: Evidence from the Summer Literacy Schools evaluation, *Educational Research*, 40, 1, 73–81

Salway, S., Allmark, P., Barley, R., Higinbottom, G., Gerrish, K. and Ellison, G. (2010) Researching ethnic inequalities, *Social Research Update*, 58, 1–4

Sanders, W. (2000) Value-added assessment from pupil achievement data, *Journal of Personnel Evaluation in Education*, 14, 4, 329–339

Sanders, W. and Horn, S. (1998) Research findings from the Tennessee Value-Added Assessment System (TVAAS) database, *Journal of Personnel Evaluation in Education*, 12, 3, 247–256

Sanders, W. and Rivers, J. (1996) *Cumulative and residual effects of teachers on future pupil academic achievement*, University of Tennessee: Value-Added Research and Assessment Center

Schlechter, M. and Milevsky, A. (2010) Parental level of education: Associations with psychological well-being, academic achievement and reasons for pursuing Higher Education in adolescence, *Educational Psychology*, 30, 1, 1–10

Schneider, S. and Tieben, N. (2011) A healthy sorting machine? Social inequality in the transition to upper secondary education in Germany, *Oxford Review of Education*, 37, 2, 139–166

Schofield, C. and Dismore, H. (2010) Predictors of retention and achievement of higher education students within a further education context, *Journal of Further and Higher Education*, 34, 2, 207–221

Scholastic Research (2008) *Desert sands unified school district, CA*, New York: Scholastic Inc.

Schutz, G., Ursprung, H. and Wobmann, L. (2008) Education policy and equality of opportunity, *Kyklos*, 61, 2, 279–308

Schvaneveldt, P. (2000) *The influence of parental behaviors during early adolescence on post-secondary education attainment as mediated by academic achievement, peers, and substance use*, Dissertation Abstracts International, Section A, The Humanities and Social Sciences

Schwinger, M., Steinmayr, R. and Spinath, B. (2009) How do motivational regulation strategies affect achievement: Mediated by effort management and moderated by intelligence, *Learning and Individual Differences*, 19, 4, 621–627

Scott, J. (2004) Family, gender, and educational attainment in Britain: A longitudinal study, *Journal of Comparative Family Studies*, 35, 4, 569–589

See, B. H., Gorard, S., Cooke, S. and Siddiqui, N. (2012) *Improving literacy in the transition period: What do we need to know about what works?* London: Educational Endowment Foundation

See, B. H., Torgerson, C., Ainsworth, H., Gorard, S., Low. G. and Wright, K. (2011) The factors that promote high post-16 participation of some ethnic minority groups in England: A systematic review of the UK-based literature, *Research in Post-compulsory Education*, 16, 1, 85–100

Sektnan, M., McClelland, M., Acock, A. and Morrison, F. (2010) Relations between early family risk, children's behavioral regulation, and academic achievement, *Early Childhood Research Quarterly*, 25, 4, 464–479

Selwyn, N., Gorard, S. and Furlong, J. (2006) *Adult learning in the digital age*, London: Routledge

Senler, B. and Sungur, S. (2009) Parental influences on students' self-concept, task value beliefs, and achievement in science, *The Spanish Journal of Psychology*, 12, 1, 106–117

Shadish, W., Cook, T. and Campbell, D. (2002) *Experimental and quasi-experimental designs for generalized causal inference*, Boston, MA: Houghton Mifflin

Shaver, A. and Walls, R. (1998) Effect of parent involvement on student reading and mathematics achievement, *Journal of Research and Development in Education*, 31, 2, 90–97

Shepherd, J. and Rogers, S. (2012) Church schools shun poorest pupils, *The Guardian*, 5 March 2012

Shin, Y. (2007) Peer relationships, social behaviours, academic performance and loneliness in Korean primary school children, *School Psychology International*, 28, 2, 220–236

Shulruf, B., Tumen, S. and Tolley, H. (2008) Extracurricular activities in school, do they matter? *Children and Youth Services Review*, 30, 4, 418–426

Simpson, L. (2004) Statistics of racial segregation: Measures, evidence and policy, *Urban Studies*, 41, 3, 661–681

Sinclair, M., Christenson, S. and Thurlow, M. (2005) Promoting school completion of urban secondary youth with emotional or behavioral disabilities, *Exceptional Children*, 71, 4, 465–82

Singh, K. and Ozturk, M. (2000) Effect of part-time work on high school math and science course taking, *The Journal of Educational Research*, 94, 2, 67–74

Singh, K., Granville, M. and Dika, S. (2002), Mathematics and science achievement: Effects of motivation, interest, and academic engagement, *Journal of Educational Research*, 95, 6, 323–32

Siraj-Blatchford, I. (2010) Learning in the home and at school: How working class children 'succeed against the odds', *British Educational Research Journal*, 36, 3, 463–482

Sirvani, H. (2007) The effect of teacher communication with parents on students' mathematics achievement, *American Secondary Education*, 36, 1, 31–46

Skaalvik, E. and Skaalvik, S. (2009) Self-concept and self-efficacy in mathematics: Relation with mathematics motivation and achievement, *Journal of Education Research*, 3, 3, 255–278

Skaliotis, E. (2010) Changes in parental involvement in secondary education: An exploration study using the longitudinal study of young people in England, *British Educational Research Journal*, 36, 6, 975–994

Skokut, M. (2010) *Educational resilience among English language learners: Examining factors associated with high school completion and post-secondary school attendance*, Dissertation Abstracts International, Section A, The Humanities and Social Sciences

Smith, A. (2003) Citizenship education in Northern Ireland: Beyond national identity, *Cambridge Journal of Education*, 33, 1, 15–31

Smith, E. and Gorard, S. (2011) Is there a shortage of scientists? A re-analysis of supply for the UK, *British Journal of Educational Studies*, 59, 2, 159–177

Smithers, A. and Robinson, P. (2010) *Worlds apart: Social variation among schools*, London: The Sutton Trust

Somers, C., Owens, D. and Piliawsky, M. (2009) A study of high school dropout prevention and at-risk ninth graders' role models and motivations for school completion, *Education*, 130, 2, 348–356

Somers, M-A., Corrin, W., Sepanik, S., Salinger, T., Levin, J. and Zmach, C. (2010) *The enhanced reading opportunities study final report: The impact of supplemental literacy courses for struggling ninth-grade readers*, NCEE 2010–4021, National Center for Education Evaluation and Regional Assistance

Son, S-H. C. and Strasser, K. (2002) *Direct and indirect influences of SES on home literacy activities and kindergarten reading skills: Evidence from early childhood longitudinal studies*, paper presented at the 2002 National Association for the Education of Young Children Annual Conference, 20–23 November (New York)

Speed, E. (1998) *Gender issues and differential achievement in education and vocational training: A research review*, Manchester: Equal Opportunities Commission

Speight, N. (2010) *The relationship between self-efficacy, resilience and academic achievement among African-American urban adolescent students*, Dissertation Abstracts International, Section B, The Sciences and Engineering

Spencer, M., Noll, E. and Cassidy, E. (2005) Monetary incentives in support of academic achievement: Results of a randomized field trial involving high-achieving, low-resource, ethnically diverse urban adolescents, *Evaluation Review*, 29, 3, 199–222

Spoth, R., Randall, G. and Shin, C. (2008) Increasing school success through partnership-based family competency training: Experimental study of long-term outcomes, *School Psychology Quarterly*, 23, 1, 70–89

Sprague, K., Hamilton, J., Coffey, D., Loadman, W., Lomax, R., Moore, R., Faddis, B. and Beam, M. (2010) *Using randomized clinical trials to determine the impact of reading intervention on struggling adolescent readers: Reports of research from five nationally funded striving readers grants*, papers presented at the Society for Research on Educational Effectiveness Conference (no details about place and date of conference). Available at https://www.sree.org/conferences/2010/program/abstracts/208.pdf (accessed 23 February 2013)

St Clair, R. and Benjamin, A. (2011) Performing desires: The dilemma of aspirations and educational attainment, *British Educational Research Journal*, 37, 3, 501–517

Staff, J. and Mortimer, J. (2007) Educational and work strategies from adolescence to early adulthood: Consequences for educational attainment, *Social Forces*, 85, 3, 1169–1194

Staff, J., Patrick, M., Loken, E. and Maggs, J. (2008) Teenage alcohol use and educational attainment, *Journal of Studies on Alcohol and Drugs*, 69, 6, 848–858

Staff, J., Schulenberg, J. and Bachman, J. (2009) Adolescent work intensity, school performance, and academic engagement, *Sociology of Education*, 83, 3, 183–200

Starkey, P. and Klein, A. (2000) Fostering parental support for children's mathematical development: An intervention with Head Start families. *Early Education and Development*, 11, 5, 659–680

Stevens, B. (1996) *Parental influences in getting children 'ready to learn'. PhD dissertation*, Dissertation Abstracts International, Section A: The Humanities and Social Sciences

Stevens, T., To, Y., Stevenson, S. and Lochbaum, M. (2008) The importance of physical activity in the prediction of academic achievement, *Journal of Sport Behavior*, 31, 4, 368–388

Stewart, W. (2009) 'Appalling' failures of English test markers, *Times Educational Supplement*, 30 March, p.14

Stewart, W. (2010) Call for FOI to be extended to academies as research reveals wide use of 'pseudo' courses, *TES*, 21 May, p.12

Strand, S. (2007) *Minority ethnic students in the longitudinal study of young people in England*, research report DCSF-RR002/DCSF-RB002, Nottingham: Department for Education and Skills

Strand, S. (2009) *In-school factors and the White British–Black Caribbean attainment gap: Test, tiers and unintended consequences of assessment practice*, paper presented at The Annual Conference of the American Educational Research Association, 13–17 April 2009 (San Diego, CA)

Strand, S. (2011) The limits of social class in explaining ethnic gaps in educational attainment, *British Educational Research Journal*, 37, 2, 197–229

Strand, S. and Winston, J. (2008) Educational aspirations in inner city schools, *Educational Studies*, 34, 4, 249–267

Stringer, N. (2012) Setting and maintaining GCSE and GCE grading standards: The case for contextualised cohort-referencing, *Research Papers in Education*, 27, 5, 535–554

Suizzo, M. and Stapleton, L. (2007) Home-based parental involvement in young children's education: Examining the effects of maternal education across US ethnic groups, *Educational Psychology*, 27, 4, 533–556

Sullivan, A., Heath, A. and Rothon, C. (2011) Equalisation or inflation? Social class and gender differentials in England and Wales, *Oxford Review of Education*, 37, 2, 215–240

Sy, S. (2006) Family and work influences on the transition to college among Latina adolescents, *Hispanic Journal of Behavioral Sciences*, 28, 3, 368–386

Sylva, K., Melhuish, E., Sammons, P., Siraj-Blatchford, I. and Taggart, B. (2008) *Final report from the primary phase: Pre-school, school and family influences on children's development during Key Stage 2 (7–11)*, research report DfE 061, Nottingham: The Department for Education

Synder, F., Flay, B., Vuchinich, S., Acock, A., Washburn, I., Beets, M. and Li, K. (2010) Impact of a social-emotional and character development program on school-level indicators of academic achievement, absenteeism and disciplinary outcomes: A matched-pair, cluster randomised controlled trial, *Journal of Research on Educational Effectiveness*, 3, 1, 26–55

Tang, W. (2004) *Investigating the factors influencing educational attainment across ethnic and gender groups: Structural analysis of NELS:88–2000 Database*, Dissertation Abstracts International, Section A, The Humanities and Social Sciences

Taningco, M. and Pachon, H. (2008) *Computer use, parental expectations, and Latino academic achievement*, California, CA: Tomas Rivera Policy Institute

Tannock, S. (2008) The problem of education-based discrimination, *British Journal of Sociology of Education*, 29, 5, 439–449

Taylor, C. and Gorard, S. (2005) *Participation in higher education: Wales, report for independent study into devolution of the student support system: The Rees Review*, Cardiff: National Assembly for Wales

Terry, A. (2008) *Components of the authoritative parenting style: Predictors of Asian American adolescent achievement*, Dissertation Abstracts International, Section B, The Sciences and Engineering

Terzian, M. and Mbwana, K. (2009) What works for parent involvement programs for adolescents: Lessons from experimental evaluations of social interventions, *Child Trends Fact Sheet*, December 2009, p. 48

Themelis, S. (2008) Meritocracy through education and social mobility in post-war Britain: A critical examination, *British Journal of Sociology of Education*, 29, 5, 427–438

Thomas, L. (2006) *Pathways to success or failure: Factors affecting academic achievement among Black students*, Dissertation Abstracts International, Section A, The Humanities and Social Sciences

Thomas, W. and Webber, D. (2009) Choice at 16: School, parental and peer group effects, *Research in Post-Compulsory Education*, 14, 2, 119–141

Thornberg, R. (2008) School children's reasoning about school rules, *Research Papers in Education*, 23, 1, 37–52

Tieben, N. and Wolbers, M. (2010) Success and failure in secondary education: Socio-economic background effects on secondary school outcome in the Netherlands, 1927–1998, *British Journal of Sociology of Education*, 31, 3, 277–290

Tiedemann, J. (2000) Parents' gender stereotypes and teachers' beliefs as predictors of children's concept of their mathematical ability in elementary school, *Journal of Educational Psychology*, 92, 1, 144–151

Tomlinson, S. (2001) *Education in a post welfare society*, Buckingham: Open University Press

Tomlinson, S. (2012) The irresistible rise of the SEN industry, *Oxford Review of Education*, 38, 3, 267–286

Topor, D., Keane, S., Shelton, T. and Calkins, S. (2010) Parent involvement and student academic performance: A multiple mediational analysis, *Journal of Prevention & Intervention in the Community*, 38, 3, 183–197

Topping K., Kearey, N., McGee, E., and Pugh, J. (2004) Tutoring in mathematics: A generic method, mentoring and tutoring, *Partnership in Learning*, 12, 3, 353–370

Trannoy, A. (1999) Social dominance egalitarianism and utilitariaris, *Revue Economique*, 50, 4, 733–755

Trzesniewski, K., Moffitt, T., Caspi, A., Taylor, A. and Maughan, B. (2006) Revisiting the association between reading achievement and antisocial behavior: New evidence of an environmental explanation from a twin study, *Child Development*, 77, 1, 72–88

Tsikalas, K., Lee, J. and Newkirk, C. (2008) *Family computing and the academic engagement and achievement of low-income urban adolescents: Findings from the Computers for Youth Intervention*, Council of Chief State School Offices (CCSSO) National Conference on Large Scale Assessment Nashville, TN: Computers for Youth Foundation

Turkheimer, E., Haley, A., Waldron, M., D'Onofrio, B. and Gottesman, I. (2003) Socioeconomic status modifies heritability of IQ of young children, *Psychological Science*, 14, 6, 623–628

Turok, I., Kintrea, K., St Clair, R. and Benjamin, A. (2008) *Shaping aspirations: The role of parents, place and poverty: Interim report*, Glasgow: Department of Urban Studies

Tuttle, C., Teh, B-R., Nichols-Barrer, I., Gill, B. and Gleason, P. (2010) *Student characteristics and achievement in 22 KIPP middle schools: Final report*, Washington, DC: Mathematica Policy Research, Inc.

Tverborgvik, T., Clausen, L., Thorsted, B., Mikkelsen, S. and Lynge, E. (2012) Intergenerational educational mobility in Denmark, *Scandinavian Journal of Educational Research*, 10.1080/00313831.2012.696211

Twist, L., Schagen, I. and Hodgson, C. (2007) *Readers and reading: the National Report for England 2006* (PIRLS: Progress in International Reading Literacy Study), Slough: NFER

Ulrich, N. (2004) *Mature students: Access to and experience of HE part-time foreign language degrees*, Birmingham: Aston University

US Department of Education (1997) *Mathematics equals opportunity*, white paper prepared for US Secretary of Education, Richard W. Riley, Report ED415119

Van Houtte, M. and Stevens, P. (2010a) School ethnic composition and aspirations of immigrant students in Belgium, *British Educational Research Journal*, 36, 2, 209–237

Van Houtte, M. and Stevens, P. (2010b) The culture of futility and its impact on study culture in technical/vocational schools in Belgium, *Oxford Review of Education*, 36, 1, 23–44

Van Keer, H. (2004) Fostering reading comprehension in fifth grade by explicit instruction in reading strategies and peer tutoring, *British Journal of Educational Psychology*, 74, 1, 37–70

Van Voorhis, F. (2001) Interactive science homework: An experiment in home school connections, *NASSP Bulletin*, 85, 627, 20–32

Vandell, D., Reisner, E. and Pierce, K. (2007) *Outcomes linked to high-quality afterschool programs: Longitudinal findings from the study of promising afterschool programs*, report ED501882, Flint, MI: Charles Stewart Mott Foundation

Vaughan, R. (2009) How to be top, *Times Educational Supplement*, 30 October, p.19

Vignoles, A. and Meschi, E. (2010) *The determinants of non-cognitive and cognitive schooling outcomes*, report to the Department of Children, Schools and Families, Special Report 004, London: The Centre for the Economics of Education

Vincson, J. (2008) *An 18-year study of the academic motivational environment of mother–child interaction*, Dissertation Abstracts International, Section A, The Humanities and Social Sciences

Vitaro, F., Brendgen, M., Larose, S. and Trembaly, R. (2005) Kindergarten disruptive behaviors, protective factors, and educational achievement by early adulthood, *Journal of Educational Psychology*, 97, 4, 617–629

Vyverman, V. and Vettenburg, N. (2009) School well-being among young people: Is it influenced by the parents' socioeconomic background? *Educational Studies*, 35, 2, 191–204

Walford, G. (2004) No discrimination on the basis of irrelevant qualifications, *Cambridge Journal of Education*, 34, 3, 353–361

Wang, J., Wildman, L. and Calhoun, G. (1996) The relationship between parental influences and student achievement in seventh grade maths, *School Science and Mathematics*, 96, 8, 395–400

Waxman, H., Lin, M. and Michko, G. (2003) *A meta-analysis of the effectiveness of teaching and learning with technology on pupil outcomes*, North Central Regional Educational Laboratory. Available at http://www.ncrel.org/tech/effects2/waxman.pdf (accessed 28 February 2006)

Welsh Assembly Government (2009) *The Foundation Phase*. Available at http://wales.gov.uk/topics/educationandskills/policy_strategy_and_planning/104009-wag/foundation_phase/?lang=en (accessed 23/9/09)

West, A., Barham, E. and Hind, A. (2011) Secondary school admissions in England 2001 to 2008: Changing legislation, policy and practice, *Oxford Review of Education*, 37, 1, 1–20

Wheldall, K. (2000) Does rainbow repeated reading add value to an intensive literacy intervention programme for low-progress readers? An experimental evaluation, *Educational Review*, 52, 1, 29–36

White, P. (2012) Modelling the 'learning divide': Predicting participation in adult learning 2002 and 2010, *British Educational Research Journal*, 38, 1, 3–22

White, P. and Selwyn, N. (2011) Learning online? Educational internet use and participation in adult learning, 2002 to 2010, *Educational Review*, 64, 4, 451–469

White, R., Haslam, M. and Hewes, G. (2006) *Improving student literacy: READ 180 in the Phoenix Union high school district, 2003–2004 and 2004–2005*, Washington, DC: Policy Studies Associates

White, R., Williams, I. and Haslem, M. (2005) *Performance of district 23 students participating in Scholastic READ 180*, Washington, DC: Policy Studies Associates. Evaluated in WWC (2009) *READ 180. What Works Clearing House intervention report*, Washington: US Department of Education, Institute of Education Sciences

Whitehead, M. (1991) The concepts and principles of equity and health, *Health Promotion International*, 6, 3, 217–228

Whitesell, N., Mitchell, C., Spicer, P. and The Voices of Indian Teens Project Team (2009) A longitudinal study of self-esteem, cultural identity, and academic success among American Indian adolescents, cultural diversity and ethnic minority, *Psychology*, 15, 1, 38–50

Wiley, R. (2006) *Exploring the impact of grade retention on students' aspirations and educational outcomes*, Dissertation Abstracts International, Section A, The Humanities and Social Sciences

Williams, M. and Husk, K. (2012) Can we, should we, measure ethnicity? *International Journal of Social Research Methodology*, iFirst 10.1080/13645579.2012.682794

Wilson, W. (1987) *The truly disadvantaged*, Chicago: Chicago University Press

Wobmann, L., (2003) Schooling resources, educational institutions and student performance: The international evidence. *Oxford Bulletin of Economics and Statistics*, 65, 2, 117–170

Woods, D. (2007) *An investigation of the effects of a middle school reading intervention on school dropout rates*, unpublished doctoral dissertation, Virginia Polytechnic Institute and State University (Blacksburg, VA)

Woodworth, K., David, J., Guha, R., Wang, H. and Lopez-Torkos, A. (2008) *San Francisco Bay Area KIPP schools: A study of early implementation and achievement, final report*, Menlo Park, CA: SRI International

Wright, P., Li, W., Ding, S. and Pickering, M. (2010) Integrating a personal and social responsibility program into a Wellness course for urban high school students: Assessing implementation and educational outcomes, *Sport, Education and Society*, 15, 3, 277–298

WWC (2009) *READ 180. What Works Clearing House intervention report*, Washington, DC: US Department of Education, Institute of Education Sciences

WWC (2010) *Project CRISS® (CReating Independence through Student-owned Strategies), What Works Clearing House intervention report*, Washington, DC: US Department of Education, Institute of Education Sciences

WWC (2012) *Peer-Assisted Learning Strategies. What Works Clearing House intervention report*, Washington: US Department of Education, Institute of Education Sciences

Yailagh, M. (2003) Role of motivation and cognition on school performance of high-school students: A structural analysis, *Indian Journal of Social Work*, 64, 1, 50–64

Yan, W. and Lin, Q. (2005) Parent involvement and mathematics achievement: Contrast across racial and ethnic groups, *Journal of Educational Research*, 99, 2, 116

Yu, C. H. (2012) Examining the relationships among academic self-concept, instrumental motivation, and TIMSS 2007 science scores, *Educational Research and Evaluation*, 18, 8, 713–731

Zand, D. and Thomson, N. (2005) Academic achievement among African American adolescents: Direct and indirect effects of demographic, individual, and contextual variables, *Journal of Black Psychology*, 31, 4, 352–368

Zanobini, M. and Usai, M. (2010) Domain self-concept and achievement motivation in the transition from primary to low middle school, *Educational Psychology*, 22, 2, 203–217

Zepke, N. and Leach, L. (2011) Beyond hard outcomes: 'Soft' outcomes and engagement as student success, *Teaching in Higher Education*, 15, 6, 661–673

Zevenbergen, A., Whitehurst, G. and Zevenbergen, J. (2003) Effects of a shared-reading intervention on the inclusion of evaluative devices in narratives of children from low-income families, *Journal of Applied Developmental Psychology*, 24, 1, 1–15.

Zhai, F., Brooks-Gunn, J. and Waldfogel, J. (2011) Head Start and urban children's school readiness: A birth cohort study in 18 cities, *Developmental Psychology*, 47, 1, 134–152

Zill, N. (1994) Understanding why children in stepfamilies have more learning and behaviour problems than children in nuclear families. In A. Booth and J. Dunn (Eds) *Stepfamilies: Who benefits? Who does not?* (pp. 97–106), Hillsdale, NJ: Erlbaum

Zimmerman, B., Bandura, A. and Martinez-Pons, M. (1992) Self-motivation for academic attainment: The role of self-efficacy beliefs and personal goal setting, *American Educational Research Journal*, 29, 3, 663–676

Zins, J., Bloodworth, M., Weissberg, R. and Walberg, H. (2004) The scientific base linking social and emotional learning to school success. In J. Zins, R. Weissberg, M. Wang and H. Walberg (Eds) *Building academic success on social and emotional learning: What does the research say?* (pp. 2–22) New York: Teacher College Press

Index